WORLD OF TANKS
CITADEL ™

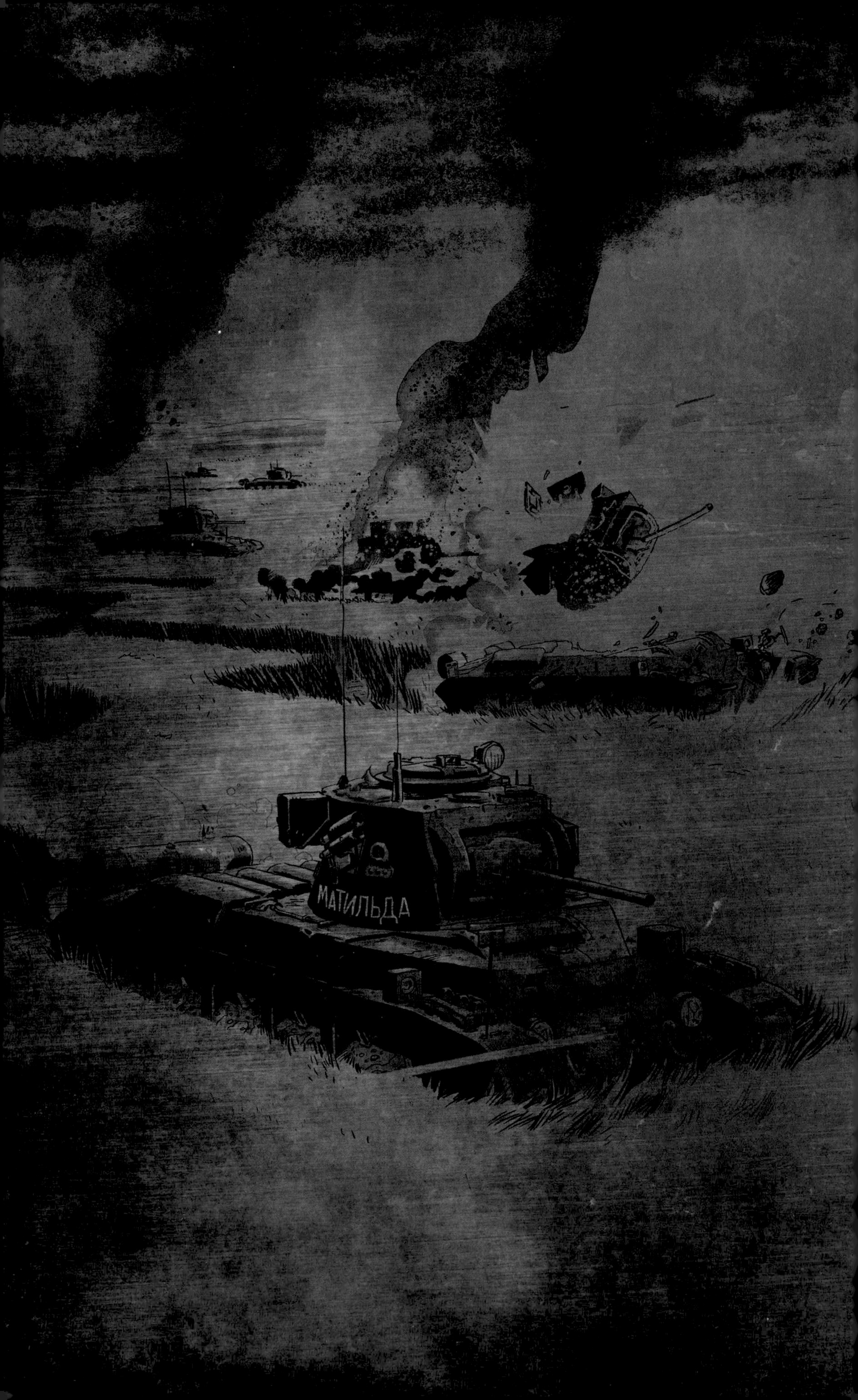
МАТИЛЬДА

WORLD OF TANKS™

CITADEL™

Script by
GARTH ENNIS

Art by
P.J. HOLDEN

Colors by
MICHAEL ATIYEH

Letters by
ROB STEEN

Cover and Chapter Break Art by
ISAAC HANNAFORD

Dark Horse Books

President and Publisher
MIKE RICHARDSON

Editor
SHANTEL LaROCQUE

Assistant Editor
BRETT ISRAEL

Digital Art Technician
JOSIE CHRISTENSEN

Collection Designer
LIN HUANG

NEIL HANKERSON Executive Vice President · **TOM WEDDLE** Chief Financial Officer · **RANDY STRADLEY** Vice President of Publishing · **NICK McWHORTER** Chief Business Development Officer · **DALE LaFOUNTAIN** Chief Information Officer · **MATT PARKINSON** Vice President of Marketing · **CARA NIECE** Vice President of Production and Scheduling · **MARK BERNARDI** Vice President of Book Trade and Digital Sales · **KEN LIZZI** General Counsel · **DAVE MARSHALL** Editor in Chief · **DAVEY ESTRADA** Editorial Director · **CHRIS WARNER** Senior Books Editor · **CARY GRAZZINI** Director of Specialty Projects · **LIA RIBACCHI** Art Director · **VANESSA TODD-HOLMES** Director of Print Purchasing · **MATT DRYER** Director of Digital Art and Prepress · **MICHAEL GOMBOS** Director of International Publishing and Licensing · **KARI YADRO** Director of Custom Programs · **KARI TORSON** Director of International Licensing

Published by Dark Horse Books
A division of Dark Horse Comics, Inc.
10956 SE Main Street, Milwaukie, OR 97222

First edition: January 2019
ISBN 978-1-50670-752-5

10 9 8 7 6 5 4 3 2 1
Printed in China

Comic Shop Locator Service: comicshoplocator.com

Special thanks to **TJ WAGNER**, **JJ BAKKEN**, and **JULIEN RAMETTE** at Wargaming and **BRYAN NUNES**, **ALEX BREWER-DISARUFINO**, and **SHEKHAR DHUPELIA**.

World of Tanks: Citadel

This volume collects and reprints the comic book series *World of Tanks: Citadel* #1–#5.

Library of Congress Cataloging-in-Publication Data

Names: Ennis, Garth, author. | Holden, P. J., artist. | Atiyeh, Michael, colourist. | Steen, Rob, 1964- letterer. | Hannaford, Isaac, artist.
Title: Citadel / script by Garth Ennis ; art by P.J. Holden ; colors by Michael Atiyeh ; letters by Rob Steen ; cover and chapter break art by Isaac Hannaford.
Description: First edition. | Milwaukie, OR : Dark Horse Books, January 2019. | Series: World of tanks ; 2 | "This volume collects and reprints the comic book series World of Tanks: Citadel #1-#5."
Identifiers: LCCN 2018035801 | ISBN 9781506707525 (paperback)
Subjects: LCSH: World War, 1939-1945--Comic books, strips, etc. | Tanks--Comic books, strips, etc. | Comic books, strips, etc. | BISAC: COMICS & GRAPHIC NOVELS / Media Tie-In. | COMICS & GRAPHIC NOVELS / General.
Classification: LCC PN6728.W68 E53 2019 | DDC 741.5/973--dc23
LC record available at https://lccn.loc.gov/2018035801

WORLD OF TANKS™

CITADEL™

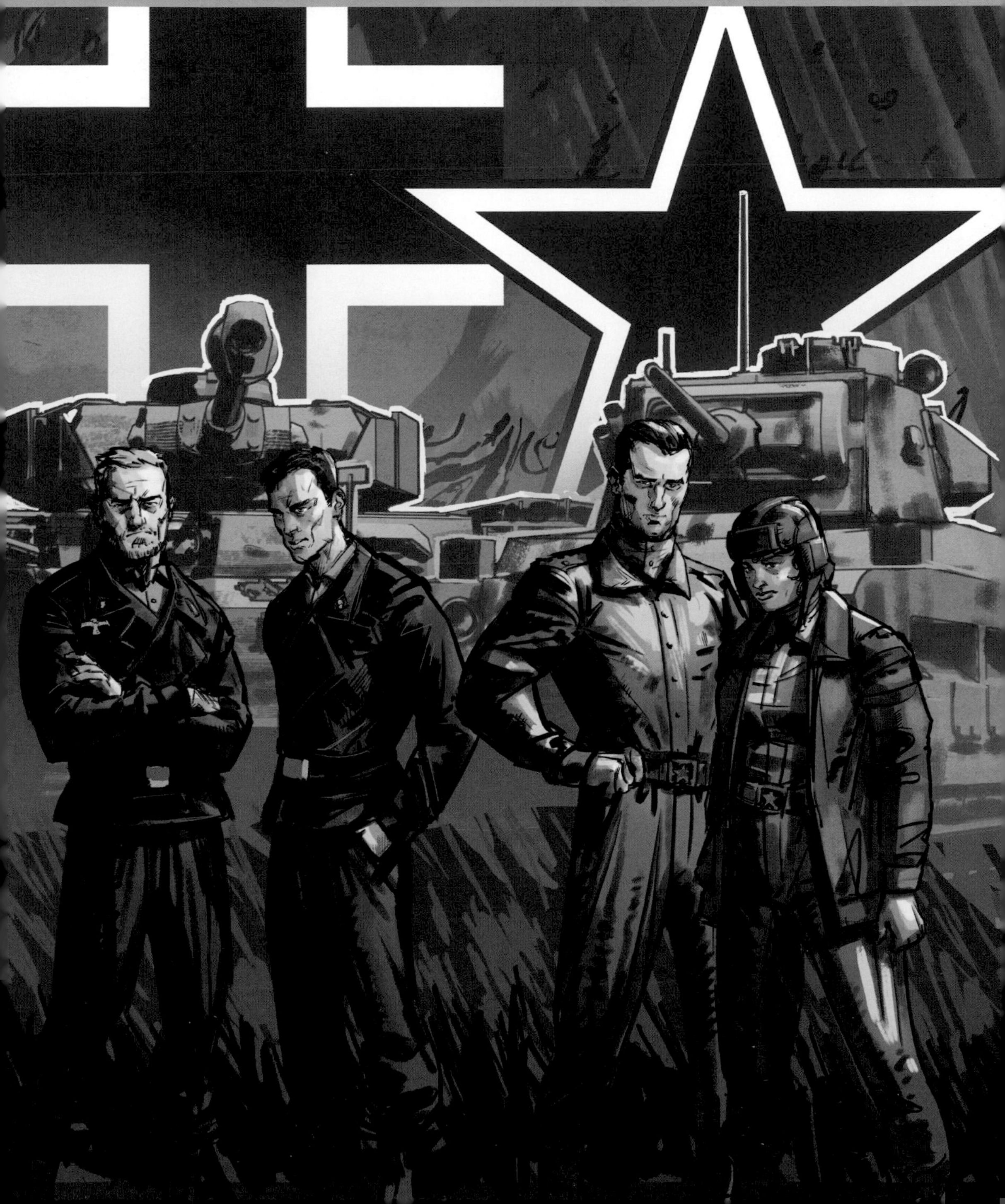

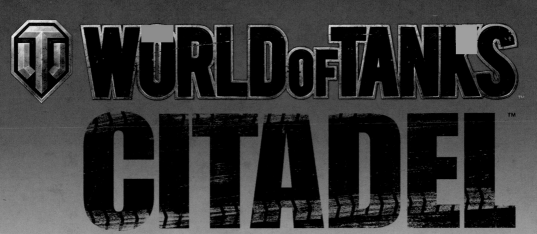

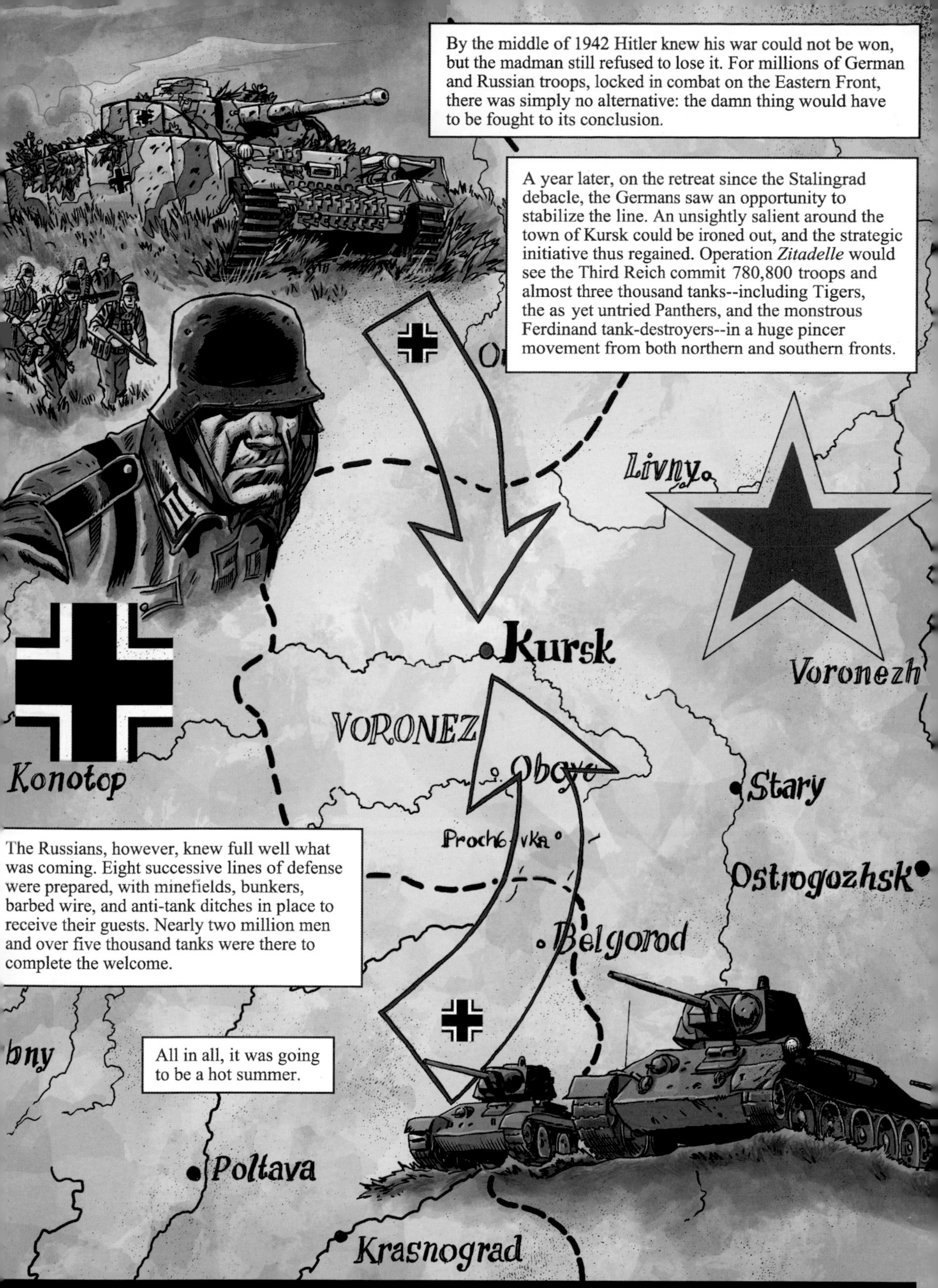
By the middle of 1942 Hitler knew his war could not be won, but the madman still refused to lose it. For millions of German and Russian troops, locked in combat on the Eastern Front, there was simply no alternative: the damn thing would have to be fought to its conclusion.
A year later, on the retreat since the Stalingrad debacle, the Germans saw an opportunity to stabilize the line. An unsightly salient around the town of Kursk could be ironed out, and the strategic initiative thus regained. Operation *Zitadelle* would see the Third Reich commit 780,800 troops and almost three thousand tanks--including Tigers, the as yet untried Panthers, and the monstrous Ferdinand tank-destroyers--in a huge pincer movement from both northern and southern fronts.
Livny
Kursk
Voronezh
VORONEZ
Konotop
Stary
The Russians, however, knew full well what was coming. Eight successive lines of defense were prepared, with minefields, bunkers, barbed wire, and anti-tank ditches in place to receive their guests. Nearly two million men and over five thousand tanks were there to complete the welcome.
Ostrogozhsk
Belgorod
All in all, it was going to be a hot summer.
Poltava
Krasnograd

1: FROM BOTH ENDS AT ONCE

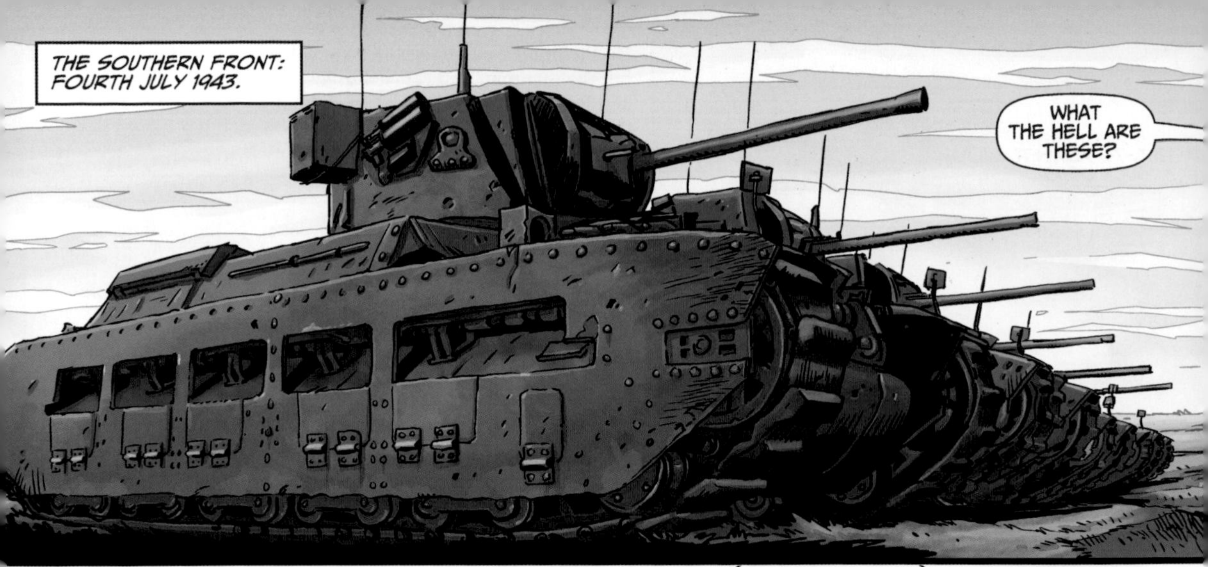
THE SOUTHERN FRONT: FOURTH JULY 1943.
WHAT THE HELL ARE THESE?

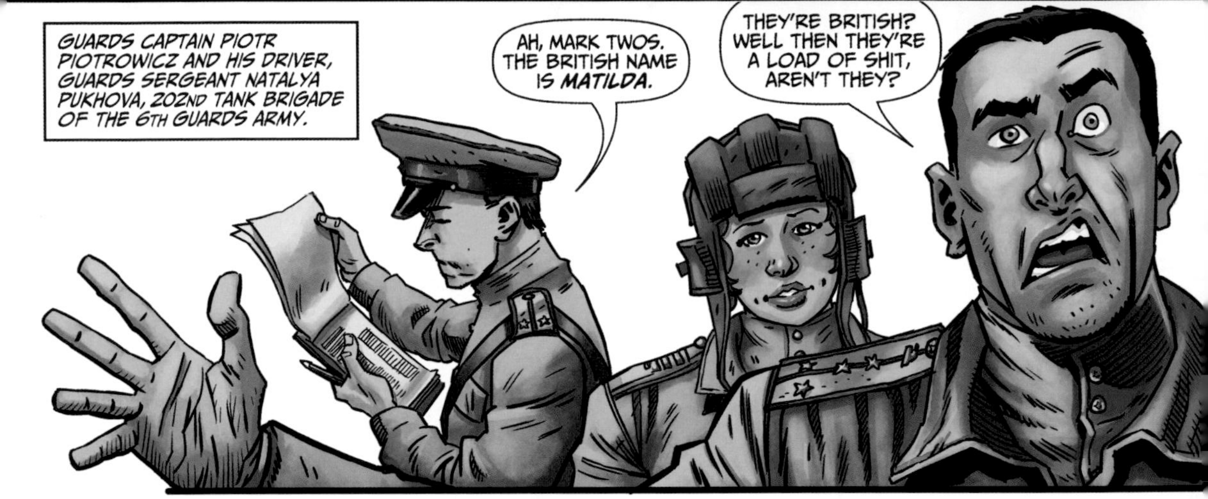
GUARDS CAPTAIN PIOTR PIOTROWICZ AND HIS DRIVER, GUARDS SERGEANT NATALYA PUKHOVA, 202ND TANK BRIGADE OF THE 6TH GUARDS ARMY.
AH, MARK TWOS. THE BRITISH NAME IS *MATILDA*.
THEY'RE BRITISH? WELL THEN THEY'RE A LOAD OF SHIT, AREN'T THEY?

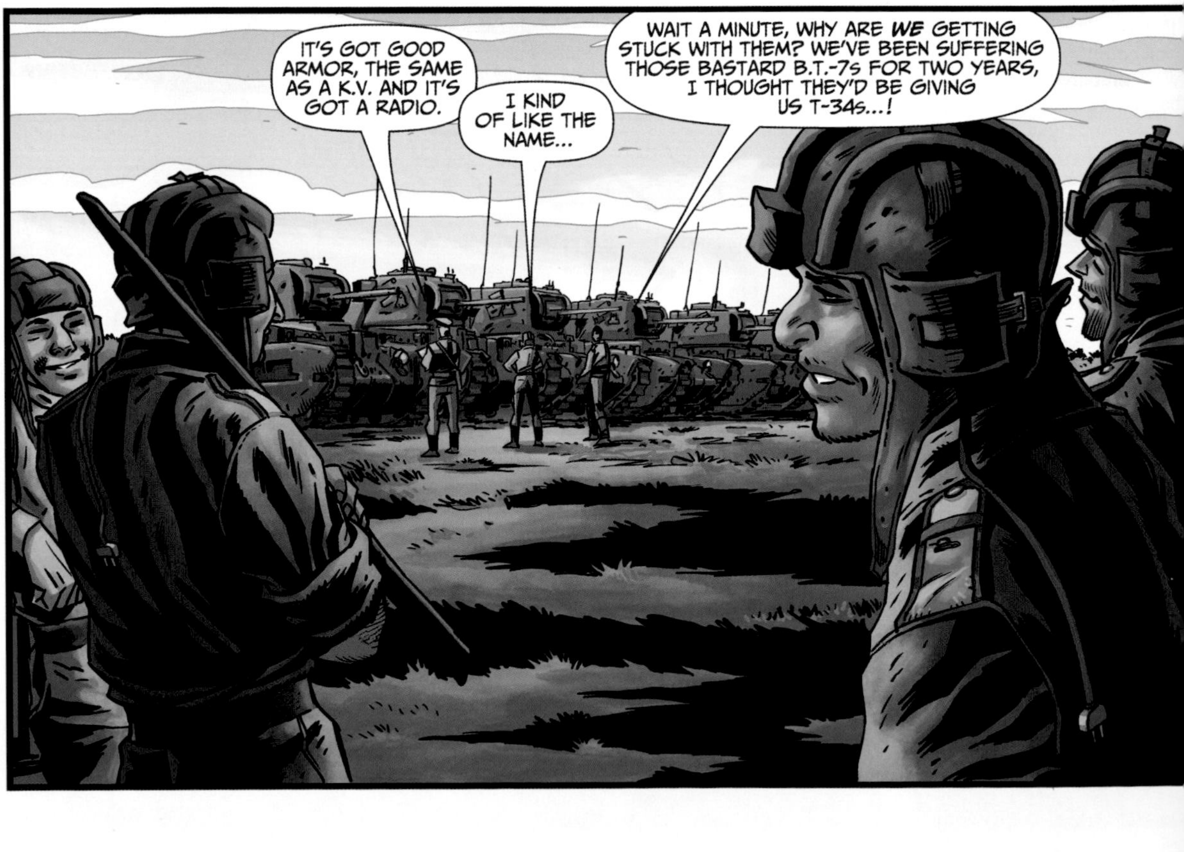
IT'S GOT GOOD ARMOR, THE SAME AS A K.V. AND IT'S GOT A RADIO.
I KIND OF LIKE THE NAME...
WAIT A MINUTE, WHY ARE ***WE*** GETTING STUCK WITH THEM? WE'VE BEEN SUFFERING THOSE BASTARD B.T.-7S FOR TWO YEARS, I THOUGHT THEY'D BE GIVING US T-34S...!

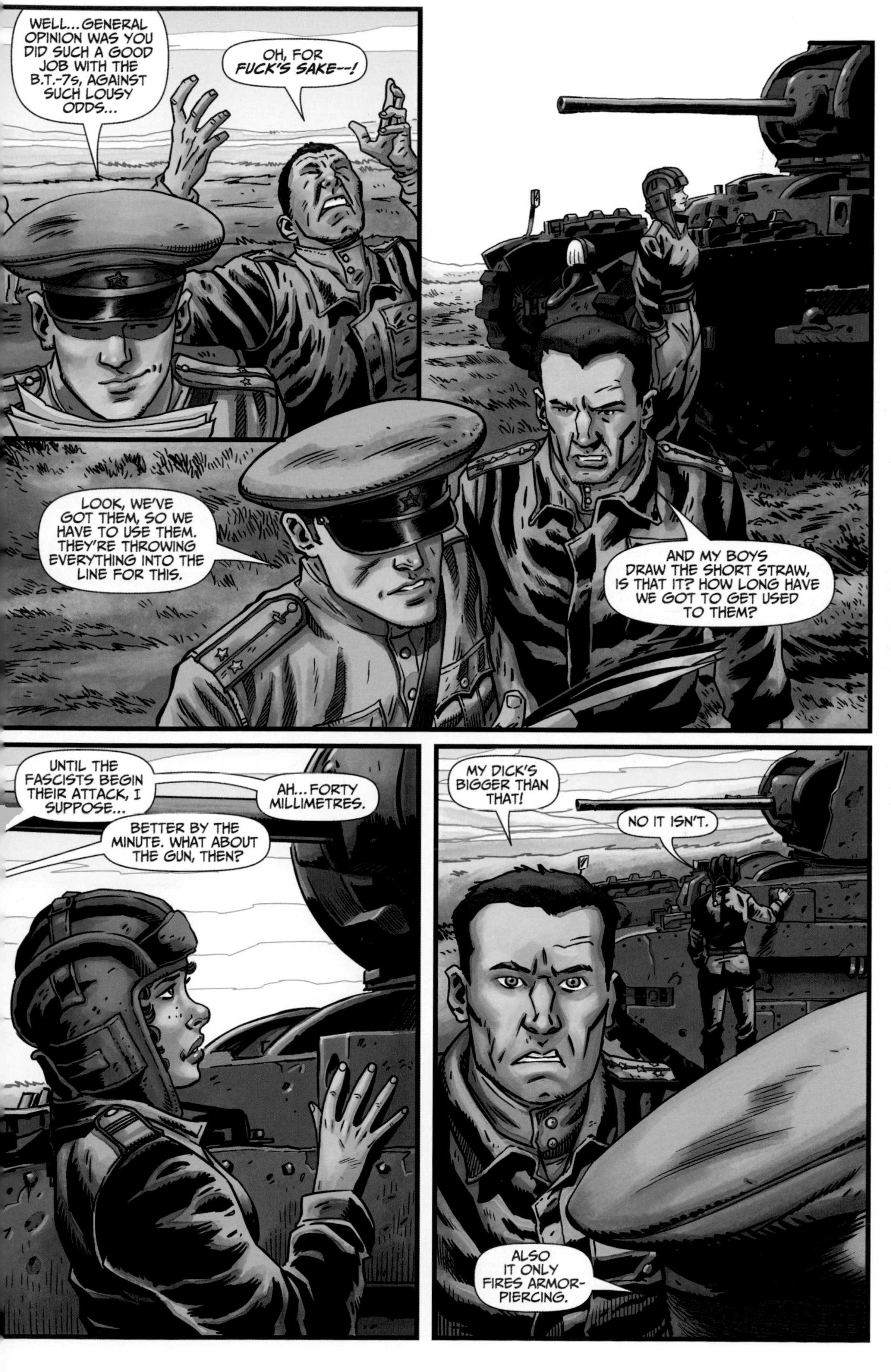
WELL... GENERAL OPINION WAS YOU DID SUCH A GOOD JOB WITH THE B.T.-7s, AGAINST SUCH LOUSY ODDS...
OH, FOR *FUCK'S SAKE*--!
LOOK, WE'VE GOT THEM, SO WE HAVE TO USE THEM. THEY'RE THROWING EVERYTHING INTO THE LINE FOR THIS.
AND MY BOYS DRAW THE SHORT STRAW, IS THAT IT? HOW LONG HAVE WE GOT TO GET USED TO THEM?
UNTIL THE FASCISTS BEGIN THEIR ATTACK, I SUPPOSE...
BETTER BY THE MINUTE. WHAT ABOUT THE GUN, THEN?
AH... FORTY MILLIMETRES.
MY DICK'S BIGGER THAN THAT!
NO IT ISN'T.
ALSO IT ONLY FIRES ARMOR-PIERCING.

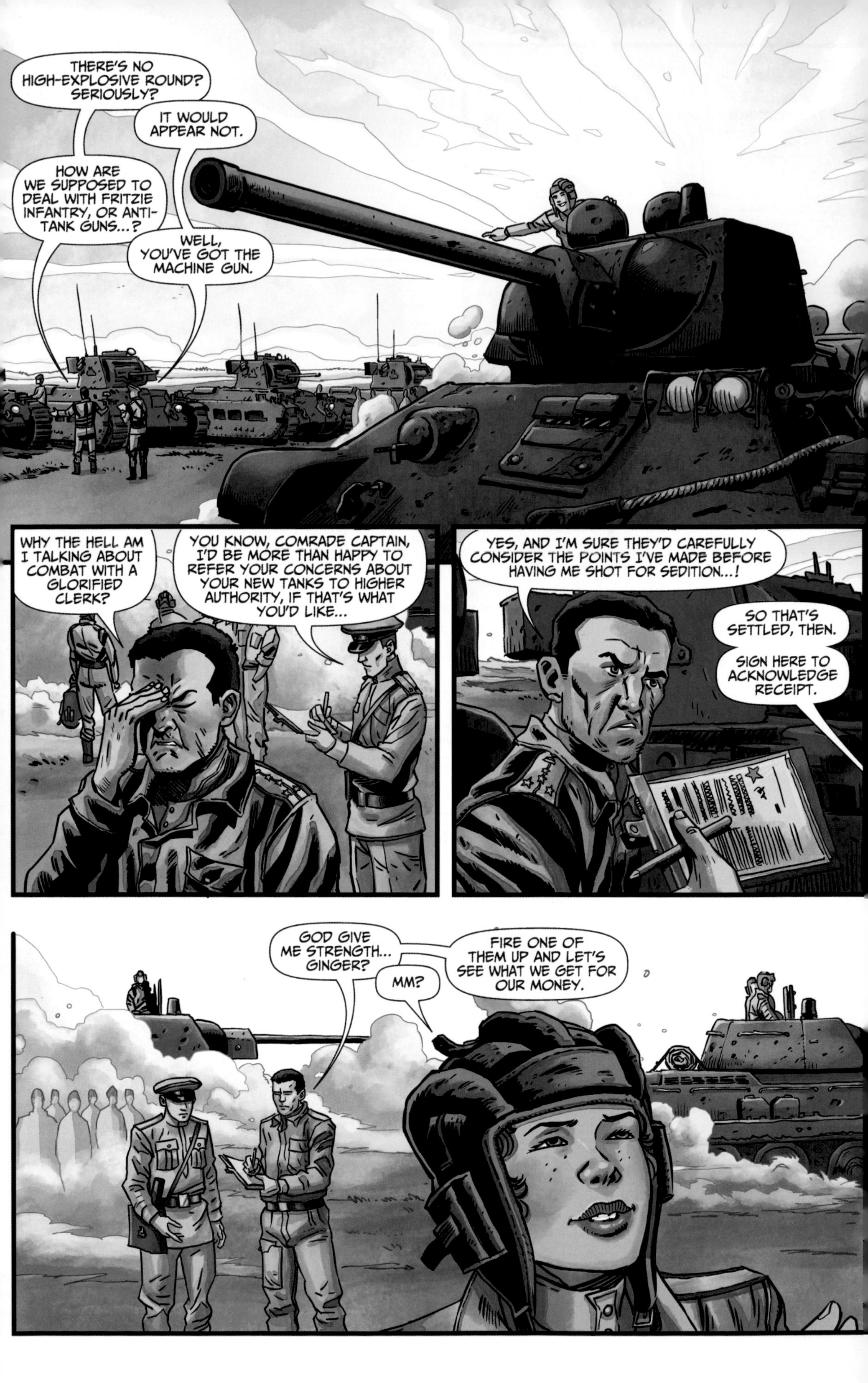
THERE'S NO HIGH-EXPLOSIVE ROUND? SERIOUSLY?
IT WOULD APPEAR NOT.
HOW ARE WE SUPPOSED TO DEAL WITH FRITZIE INFANTRY, OR ANTI-TANK GUNS...?
WELL, YOU'VE GOT THE MACHINE GUN.
WHY THE HELL AM I TALKING ABOUT COMBAT WITH A GLORIFIED CLERK?
YOU KNOW, COMRADE CAPTAIN, I'D BE MORE THAN HAPPY TO REFER YOUR CONCERNS ABOUT YOUR NEW TANKS TO HIGHER AUTHORITY, IF THAT'S WHAT YOU'D LIKE...
YES, AND I'M SURE THEY'D CAREFULLY CONSIDER THE POINTS I'VE MADE BEFORE HAVING ME SHOT FOR SEDITION...!
SO THAT'S SETTLED, THEN.
SIGN HERE TO ACKNOWLEDGE RECEIPT.
GOD GIVE ME STRENGTH... GINGER?
MM?
FIRE ONE OF THEM UP AND LET'S SEE WHAT WE GET FOR OUR MONEY.

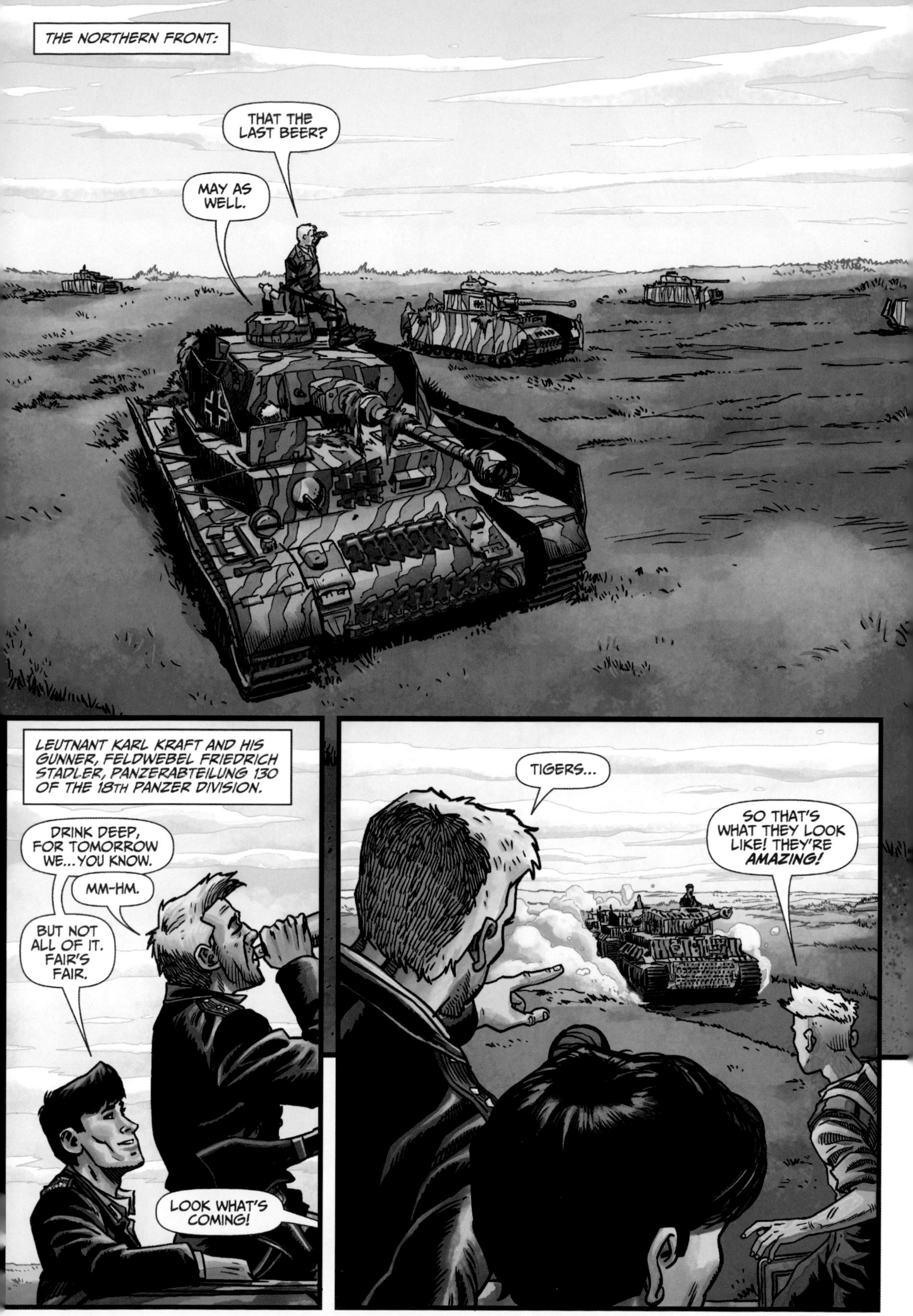

THE NORTHERN FRONT:
THAT THE LAST BEER?
MAY AS WELL.
LEUTNANT KARL KRAFT AND HIS GUNNER, FELDWEBEL FRIEDRICH STADLER, PANZERABTEILUNG 130 OF THE 18TH PANZER DIVISION.
DRINK DEEP, FOR TOMORROW WE...YOU KNOW.
MM-HM.
BUT NOT ALL OF IT. FAIR'S FAIR.
LOOK WHAT'S COMING!
TIGERS...
SO THAT'S WHAT THEY LOOK LIKE! THEY'RE AMAZING!

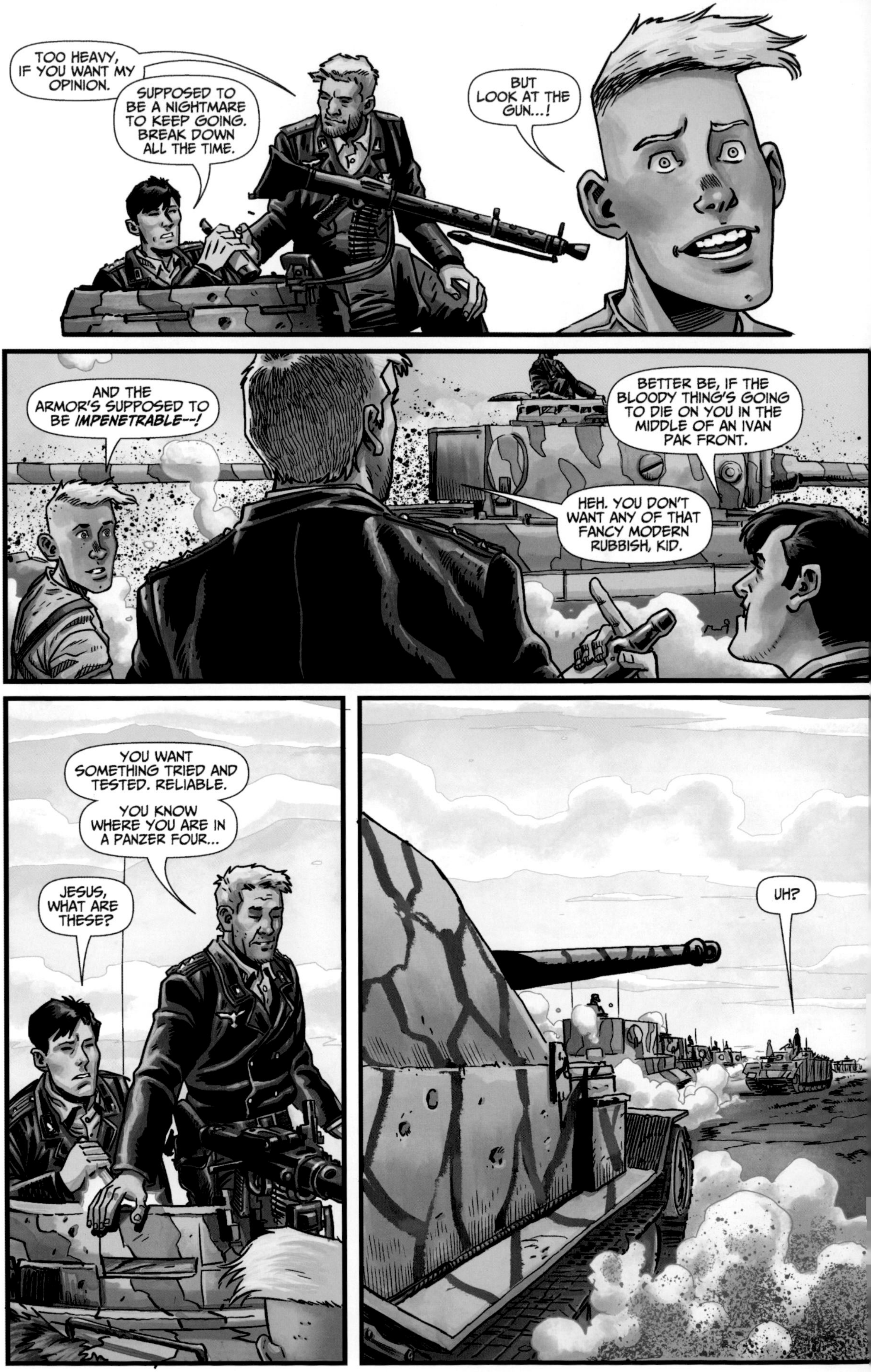
TOO HEAVY, IF YOU WANT MY OPINION.
SUPPOSED TO BE A NIGHTMARE TO KEEP GOING. BREAK DOWN ALL THE TIME.
BUT LOOK AT THE GUN...!
AND THE ARMOR'S SUPPOSED TO BE *IMPENETRABLE--!*
BETTER BE, IF THE BLOODY THING'S GOING TO DIE ON YOU IN THE MIDDLE OF AN IVAN PAK FRONT.
HEH. YOU DON'T WANT ANY OF THAT FANCY MODERN RUBBISH, KID.
YOU WANT SOMETHING TRIED AND TESTED. RELIABLE.
YOU KNOW WHERE YOU ARE IN A PANZER FOUR...
JESUS, WHAT ARE THESE?
UH?

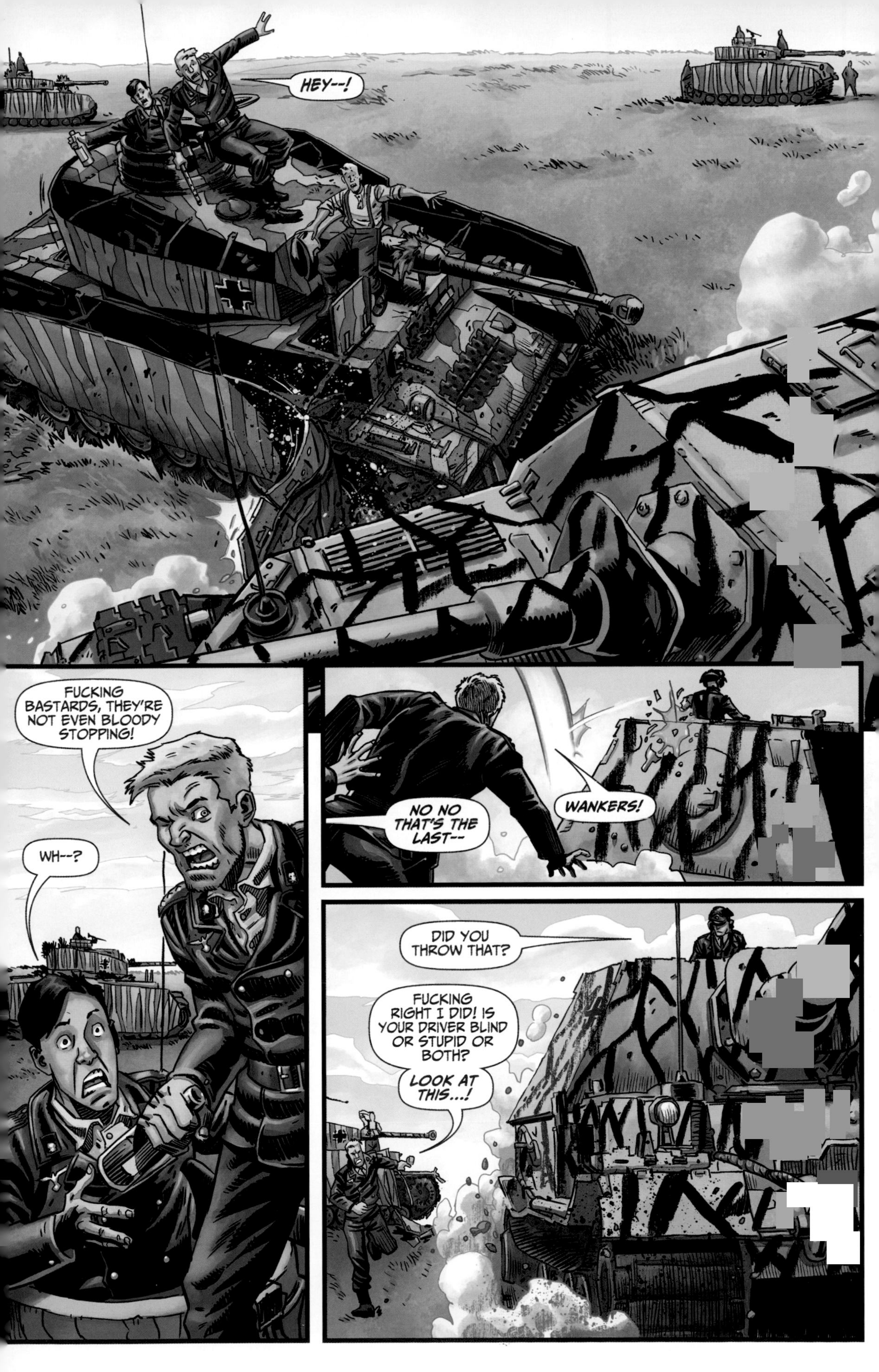
HEY--!
FUCKING BASTARDS, THEY'RE NOT EVEN BLOODY STOPPING!
WH--?
NO NO THAT'S THE LAST--
WANKERS!
DID YOU THROW THAT?
FUCKING RIGHT I DID! IS YOUR DRIVER BLIND OR STUPID OR BOTH?
LOOK AT THIS...!

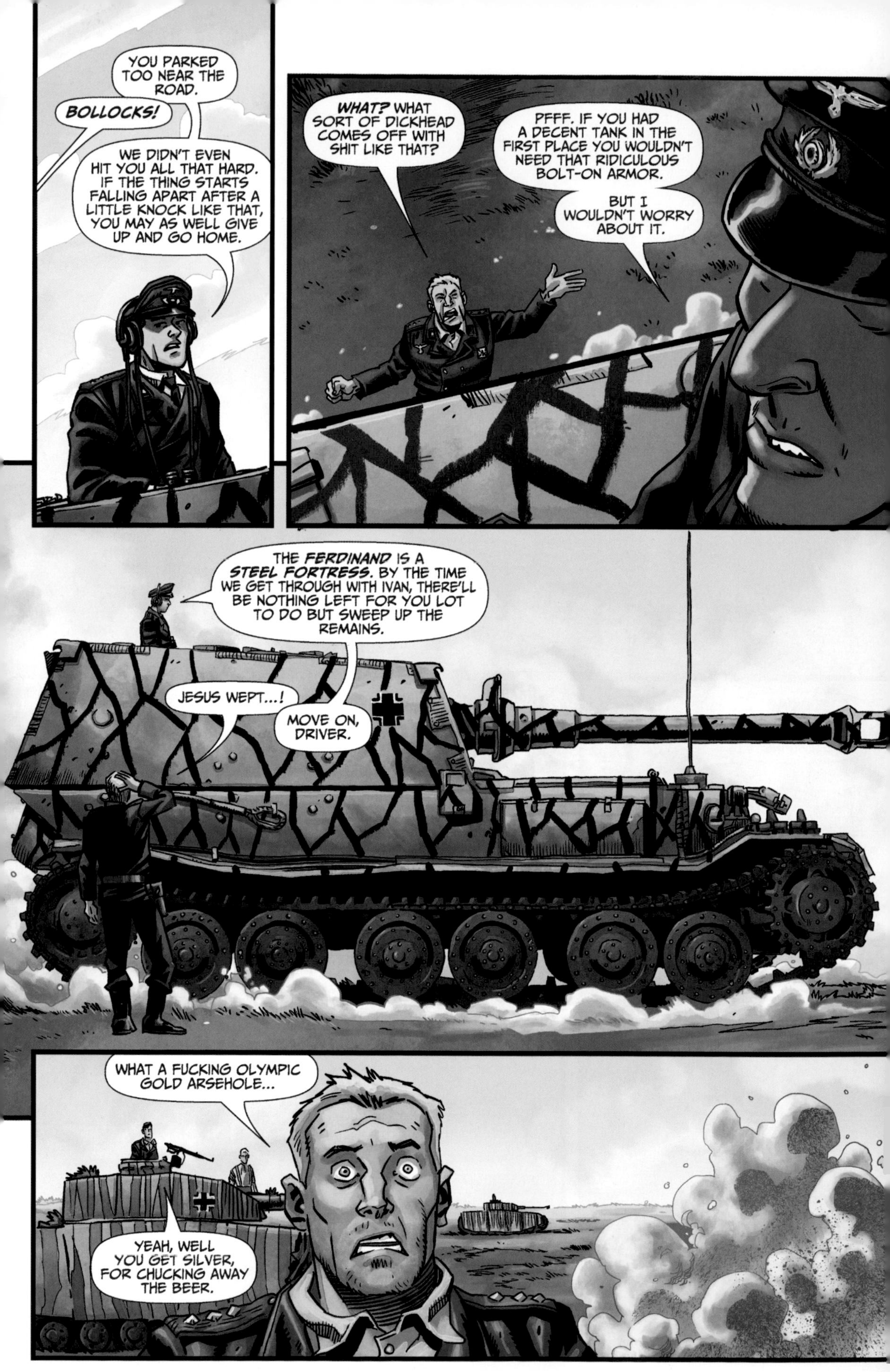

YOU PARKED TOO NEAR THE ROAD.
BOLLOCKS!
WE DIDN'T EVEN HIT YOU ALL THAT HARD. IF THE THING STARTS FALLING APART AFTER A LITTLE KNOCK LIKE THAT, YOU MAY AS WELL GIVE UP AND GO HOME.
WHAT? WHAT SORT OF DICKHEAD COMES OFF WITH SHIT LIKE THAT?
PFFF. IF YOU HAD A DECENT TANK IN THE FIRST PLACE YOU WOULDN'T NEED THAT RIDICULOUS BOLT-ON ARMOR.
BUT I WOULDN'T WORRY ABOUT IT.
THE FERDINAND IS A STEEL FORTRESS. BY THE TIME WE GET THROUGH WITH IVAN, THERE'LL BE NOTHING LEFT FOR YOU LOT TO DO BUT SWEEP UP THE REMAINS.
JESUS WEPT...!
MOVE ON, DRIVER.
WHAT A FUCKING OLYMPIC GOLD ARSEHOLE...
YEAH, WELL YOU GET SILVER, FOR CHUCKING AWAY THE BEER.

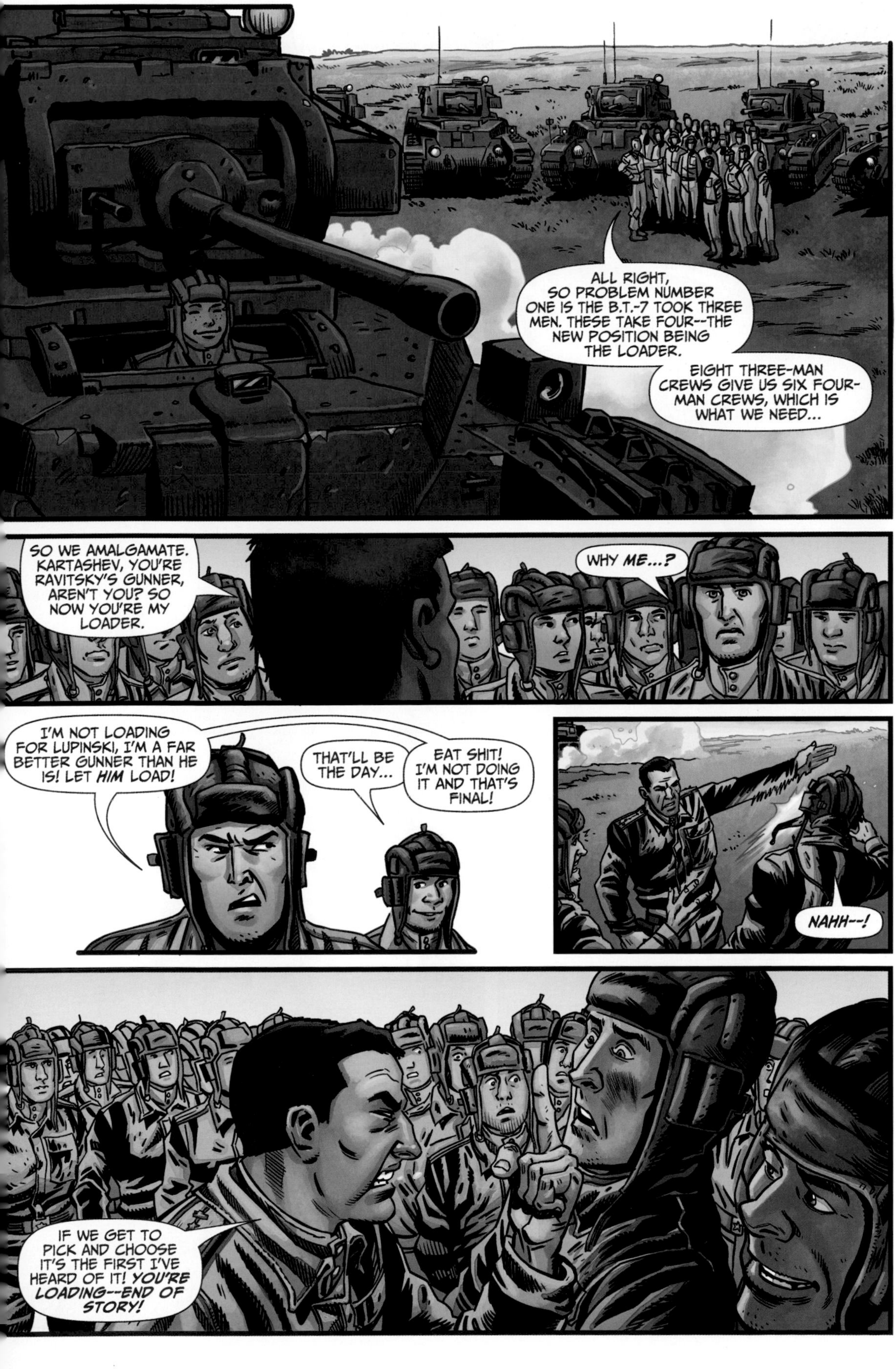
ALL RIGHT, SO PROBLEM NUMBER ONE IS THE B.T.-7 TOOK THREE MEN. THESE TAKE FOUR--THE NEW POSITION BEING THE LOADER.
EIGHT THREE-MAN CREWS GIVE US SIX FOUR-MAN CREWS, WHICH IS WHAT WE NEED...
SO WE AMALGAMATE. KARTASHEV, YOU'RE RAVITSKY'S GUNNER, AREN'T YOU? SO NOW YOU'RE MY LOADER.
WHY *ME*...?
I'M NOT LOADING FOR LUPINSKI, I'M A FAR BETTER GUNNER THAN HE IS! LET *HIM* LOAD!
THAT'LL BE THE DAY...
EAT SHIT! I'M NOT DOING IT AND THAT'S FINAL!
NAHH--!
IF WE GET TO PICK AND CHOOSE IT'S THE FIRST I'VE HEARD OF IT! *YOU'RE LOADING--END OF STORY!*

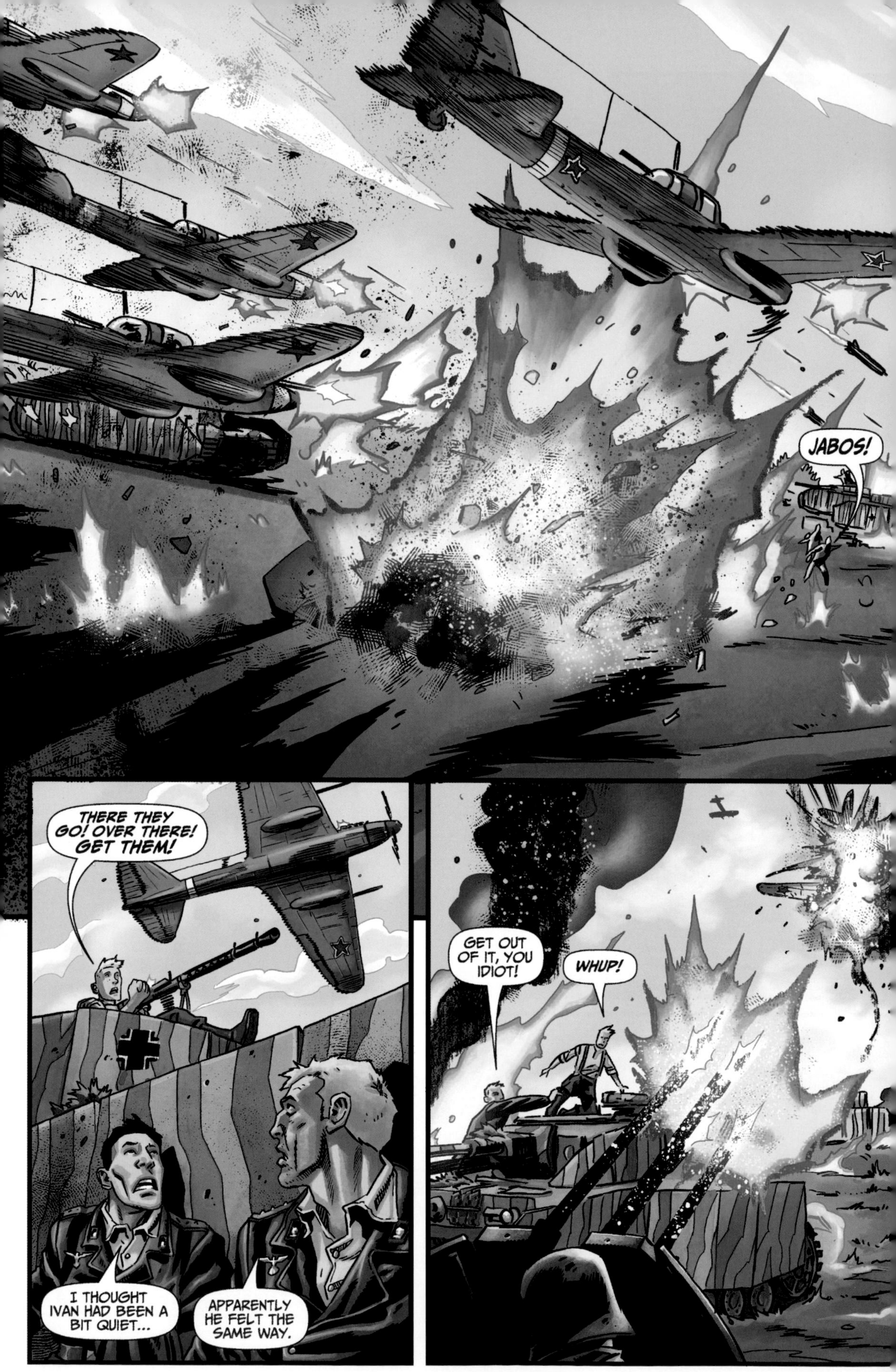
JABOS!
THERE THEY GO! OVER THERE! GET THEM!
I THOUGHT IVAN HAD BEEN A BIT QUIET...
APPARENTLY HE FELT THE SAME WAY.
GET OUT OF IT, YOU IDIOT!
WHUP!

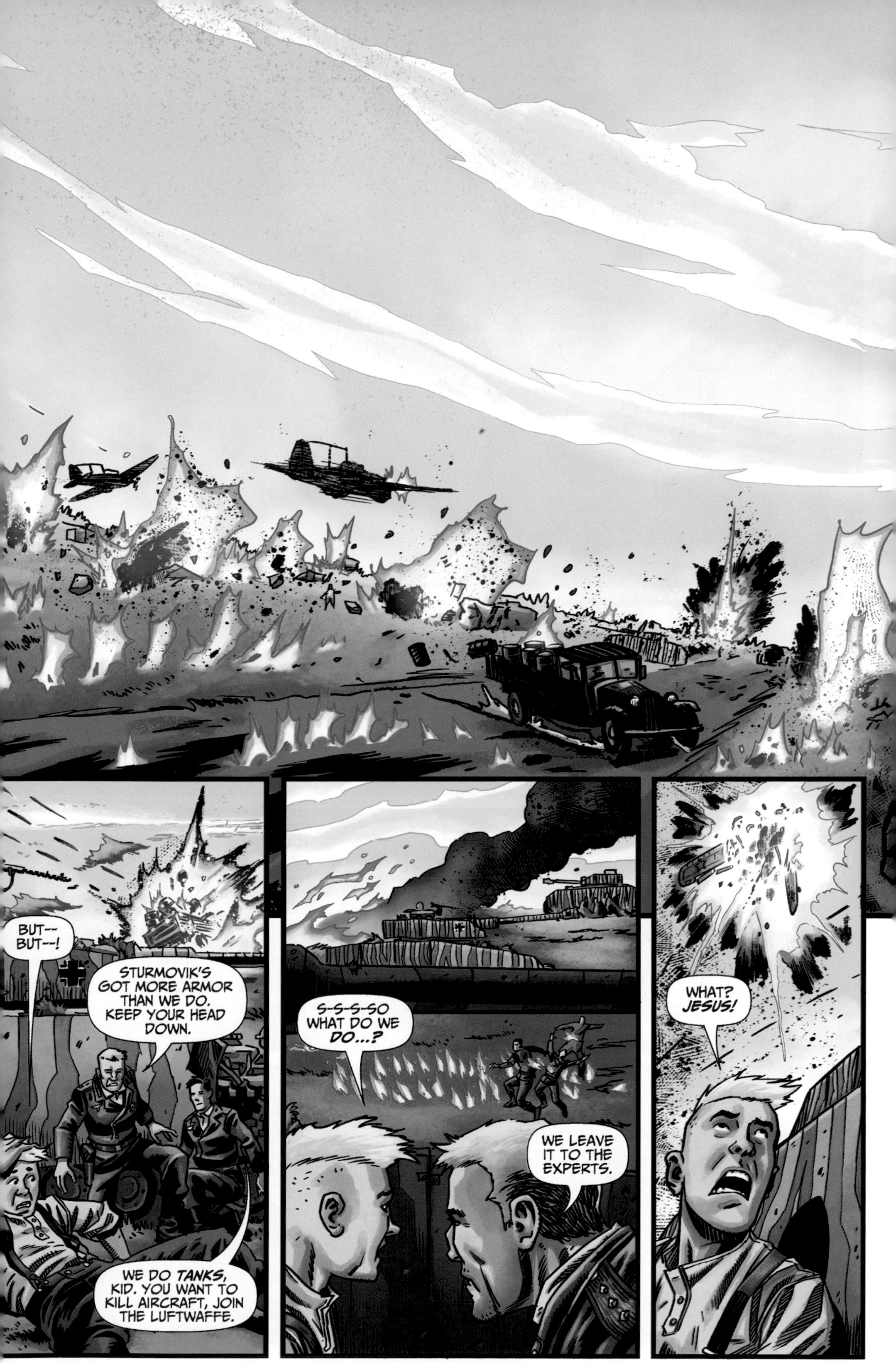
BUT--
BUT--!
STURMOVIK'S GOT MORE ARMOR THAN WE DO. KEEP YOUR HEAD DOWN.
WE DO TANKS, KID. YOU WANT TO KILL AIRCRAFT, JOIN THE LUFTWAFFE.
S-S-S-SO WHAT DO WE DO...?
WE LEAVE IT TO THE EXPERTS.
WHAT? JESUS!

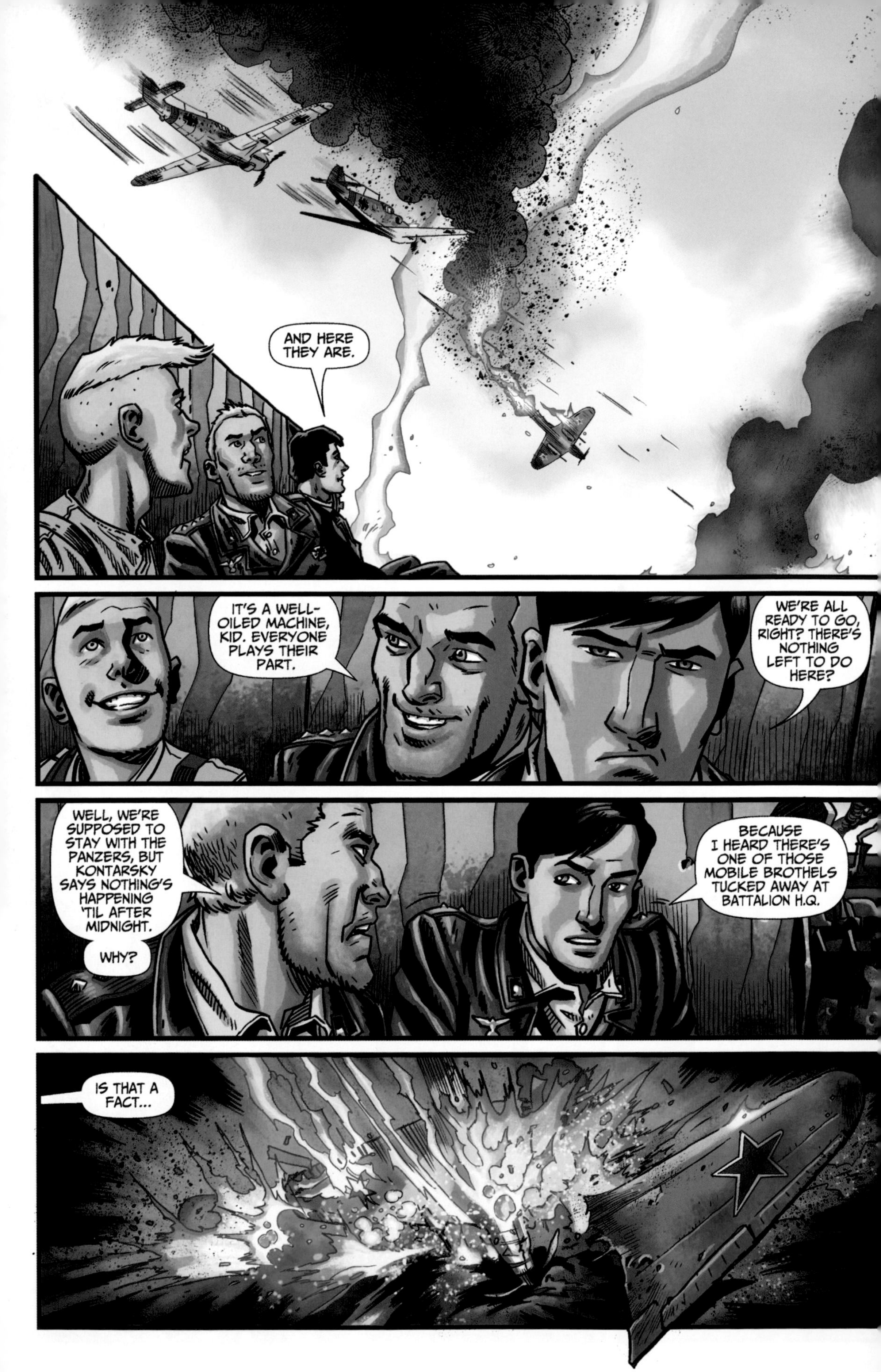
AND HERE THEY ARE.
IT'S A WELL-OILED MACHINE, KID. EVERYONE PLAYS THEIR PART.
WE'RE ALL READY TO GO, RIGHT? THERE'S NOTHING LEFT TO DO HERE?
WELL, WE'RE SUPPOSED TO STAY WITH THE PANZERS, BUT KONTARSKY SAYS NOTHING'S HAPPENING 'TIL AFTER MIDNIGHT.
WHY?
BECAUSE I HEARD THERE'S ONE OF THOSE MOBILE BROTHELS TUCKED AWAY AT BATTALION H.Q.
IS THAT A FACT...

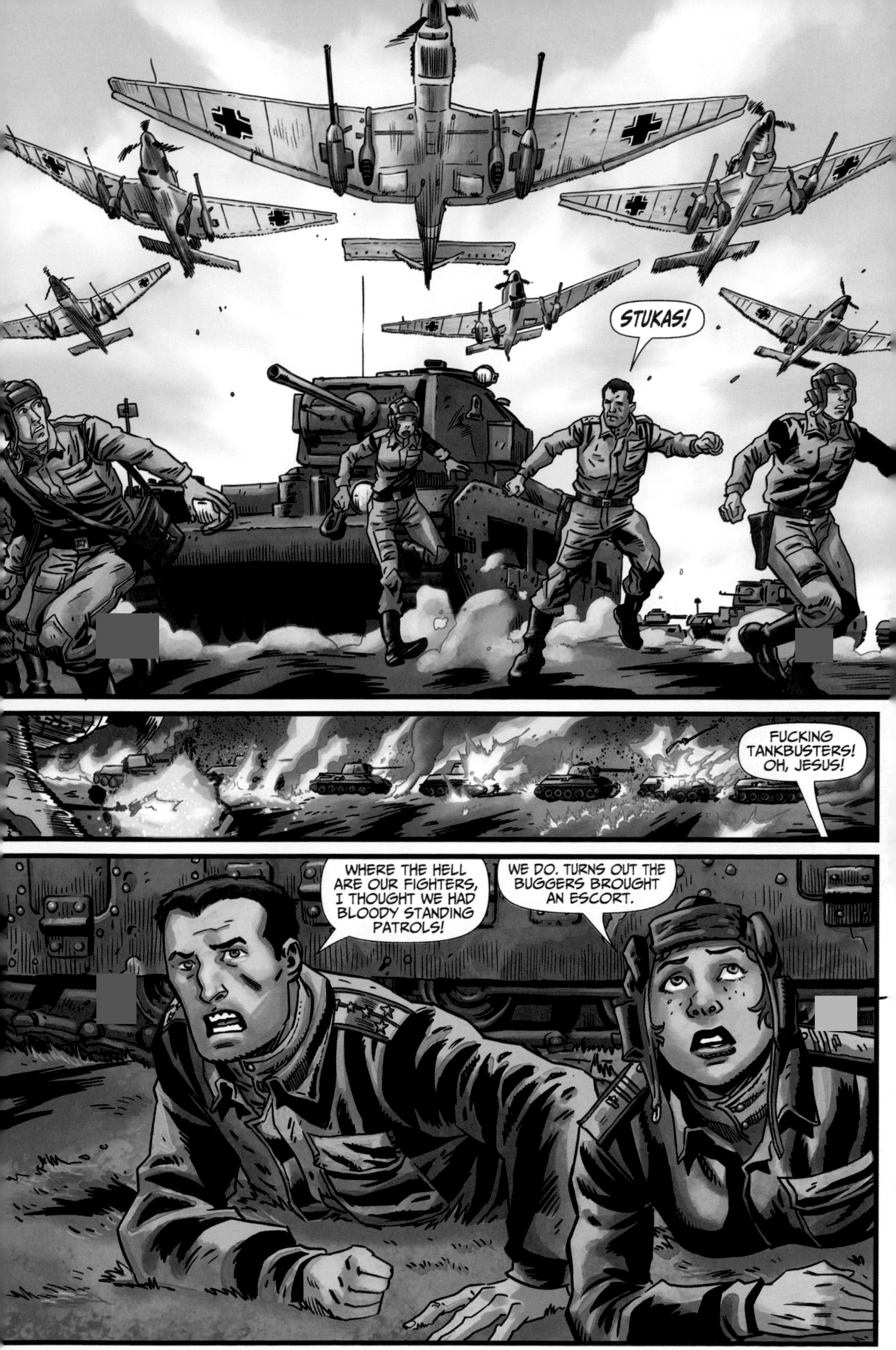
STUKAS!
FUCKING TANKBUSTERS! OH, JESUS!
WHERE THE HELL ARE OUR FIGHTERS, I THOUGHT WE HAD BLOODY STANDING PATROLS!
WE DO. TURNS OUT THE BUGGERS BROUGHT AN ESCORT.

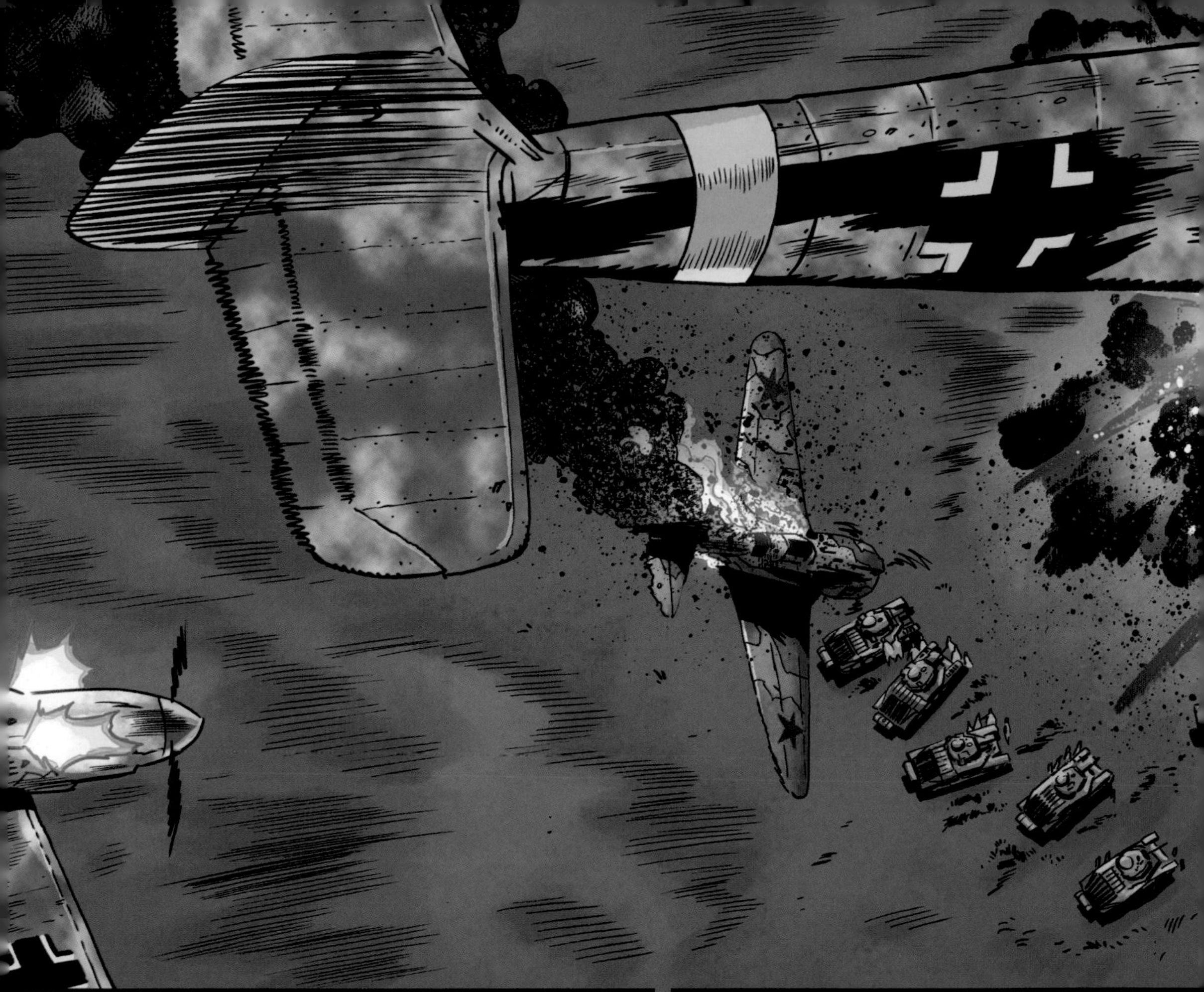

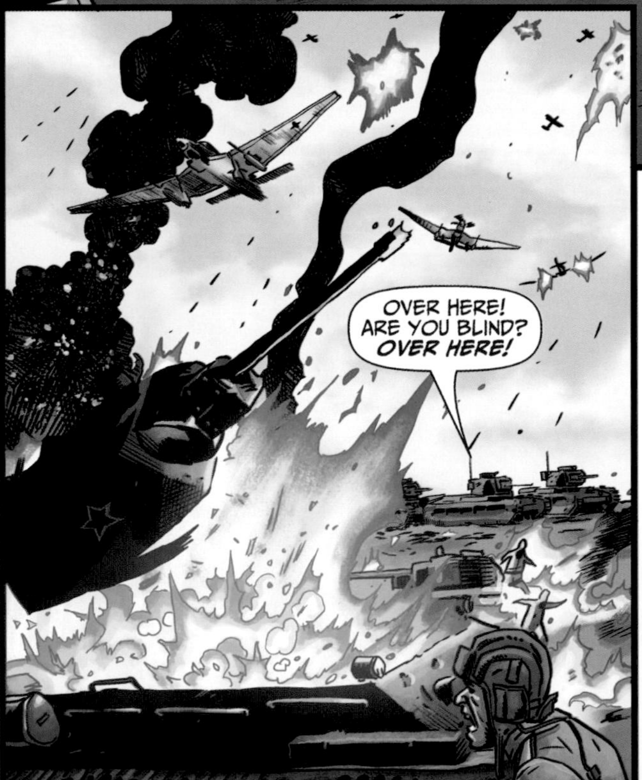
OVER HERE! ARE YOU BLIND? OVER HERE!

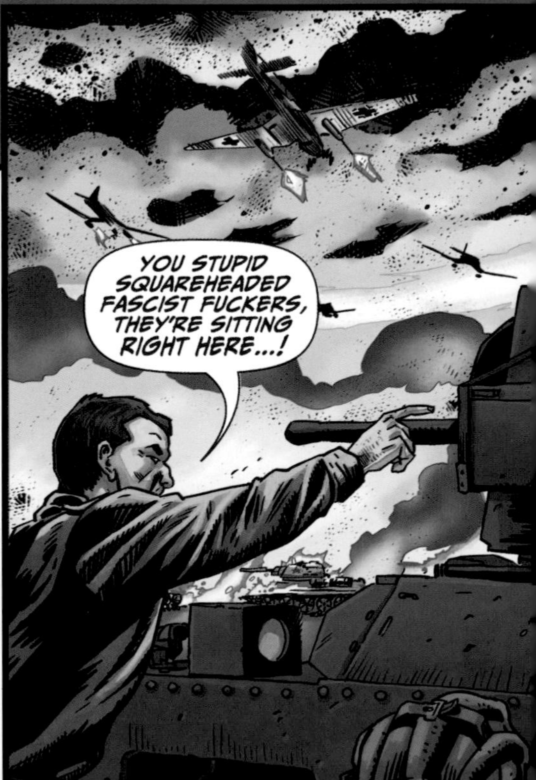
YOU STUPID SQUAREHEADED FASCIST FUCKERS, THEY'RE SITTING RIGHT HERE...!

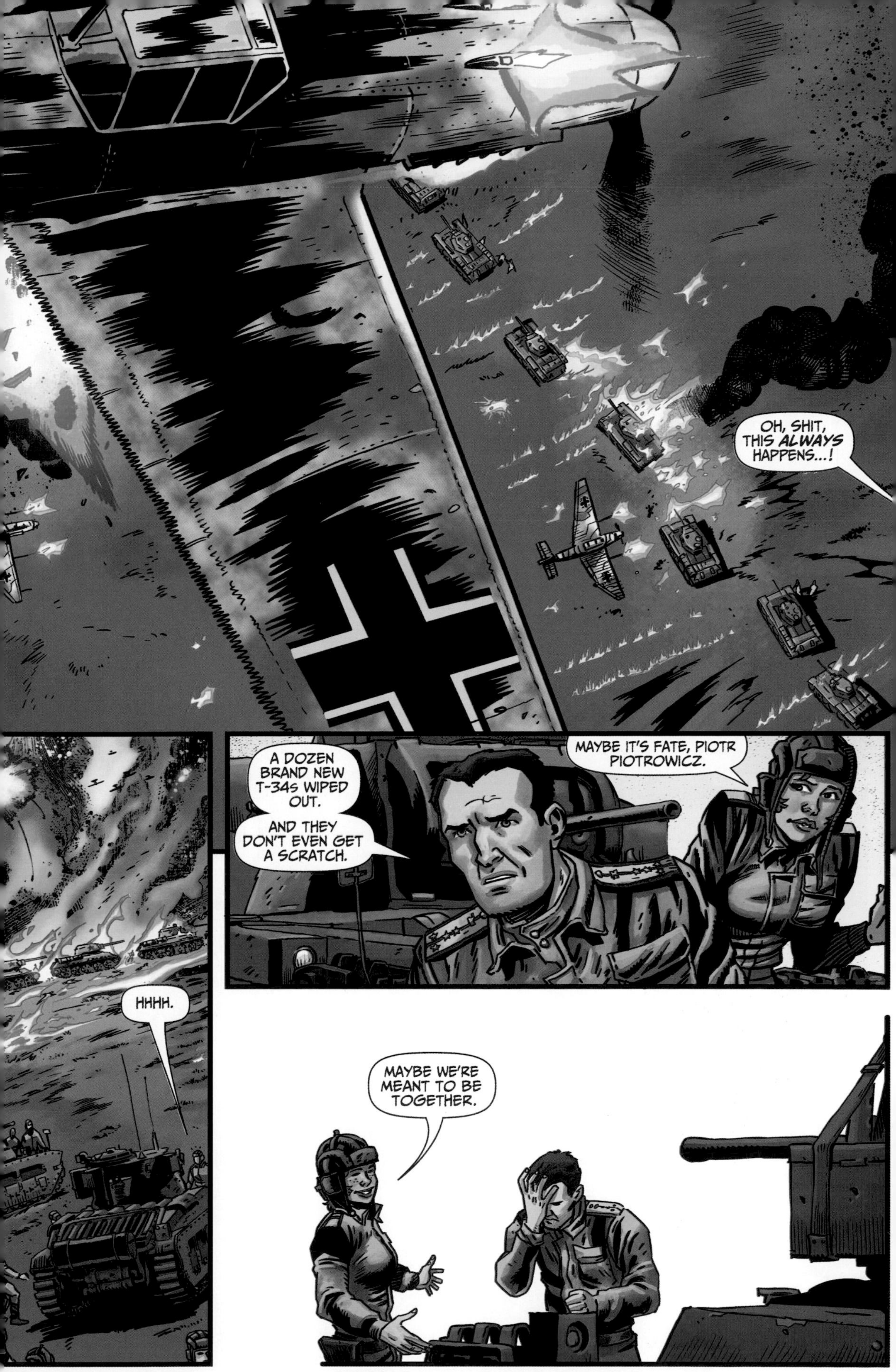
OH, SHIT, THIS ALWAYS HAPPENS...!
A DOZEN BRAND NEW T-34s WIPED OUT.
AND THEY DON'T EVEN GET A SCRATCH.
MAYBE IT'S FATE, PIOTR PIOTROWICZ.
HHHH.
MAYBE WE'RE MEANT TO BE TOGETHER.

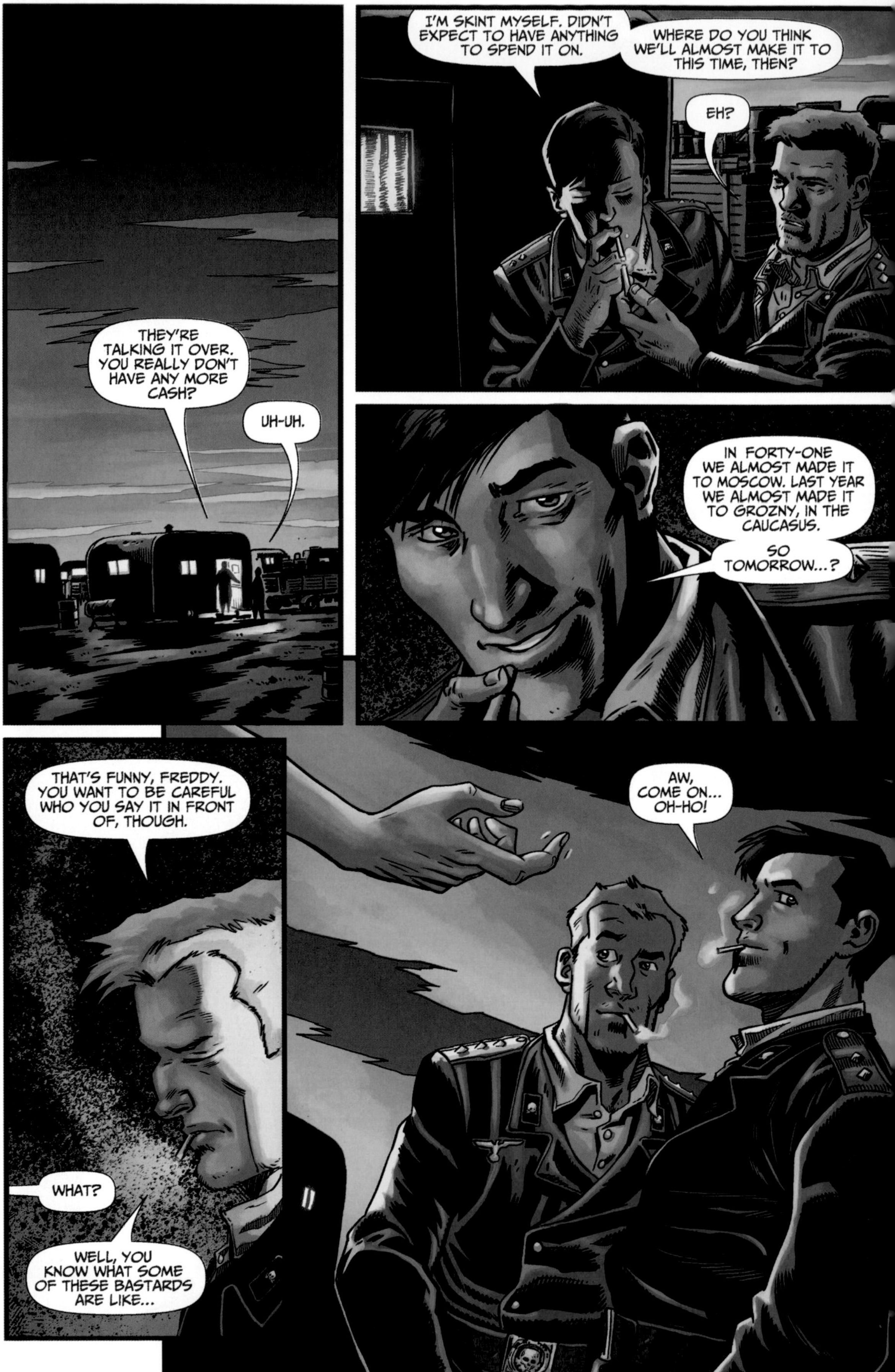
THEY'RE TALKING IT OVER. YOU REALLY DON'T HAVE ANY MORE CASH?
UH-UH.
I'M SKINT MYSELF. DIDN'T EXPECT TO HAVE ANYTHING TO SPEND IT ON.
WHERE DO YOU THINK WE'LL ALMOST MAKE IT TO THIS TIME, THEN?
EH?
IN FORTY-ONE WE ALMOST MADE IT TO MOSCOW. LAST YEAR WE ALMOST MADE IT TO GROZNY, IN THE CAUCASUS.
SO TOMORROW...?
THAT'S FUNNY, FREDDY. YOU WANT TO BE CAREFUL WHO YOU SAY IT IN FRONT OF, THOUGH.
AW, COME ON... OH-HO!
WHAT?
WELL, YOU KNOW WHAT SOME OF THESE BASTARDS ARE LIKE...

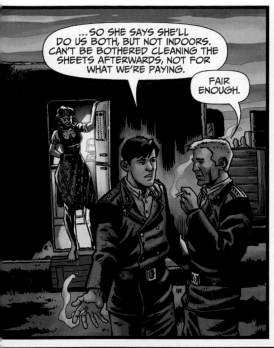

...SO SHE SAYS SHE'LL DO US BOTH, BUT NOT INDOORS. CAN'T BE BOTHERED CLEANING THE SHEETS AFTERWARDS, NOT FOR WHAT WE'RE PAYING.

FAIR ENOUGH.

AND FOR THE SAME REASON, IT'LL HAVE TO BE BOTH OF US AT ONCE. TIME IS MONEY, APPARENTLY.

NO FUCKING WAY...!

WHY NOT?

BECAUSE IF I'M WORKING AWAY AT *ANASTASIA* OVER HERE, THE LAST THING I WANT TO SEE AT THE MAGIC MOMENT IS YOUR GRINNING FUCKING MUG AT THE OTHER END!

UH...WELL... THE THING IS, I THINK IT'S GOING TO BE THIS OR NOTHING...

OH, BLOODY HELL!

AND I MEAN CONSIDERING WHAT'S HAPPENING TOMORROW, IT MIGHT BE OUR LAST CHANCE FOR QUITE A WHILE...

OH, JESUS--!

OUR LAST CHANCE ALTOGETHER, IF OUR LUCK RUNS OUT.

OH, GOD--!

WHAT D'YOU THINK?

МАТИЛЬДА

I THINK WE'RE NOT READY.

I MEANT...

THERE'VE BEEN ATTACKS REPORTED FARTHER ALONG THE LINE TODAY, WITH WAFFEN S.S. APPARENTLY INVOLVED. THIS BLOODY BATTLE'S ALREADY STARTED AND *WE'RE NOT READY*...

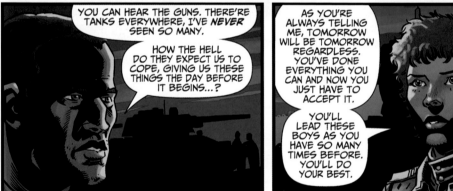

YOU CAN HEAR THE GUNS. THERE'RE TANKS EVERYWHERE, I'VE *NEVER* SEEN SO MANY.

HOW THE HELL DO THEY EXPECT US TO COPE, GIVING US THESE THINGS THE DAY BEFORE IT BEGINS...?

AS YOU'RE ALWAYS TELLING ME, TOMORROW WILL BE TOMORROW REGARDLESS. YOU'VE DONE EVERYTHING YOU CAN AND NOW YOU JUST HAVE TO ACCEPT IT.

YOU'LL LEAD THESE BOYS AS YOU HAVE SO MANY TIMES BEFORE. YOU'LL DO YOUR BEST.

PIOTR PIOTROWICZ, REALLY, WHAT ELSE IS THERE?

GINGER GINGEROVA.

WHERE WOULD I EVER BE WITHOUT YOU?

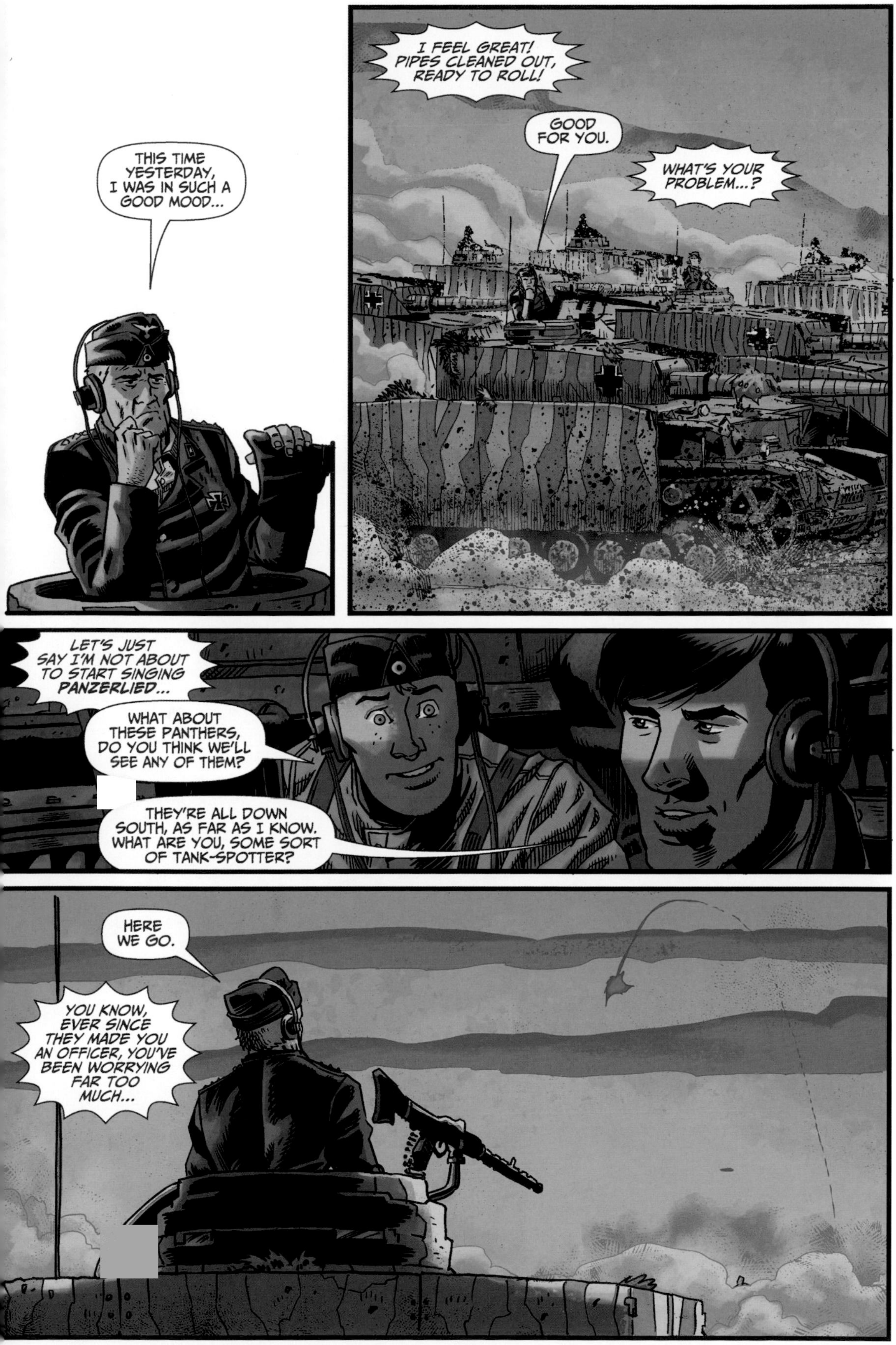
THIS TIME YESTERDAY, I WAS IN SUCH A GOOD MOOD...
I FEEL GREAT! PIPES CLEANED OUT, READY TO ROLL!
GOOD FOR YOU.
WHAT'S YOUR PROBLEM...?
LET'S JUST SAY I'M NOT ABOUT TO START SINGING PANZERLIED...
WHAT ABOUT THESE PANTHERS, DO YOU THINK WE'LL SEE ANY OF THEM?
THEY'RE ALL DOWN SOUTH, AS FAR AS I KNOW. WHAT ARE YOU, SOME SORT OF TANK-SPOTTER?
HERE WE GO.
YOU KNOW, EVER SINCE THEY MADE YOU AN OFFICER, YOU'VE BEEN WORRYING FAR TOO MUCH...

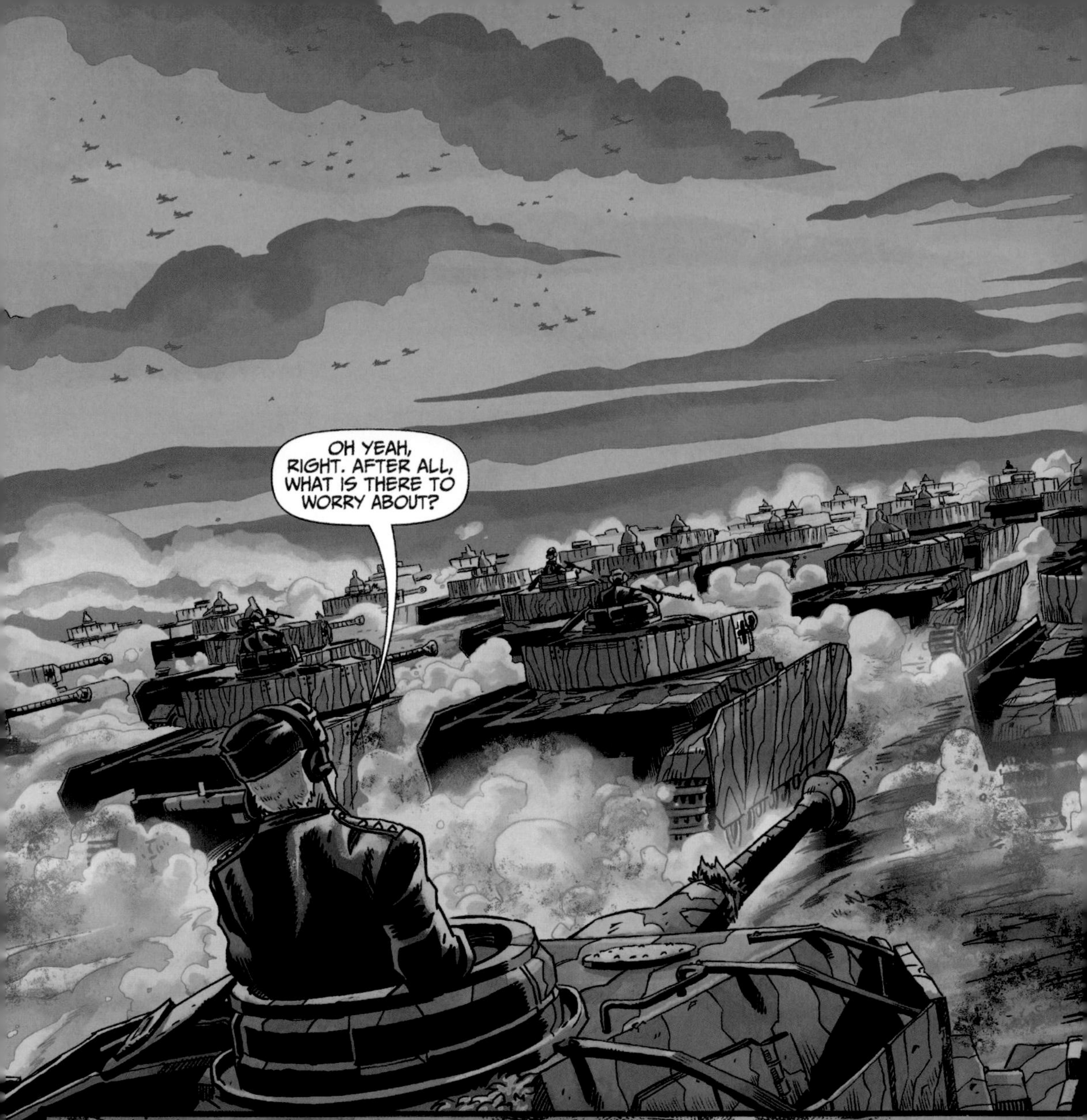
OH YEAH, RIGHT. AFTER ALL, WHAT IS THERE TO WORRY ABOUT?

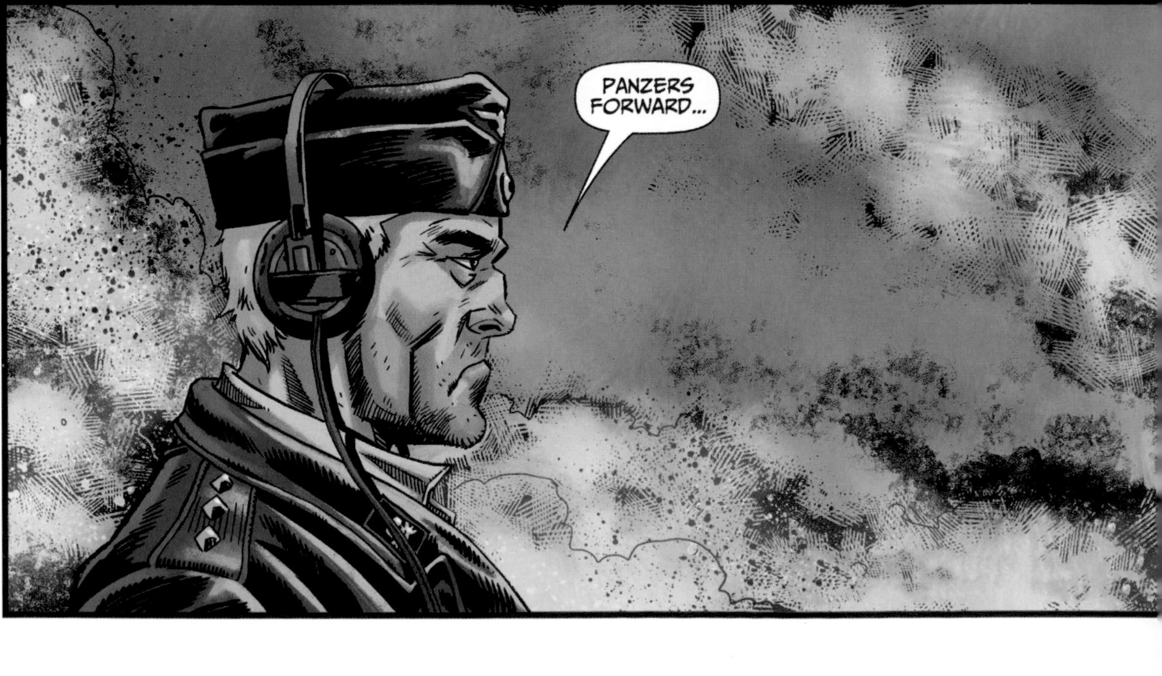
PANZERS FORWARD...

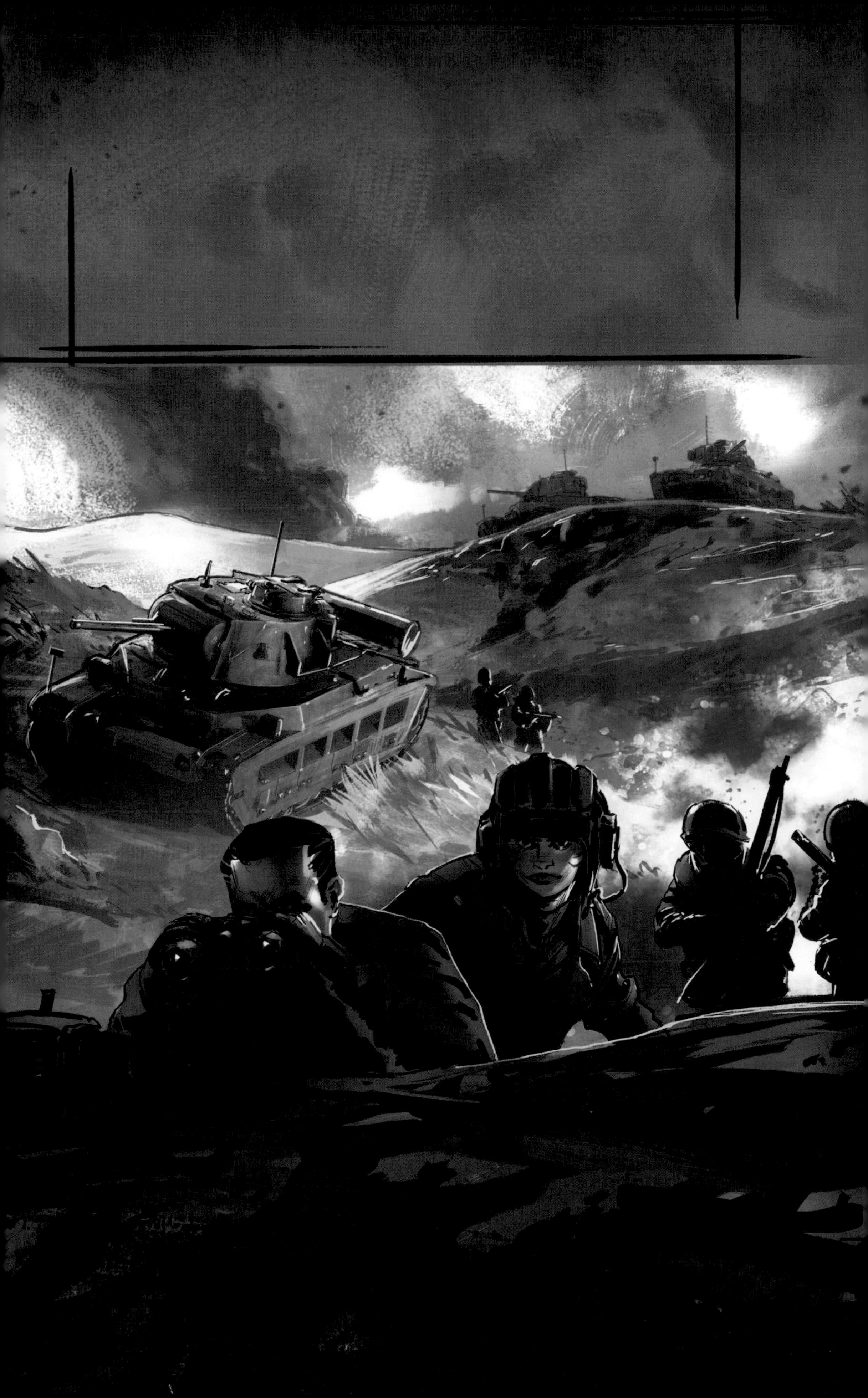

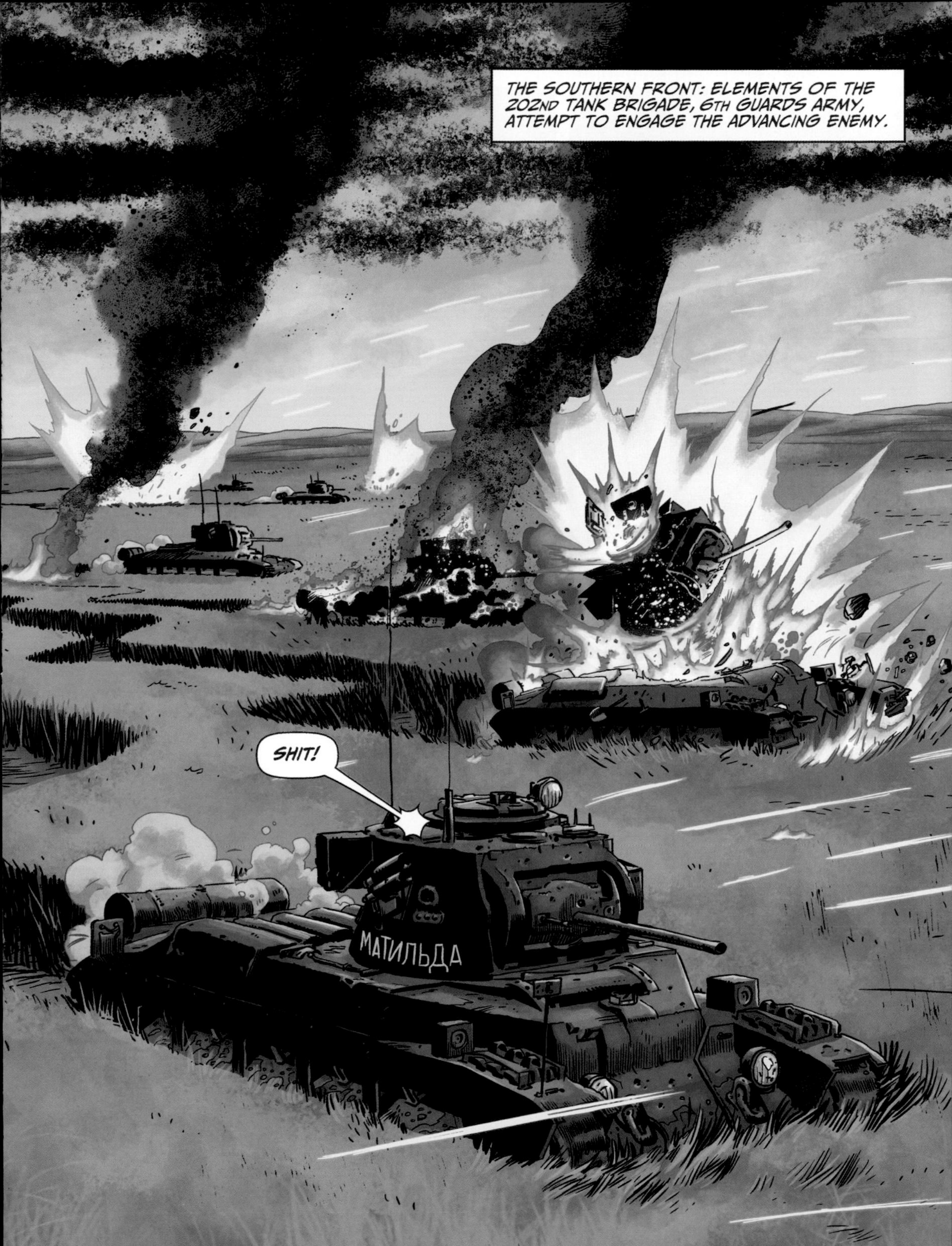
THE SOUTHERN FRONT: ELEMENTS OF THE 202ND TANK BRIGADE, 6TH GUARDS ARMY, ATTEMPT TO ENGAGE THE ADVANCING ENEMY.
SHIT!
МАТИЛЬДА

2: WALTZING MATILDA

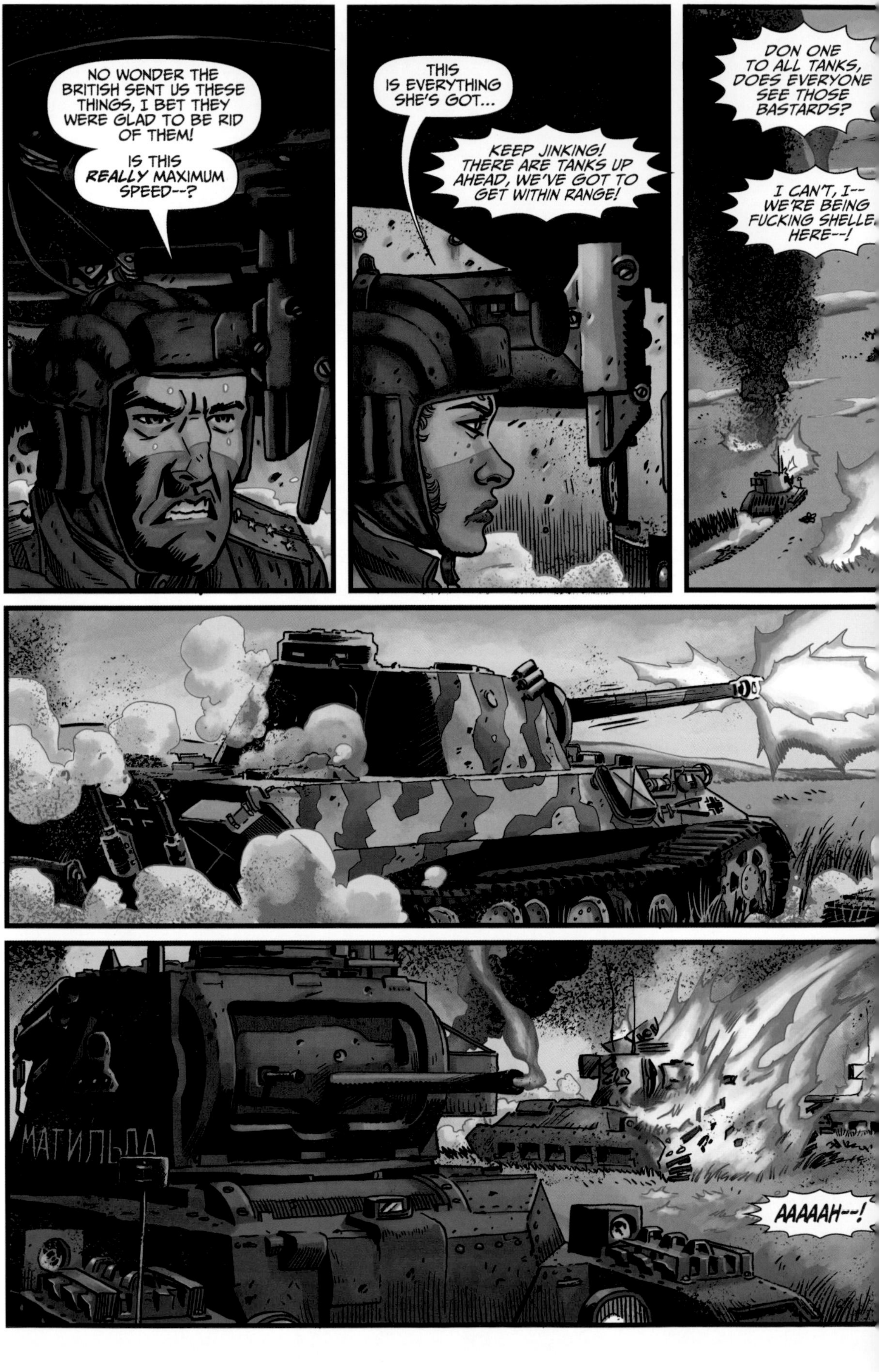
NO WONDER THE BRITISH SENT US THESE THINGS, I BET THEY WERE GLAD TO BE RID OF THEM!
IS THIS *REALLY* MAXIMUM SPEED--?
THIS IS EVERYTHING SHE'S GOT...
KEEP JINKING! THERE ARE TANKS UP AHEAD, WE'VE GOT TO GET WITHIN RANGE!
DON ONE TO ALL TANKS, DOES EVERYONE SEE THOSE BASTARDS?
I CAN'T, I-- WE'RE BEING FUCKING SHELLE HERE--!
МАТИЛЬДА
AAAAAH--!

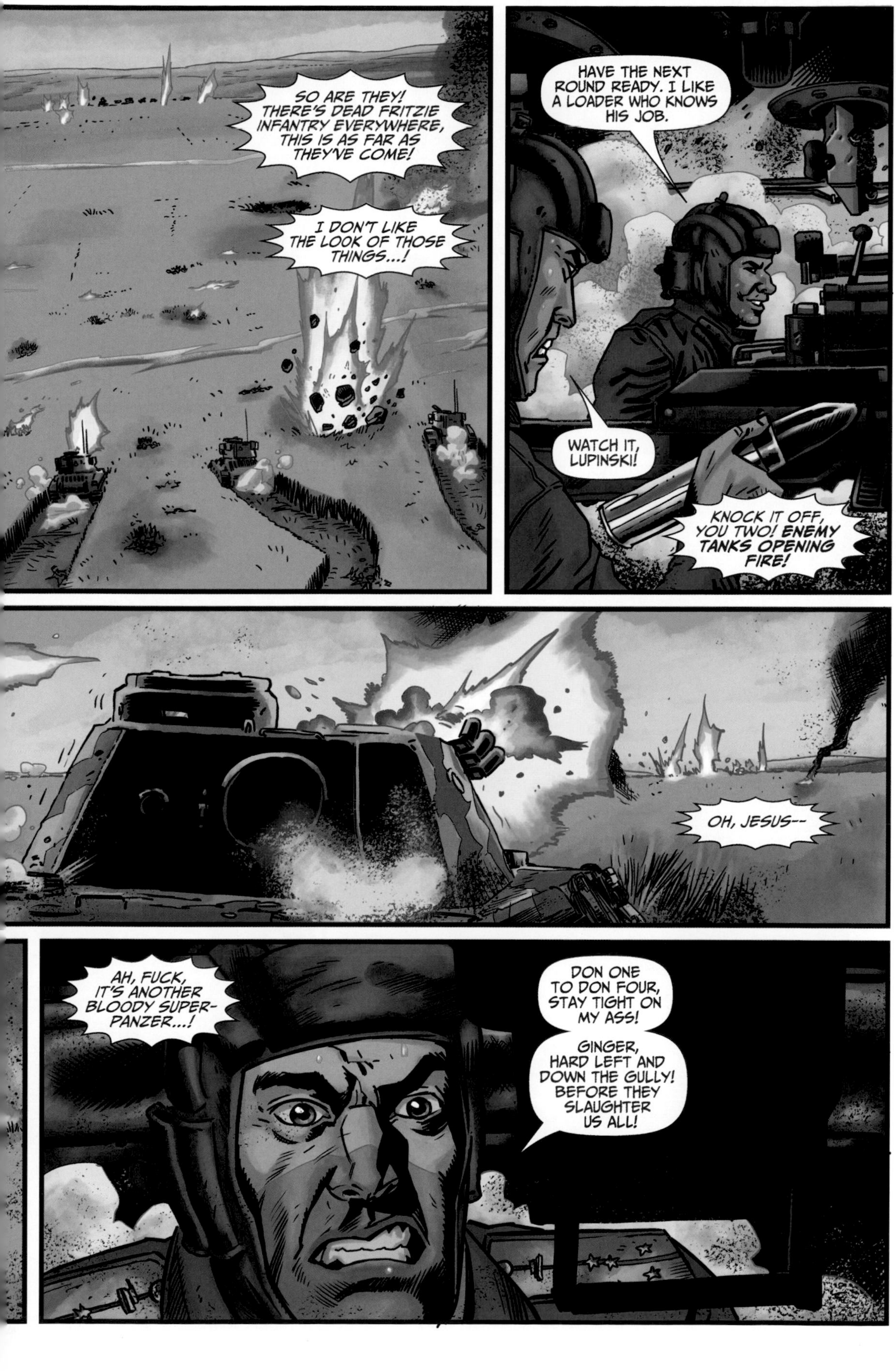
SO ARE THEY! THERE'S DEAD FRITZIE INFANTRY EVERYWHERE, THIS IS AS FAR AS THEY'VE COME!
I DON'T LIKE THE LOOK OF THOSE THINGS...!
HAVE THE NEXT ROUND READY. I LIKE A LOADER WHO KNOWS HIS JOB.
WATCH IT, LUPINSKI!
KNOCK IT OFF, YOU TWO! ENEMY TANKS OPENING FIRE!
OH, JESUS--
AH, FUCK, IT'S ANOTHER BLOODY SUPER-PANZER...!
DON ONE TO DON FOUR, STAY TIGHT ON MY ASS!
GINGER, HARD LEFT AND DOWN THE GULLY! BEFORE THEY SLAUGHTER US ALL!

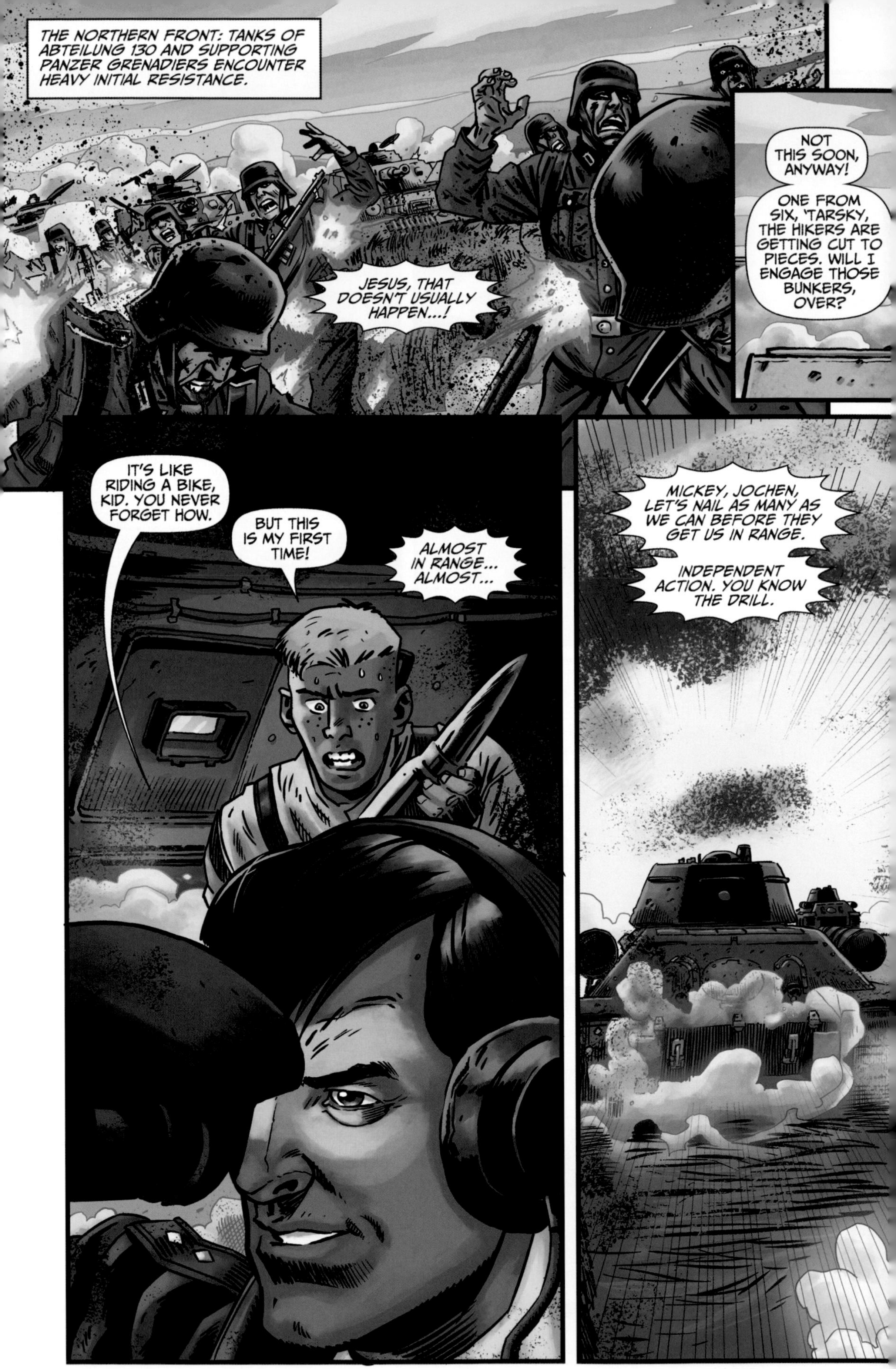
THE NORTHERN FRONT: TANKS OF ABTEILUNG 130 AND SUPPORTING PANZER GRENADIERS ENCOUNTER HEAVY INITIAL RESISTANCE.
JESUS, THAT DOESN'T USUALLY HAPPEN...!
NOT THIS SOON, ANYWAY!
ONE FROM SIX, 'TARSKY, THE HIKERS ARE GETTING CUT TO PIECES. WILL I ENGAGE THOSE BUNKERS, OVER?
IT'S LIKE RIDING A BIKE, KID. YOU NEVER FORGET HOW.
BUT THIS IS MY FIRST TIME!
ALMOST IN RANGE... ALMOST...
MICKEY, JOCHEN, LET'S NAIL AS MANY AS WE CAN BEFORE THEY GET US IN RANGE.
INDEPENDENT ACTION. YOU KNOW THE DRILL.

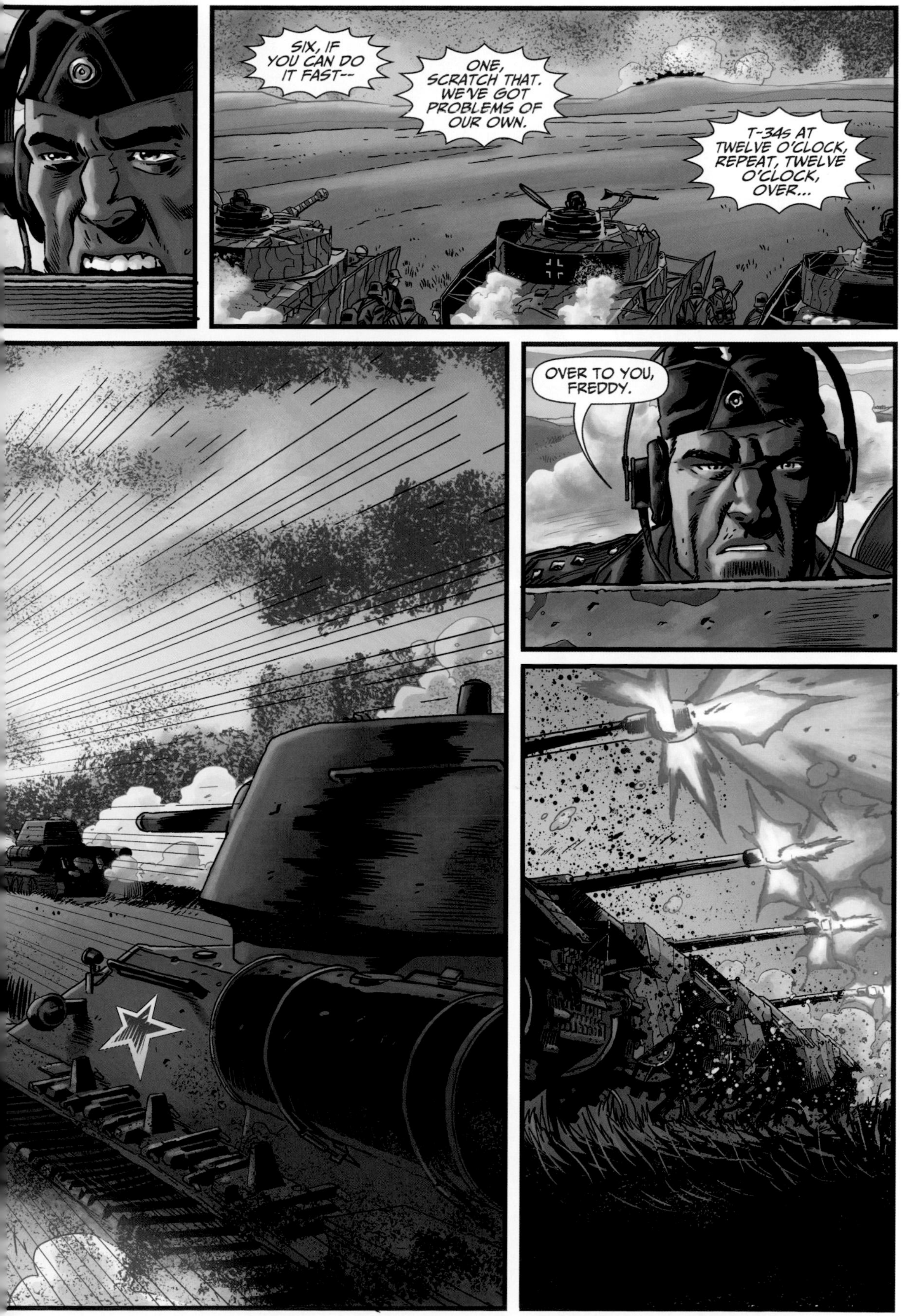
SIX, IF YOU CAN DO IT FAST--
ONE, SCRATCH THAT. WE'VE GOT PROBLEMS OF OUR OWN.
T-34s AT TWELVE O'CLOCK, REPEAT, TWELVE O'CLOCK, OVER...
OVER TO YOU, FREDDY.

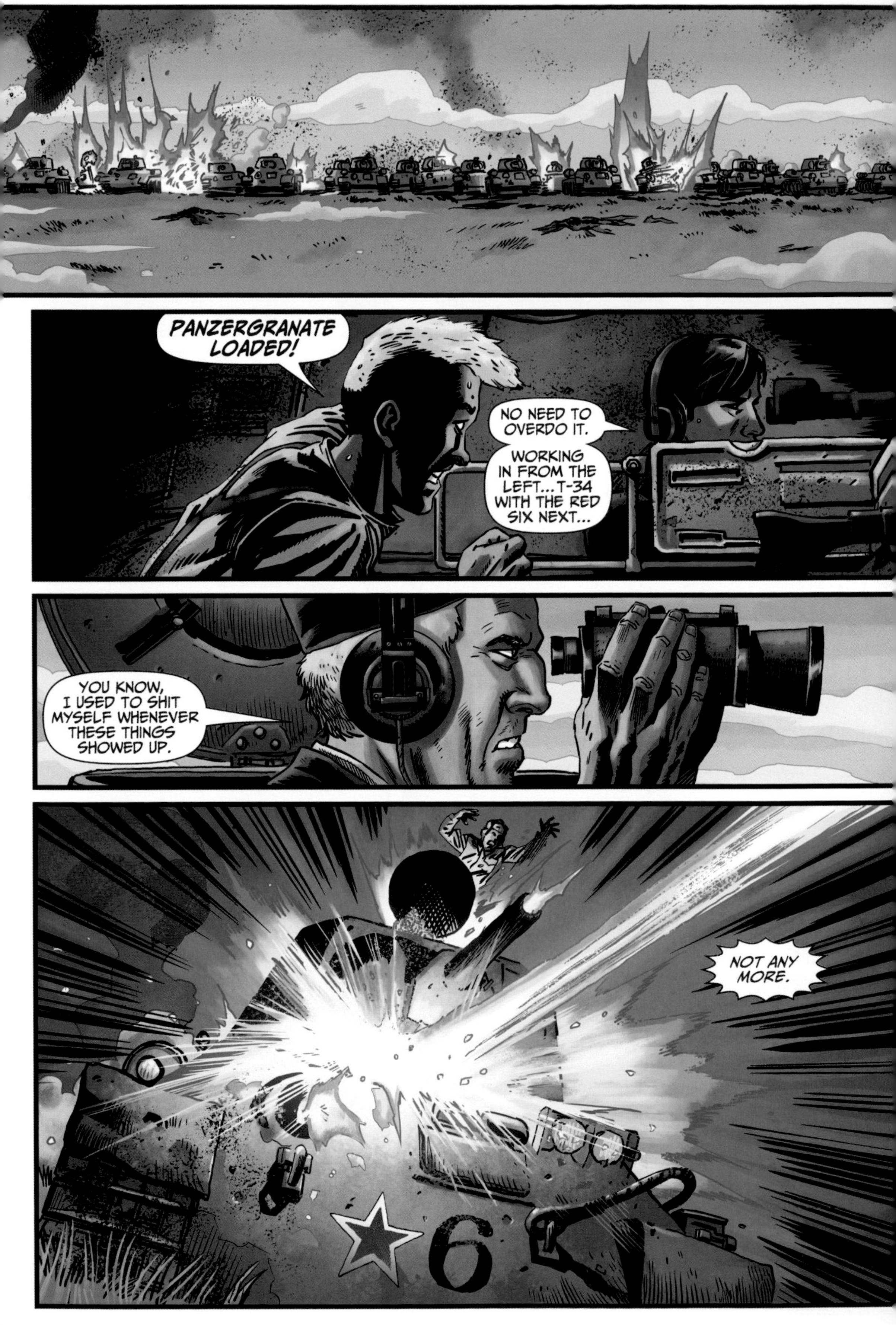
PANZERGRANATE LOADED!
NO NEED TO OVERDO IT.
WORKING IN FROM THE LEFT... T-34 WITH THE RED SIX NEXT...
YOU KNOW, I USED TO SHIT MYSELF WHENEVER THESE THINGS SHOWED UP.
NOT ANY MORE.

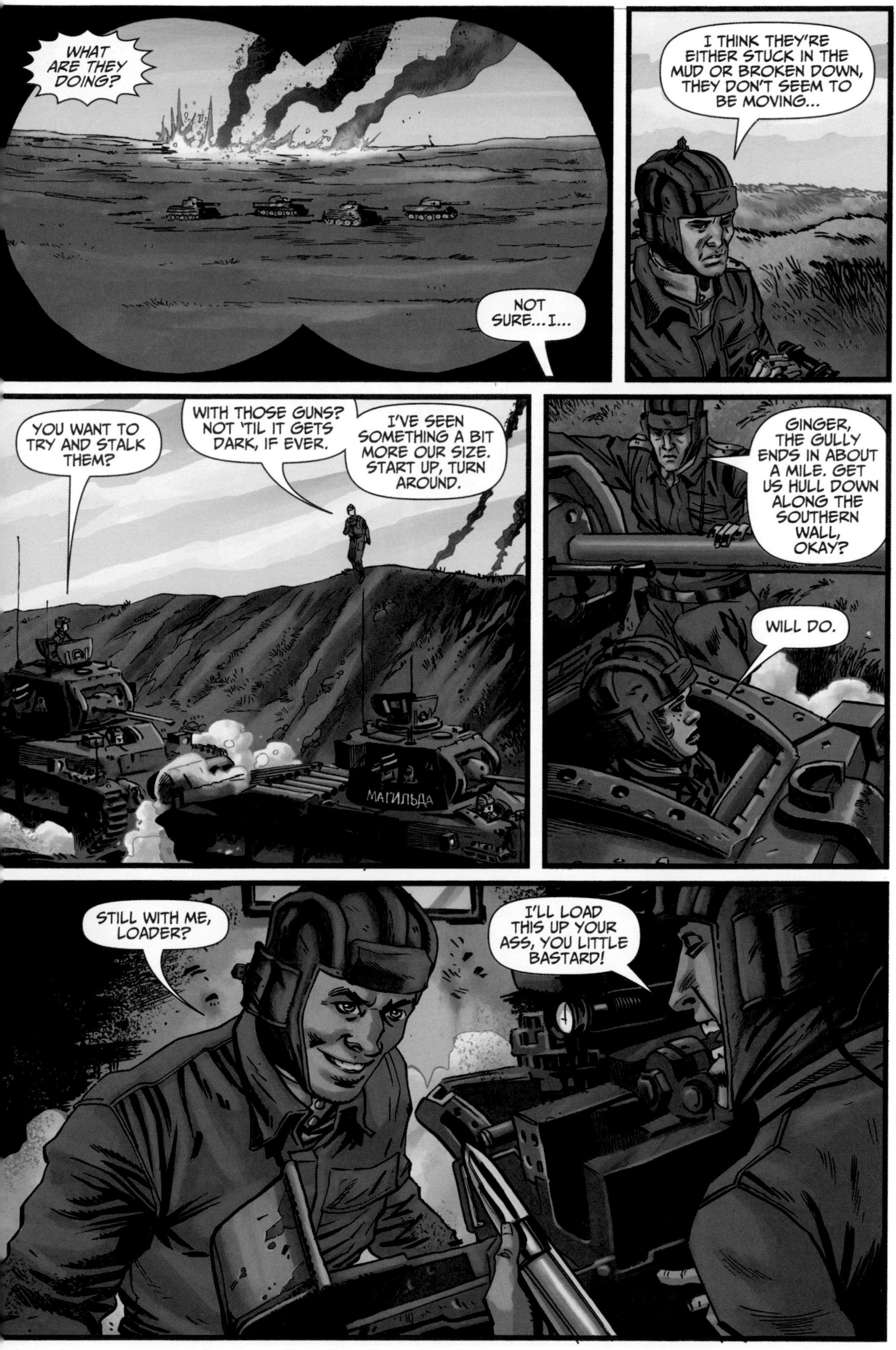
WHAT ARE THEY DOING?
NOT SURE... I...
I THINK THEY'RE EITHER STUCK IN THE MUD OR BROKEN DOWN, THEY DON'T SEEM TO BE MOVING...
YOU WANT TO TRY AND STALK THEM?
WITH THOSE GUNS? NOT 'TIL IT GETS DARK, IF EVER.
I'VE SEEN SOMETHING A BIT MORE OUR SIZE. START UP, TURN AROUND.
МАГИЛЬДА
GINGER, THE GULLY ENDS IN ABOUT A MILE. GET US HULL DOWN ALONG THE SOUTHERN WALL, OKAY?
WILL DO.
STILL WITH ME, LOADER?
I'LL LOAD THIS UP YOUR ASS, YOU LITTLE BASTARD!

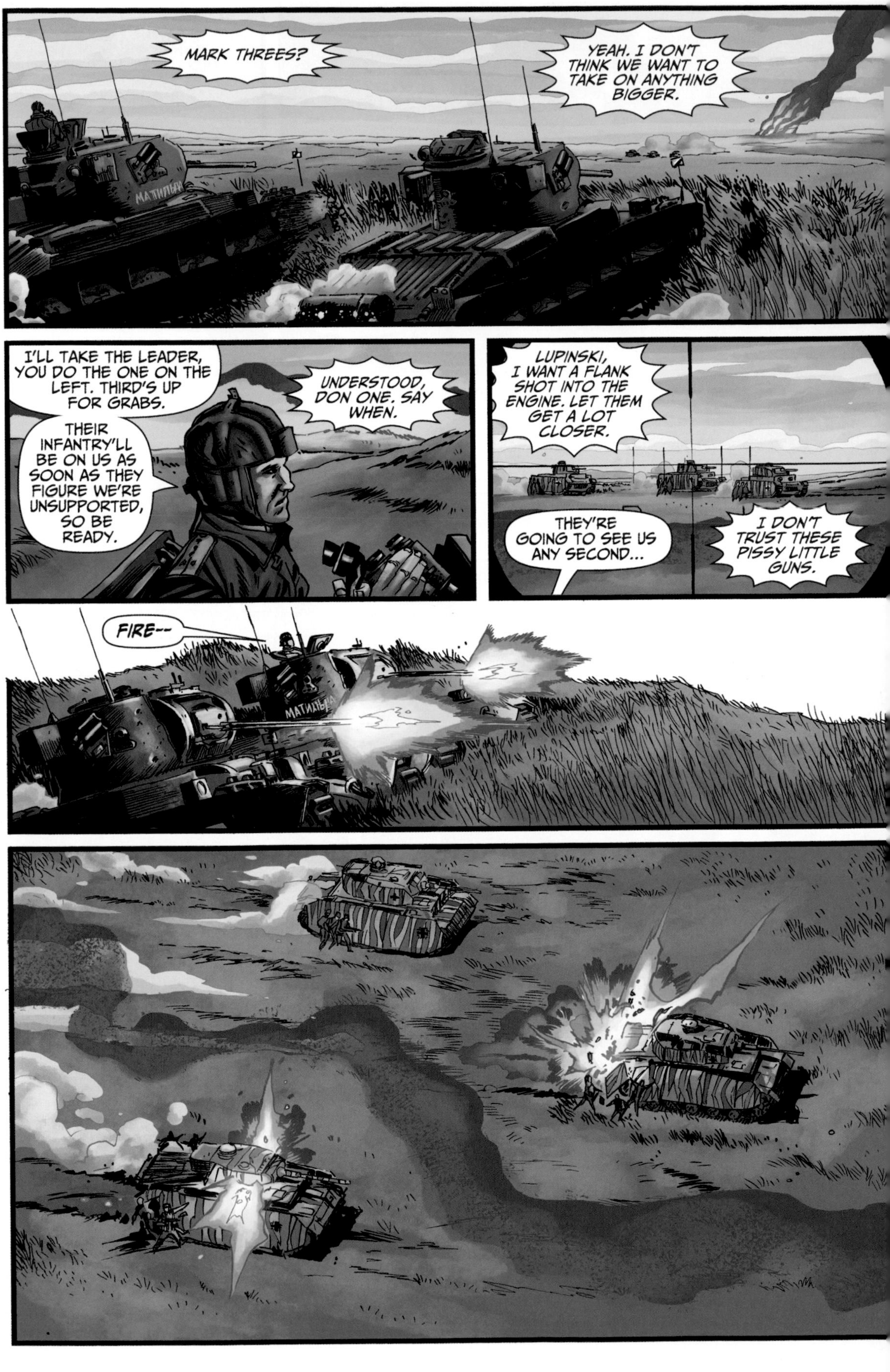
MARK THREES?
YEAH. I DON'T THINK WE WANT TO TAKE ON ANYTHING BIGGER.
I'LL TAKE THE LEADER, YOU DO THE ONE ON THE LEFT. THIRD'S UP FOR GRABS.
THEIR INFANTRY'LL BE ON US AS SOON AS THEY FIGURE WE'RE UNSUPPORTED, SO BE READY.
UNDERSTOOD, DON ONE. SAY WHEN.
LUPINSKI, I WANT A FLANK SHOT INTO THE ENGINE. LET THEM GET A LOT CLOSER.
THEY'RE GOING TO SEE US ANY SECOND...
I DON'T TRUST THESE PISSY LITTLE GUNS.
FIRE--

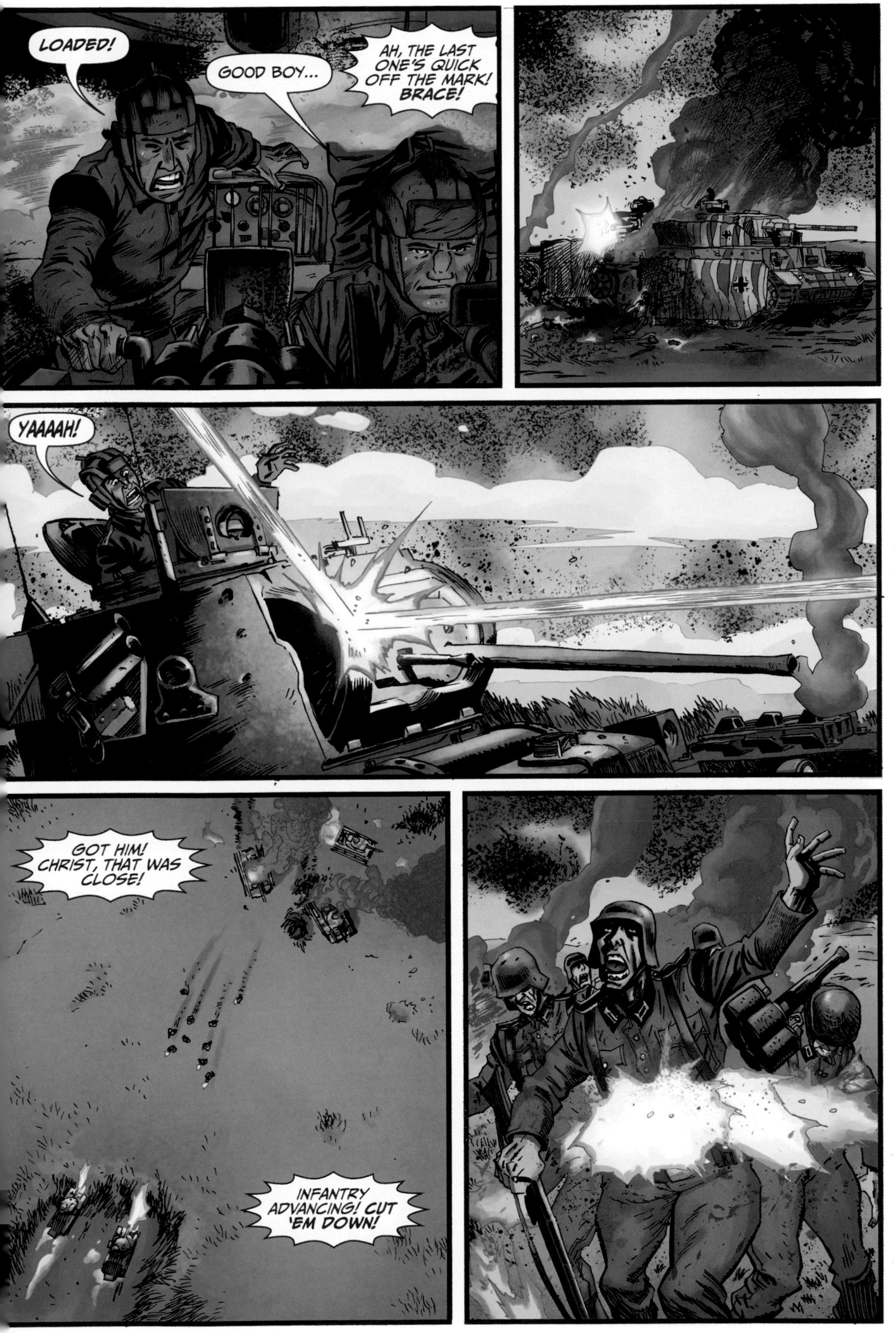
LOADED!
GOOD BOY...
AH, THE LAST ONE'S QUICK OFF THE MARK! BRACE!
YAAAAH!
GOT HIM! CHRIST, THAT WAS CLOSE!
INFANTRY ADVANCING! CUT 'EM DOWN!

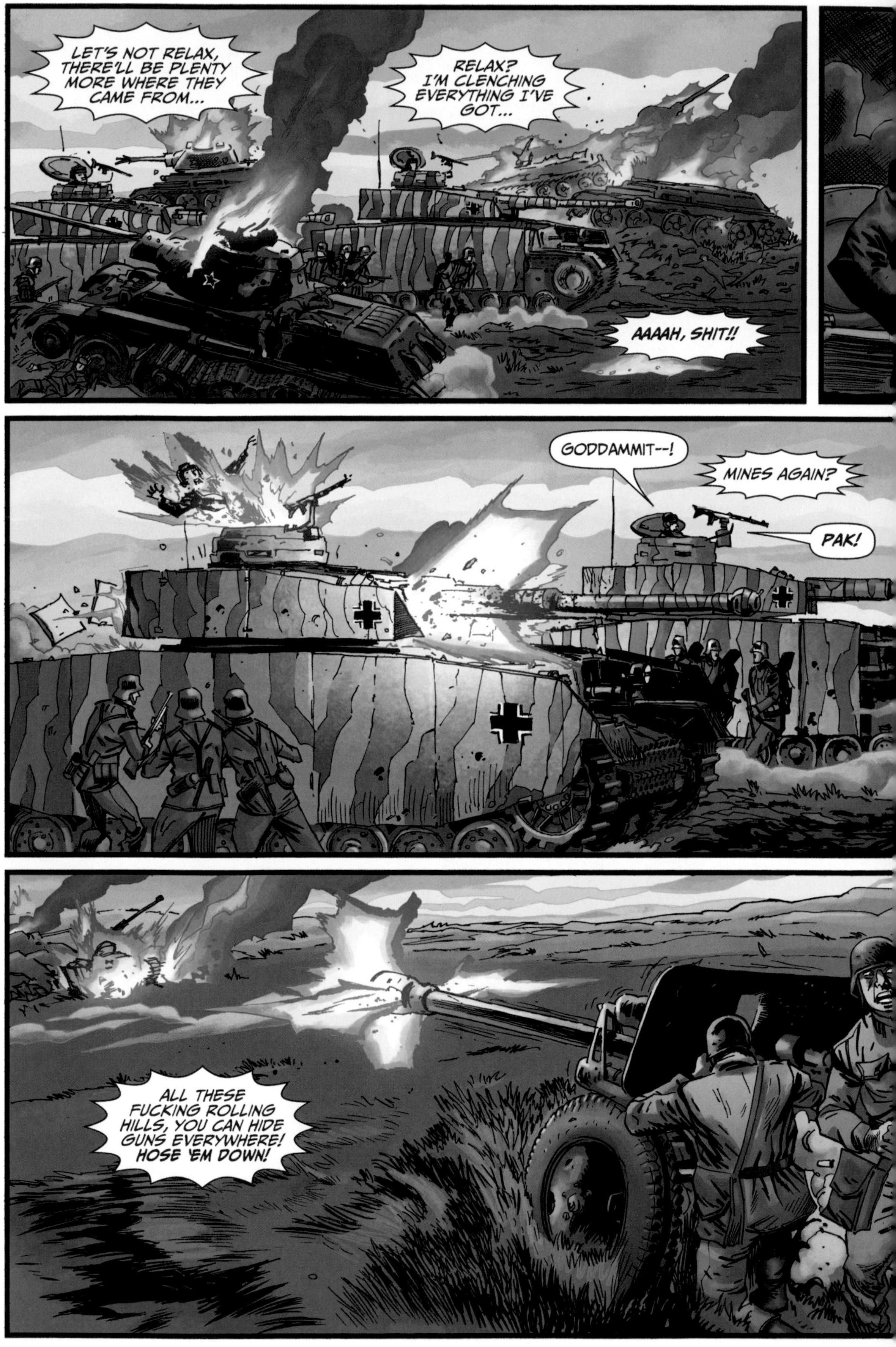
LET'S NOT RELAX, THERE'LL BE PLENTY MORE WHERE THEY CAME FROM...
RELAX? I'M CLENCHING EVERYTHING I'VE GOT...
AAAAH, SHIT!!
GODDAMMIT--!
MINES AGAIN?
PAK!
ALL THESE FUCKING ROLLING HILLS, YOU CAN HIDE GUNS EVERYWHERE! HOSE 'EM DOWN!

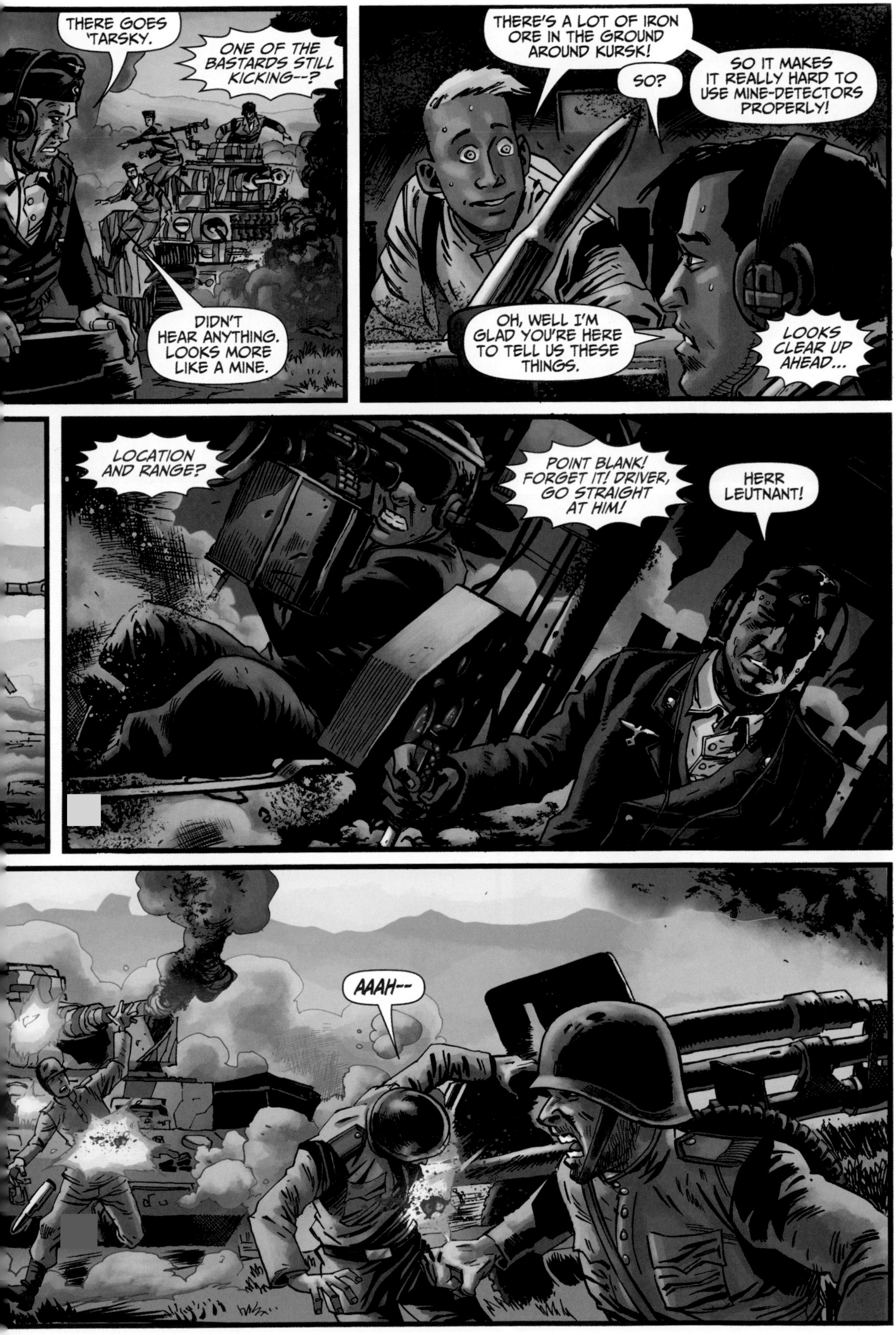
THERE GOES 'TARSKY.
ONE OF THE BASTARDS STILL KICKING--?
DIDN'T HEAR ANYTHING. LOOKS MORE LIKE A MINE.
THERE'S A LOT OF IRON ORE IN THE GROUND AROUND KURSK!
SO?
SO IT MAKES IT REALLY HARD TO USE MINE-DETECTORS PROPERLY!
OH, WELL I'M GLAD YOU'RE HERE TO TELL US THESE THINGS.
LOOKS CLEAR UP AHEAD...
LOCATION AND RANGE?
POINT BLANK! FORGET IT! DRIVER, GO STRAIGHT AT HIM!
HERR LEUTNANT!
AAAH--

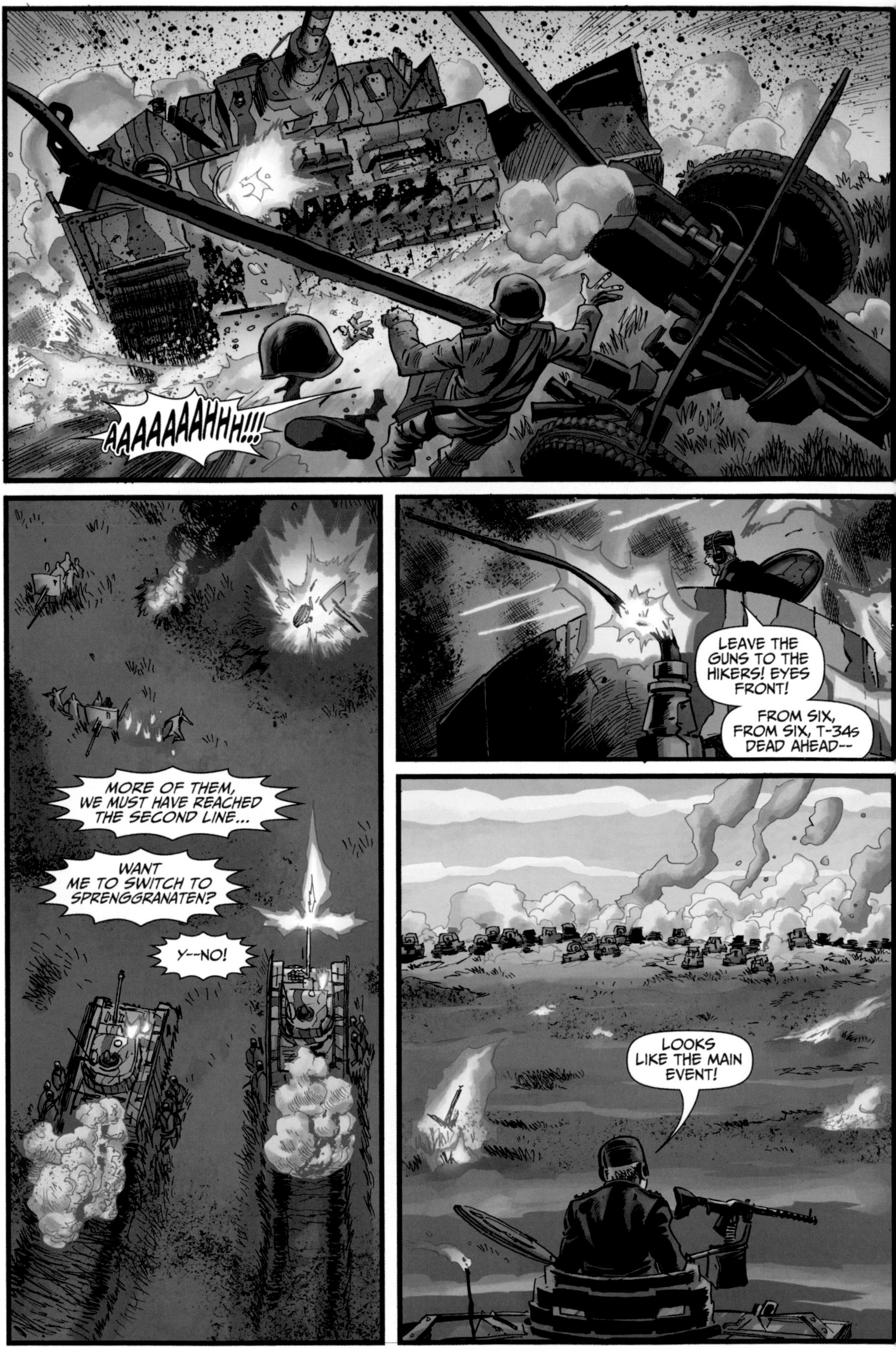
AAAAAAAHHH!!!
MORE OF THEM, WE MUST HAVE REACHED THE SECOND LINE...
WANT ME TO SWITCH TO SPRENGGRANATEN?
Y--NO!
LEAVE THE GUNS TO THE HIKERS! EYES FRONT!
FROM SIX, FROM SIX, T-34s DEAD AHEAD--
LOOKS LIKE THE MAIN EVENT!

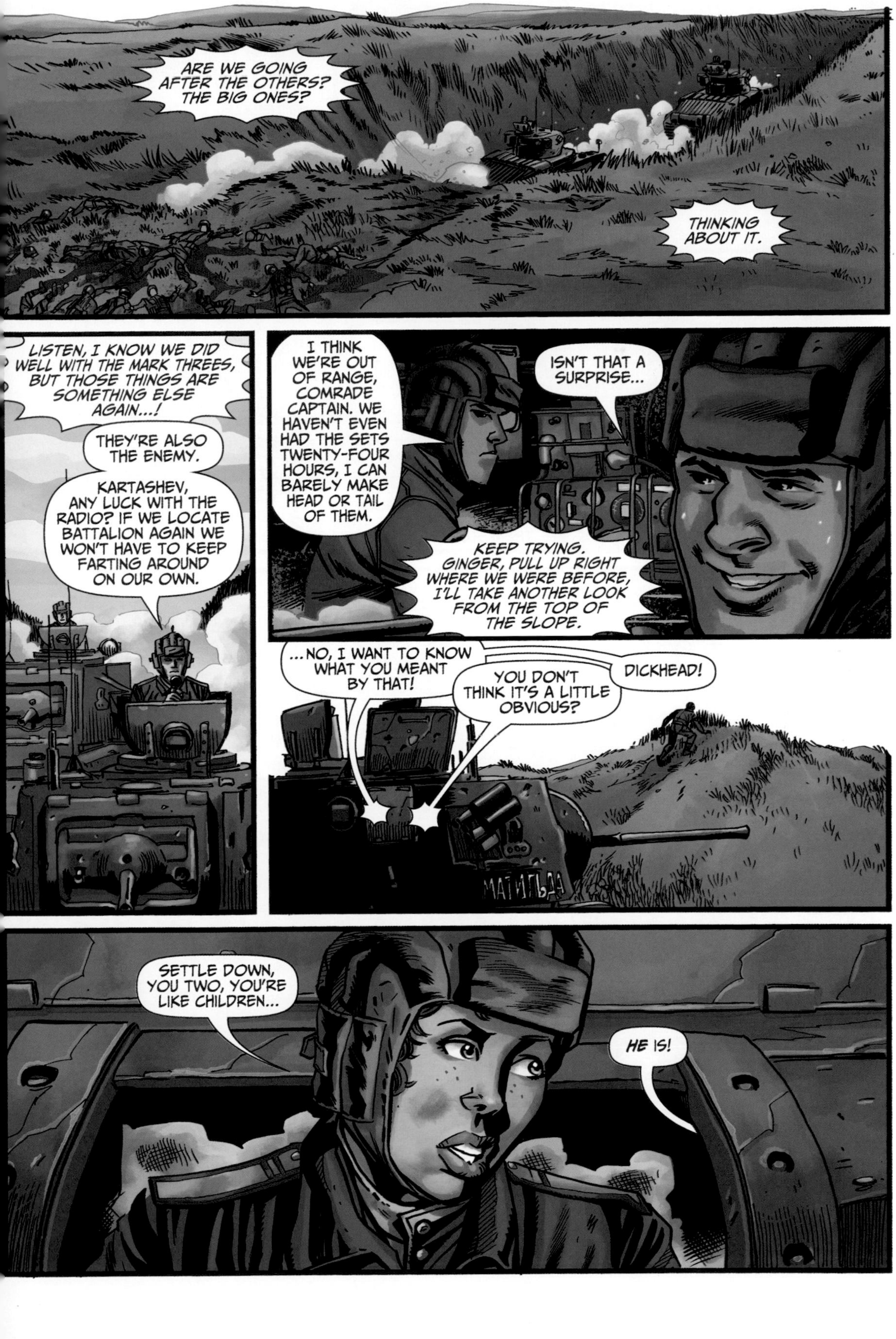

ARE WE GOING AFTER THE OTHERS? THE BIG ONES?
THINKING ABOUT IT.
LISTEN, I KNOW WE DID WELL WITH THE MARK THREES, BUT THOSE THINGS ARE SOMETHING ELSE AGAIN...!
THEY'RE ALSO THE ENEMY.
KARTASHEV, ANY LUCK WITH THE RADIO? IF WE LOCATE BATTALION AGAIN WE WON'T HAVE TO KEEP FARTING AROUND ON OUR OWN.
I THINK WE'RE OUT OF RANGE, COMRADE CAPTAIN. WE HAVEN'T EVEN HAD THE SETS TWENTY-FOUR HOURS, I CAN BARELY MAKE HEAD OR TAIL OF THEM.
ISN'T THAT A SURPRISE...
KEEP TRYING. GINGER, PULL UP RIGHT WHERE WE WERE BEFORE, I'LL TAKE ANOTHER LOOK FROM THE TOP OF THE SLOPE.
DICKHEAD!
YOU DON'T THINK IT'S A LITTLE OBVIOUS?
...NO, I WANT TO KNOW WHAT YOU MEANT BY THAT!
МАТИЛЬДА
SETTLE DOWN, YOU TWO, YOU'RE LIKE CHILDREN...
HE IS!

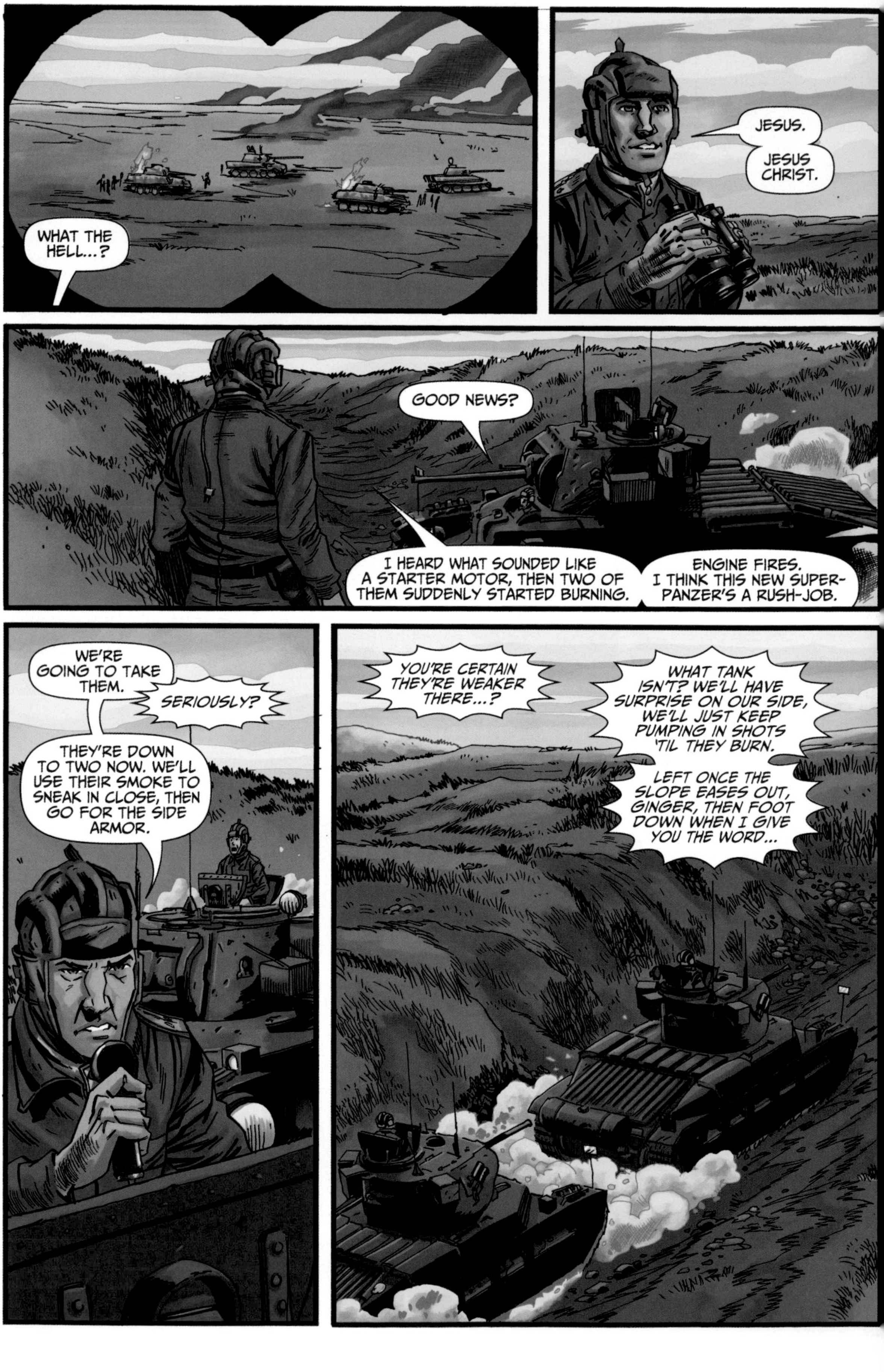
WHAT THE HELL...?
JESUS.
JESUS CHRIST.
GOOD NEWS?
I HEARD WHAT SOUNDED LIKE A STARTER MOTOR, THEN TWO OF THEM SUDDENLY STARTED BURNING.
ENGINE FIRES. I THINK THIS NEW SUPER-PANZER'S A RUSH-JOB.
WE'RE GOING TO TAKE THEM.
SERIOUSLY?
THEY'RE DOWN TO TWO NOW. WE'LL USE THEIR SMOKE TO SNEAK IN CLOSE, THEN GO FOR THE SIDE ARMOR.
YOU'RE CERTAIN THEY'RE WEAKER THERE...?
WHAT TANK ISN'T? WE'LL HAVE SURPRISE ON OUR SIDE, WE'LL JUST KEEP PUMPING IN SHOTS 'TIL THEY BURN.
LEFT ONCE THE SLOPE EASES OUT, GINGER, THEN FOOT DOWN WHEN I GIVE YOU THE WORD...

IT'S WORKING...!

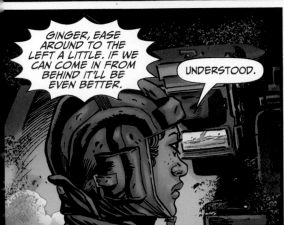

GINGER, EASE AROUND TO THE LEFT A LITTLE. IF WE CAN COME IN FROM BEHIND IT'LL BE EVEN BETTER.

UNDERSTOOD.

TRY AND KEEP UP WITH ME THIS TIME, MM? JUST RAM IT IN, DON'T WAIT TO BE TOLD...

YEAH, AS YOUR DEAR MOTHER SAYS WHEN THE FLEET'S IN TOWN!

SCHEISSE--!

ACHTUNG! ACHTUNG, PANZER!

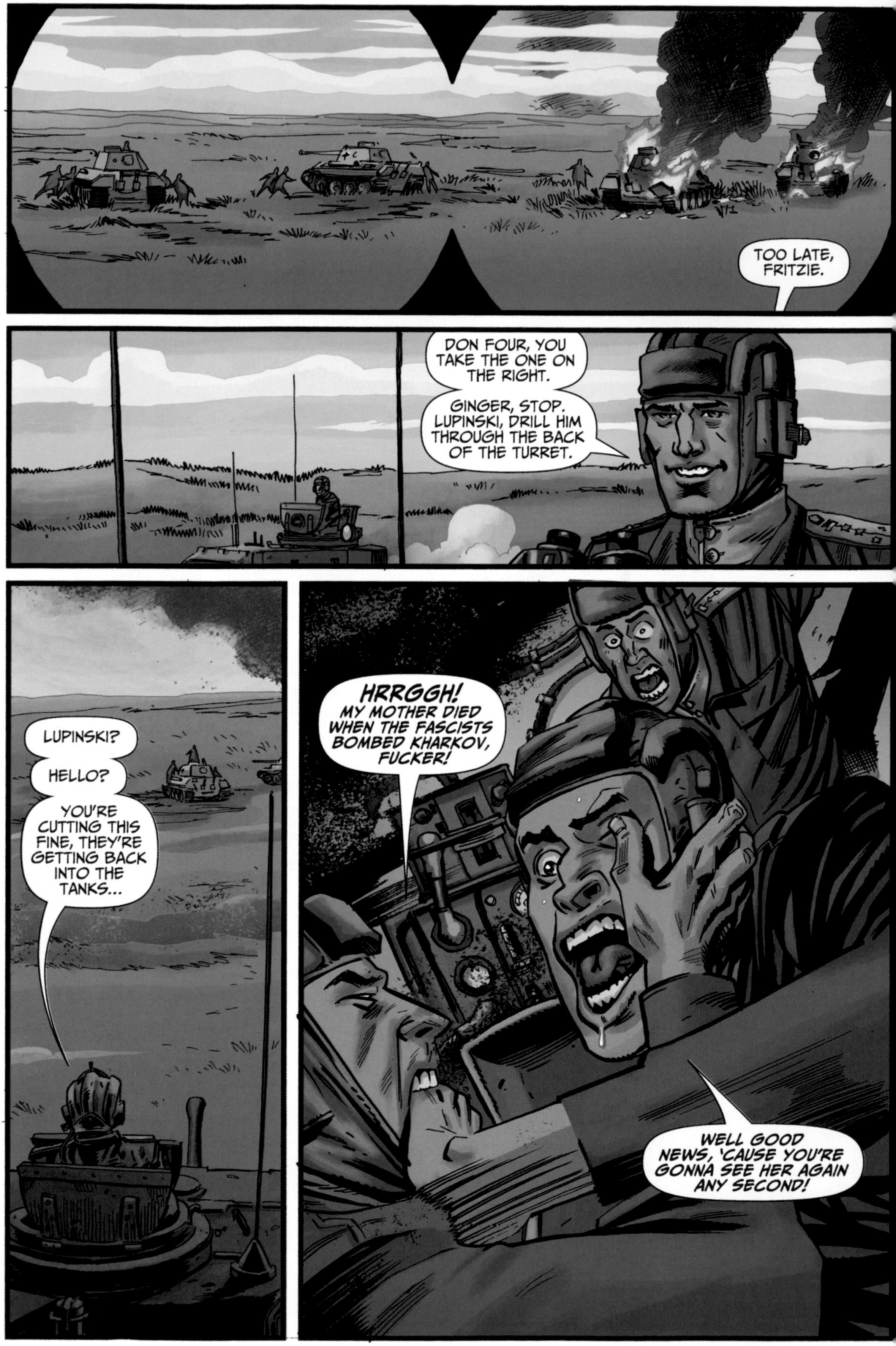
TOO LATE, FRITZIE.
DON FOUR, YOU TAKE THE ONE ON THE RIGHT.
GINGER, STOP. LUPINSKI, DRILL HIM THROUGH THE BACK OF THE TURRET.
LUPINSKI?
HELLO?
YOU'RE CUTTING THIS FINE, THEY'RE GETTING BACK INTO THE TANKS...
HRRGGH! MY MOTHER DIED WHEN THE FASCISTS BOMBED KHARKOV, FUCKER!
WELL GOOD NEWS, 'CAUSE YOU'RE GONNA SEE HER AGAIN ANY SECOND!

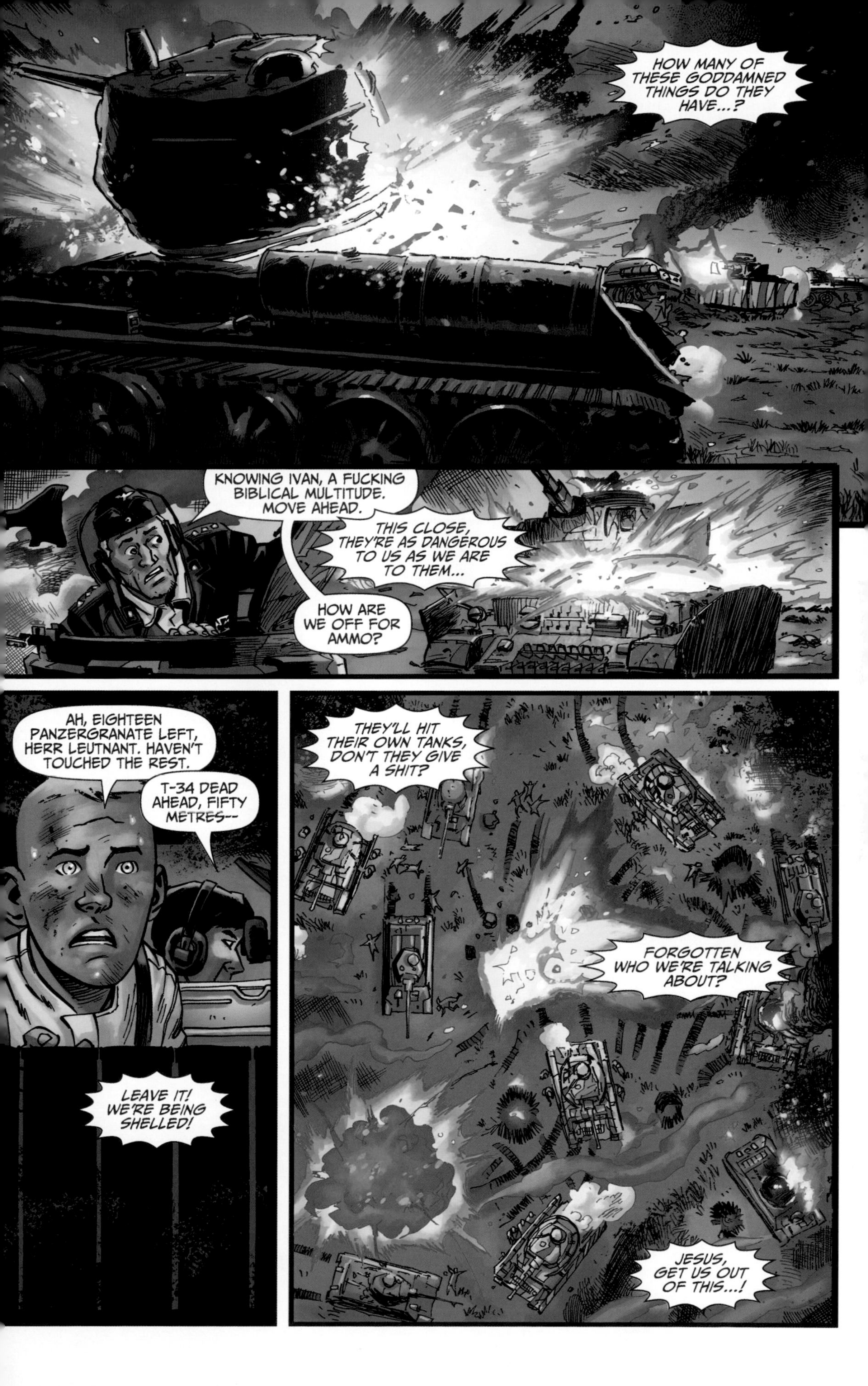
HOW MANY OF THESE GODDAMNED THINGS DO THEY HAVE...?
KNOWING IVAN, A FUCKING BIBLICAL MULTITUDE. MOVE AHEAD.
THIS CLOSE, THEY'RE AS DANGEROUS TO US AS WE ARE TO THEM...
HOW ARE WE OFF FOR AMMO?
AH, EIGHTEEN PANZERGRANATE LEFT, HERR LEUTNANT. HAVEN'T TOUCHED THE REST.
T-34 DEAD AHEAD, FIFTY METRES--
LEAVE IT! WE'RE BEING SHELLED!
THEY'LL HIT THEIR OWN TANKS, DON'T THEY GIVE A SHIT?
FORGOTTEN WHO WE'RE TALKING ABOUT?
JESUS, GET US OUT OF THIS...!

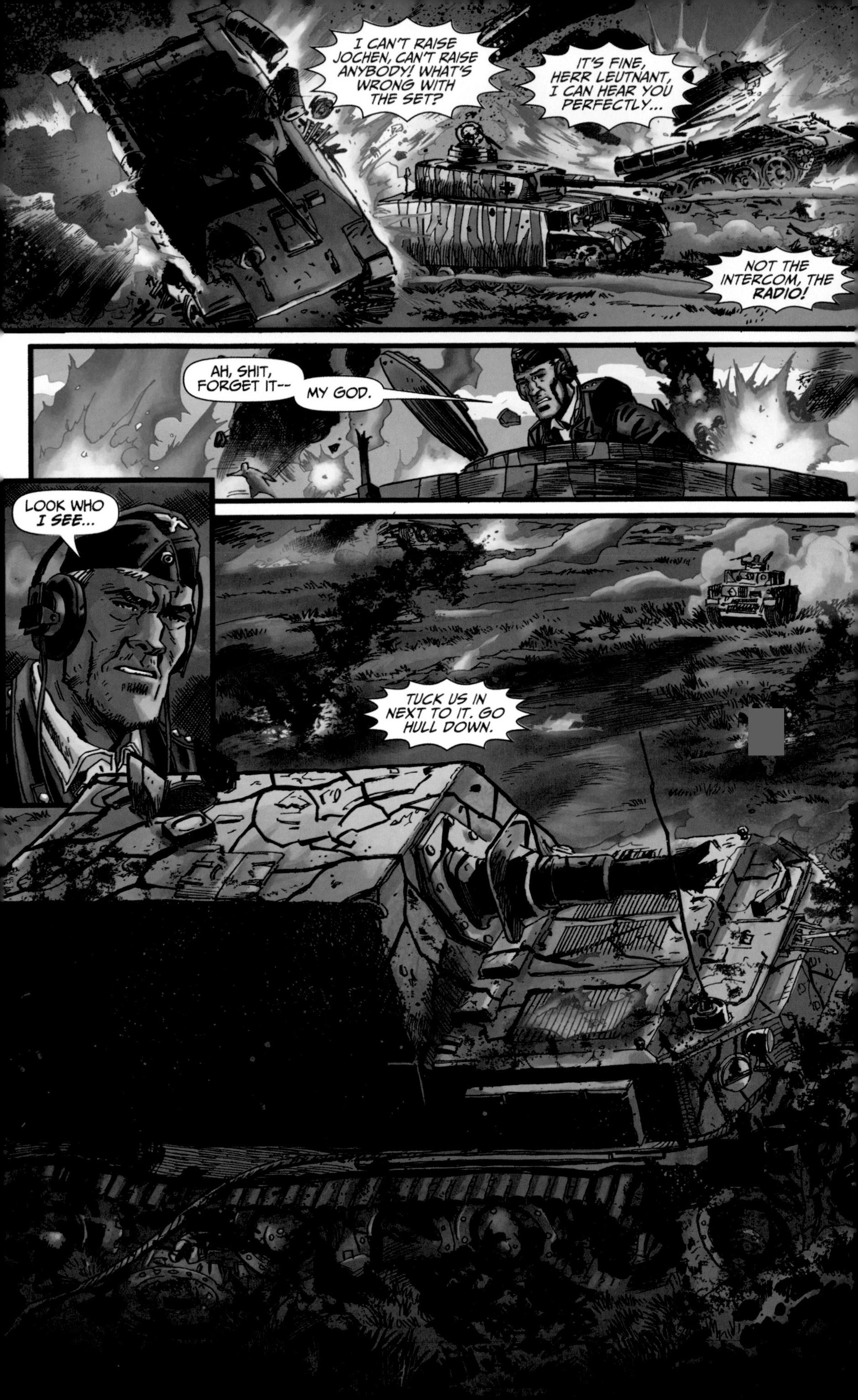
I CAN'T RAISE JOCHEN, CAN'T RAISE ANYBODY! WHAT'S WRONG WITH THE SET?
IT'S FINE, HERR LEUTNANT, I CAN HEAR YOU PERFECTLY...
NOT THE INTERCOM, THE RADIO!
AH, SHIT, FORGET IT--
MY GOD.
LOOK WHO I SEE...
TUCK US IN NEXT TO IT. GO HULL DOWN.

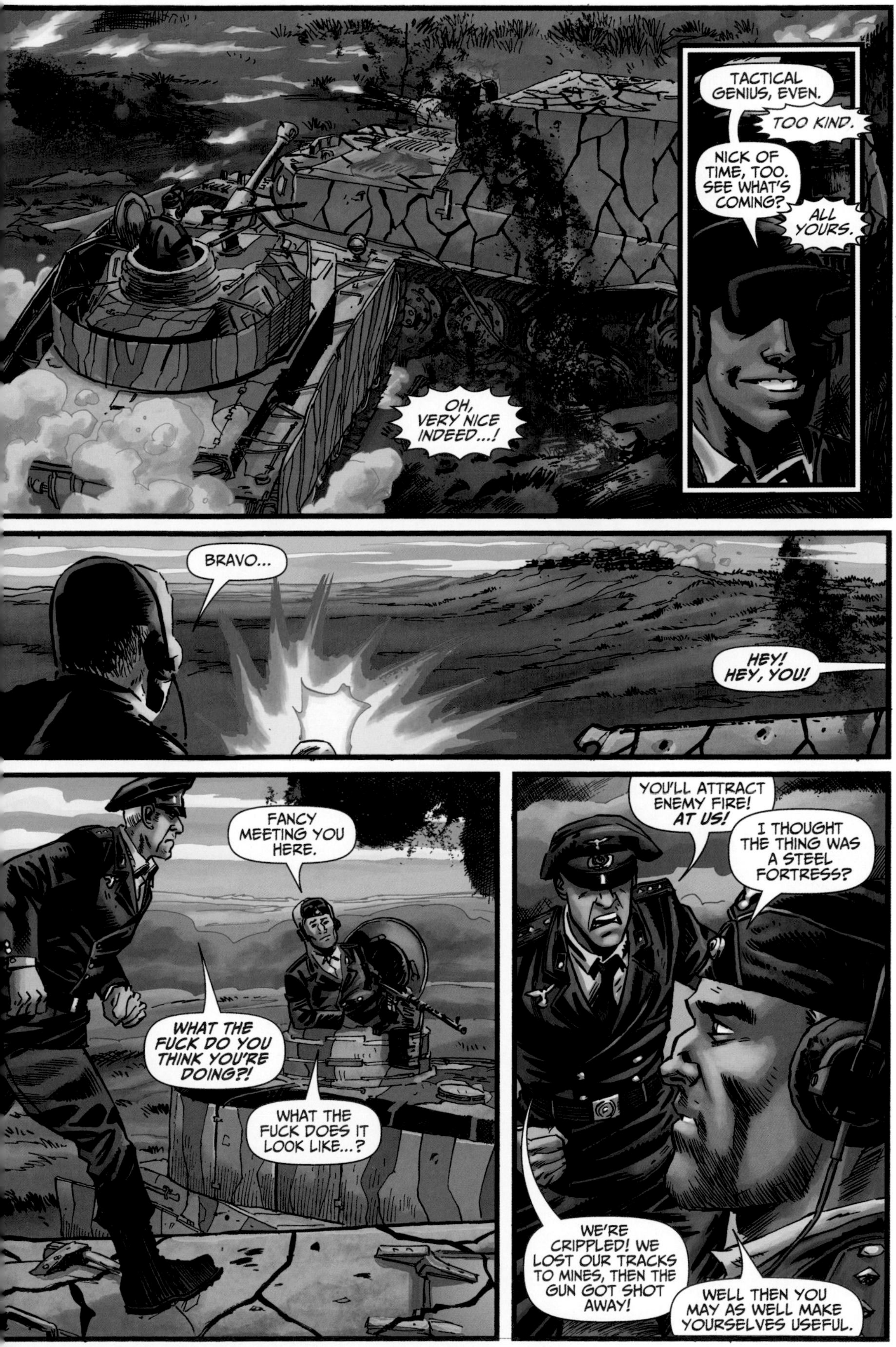
TACTICAL GENIUS, EVEN.
TOO KIND.
NICK OF TIME, TOO. SEE WHAT'S COMING?
ALL YOURS.
OH, VERY NICE INDEED...!
BRAVO...
HEY! HEY, YOU!
FANCY MEETING YOU HERE.
WHAT THE FUCK DO YOU THINK YOU'RE DOING?!
WHAT THE FUCK DOES IT LOOK LIKE...?
YOU'LL ATTRACT ENEMY FIRE! AT US!
I THOUGHT THE THING WAS A STEEL FORTRESS?
WE'RE CRIPPLED! WE LOST OUR TRACKS TO MINES, THEN THE GUN GOT SHOT AWAY!
WELL THEN YOU MAY AS WELL MAKE YOURSELVES USEFUL.

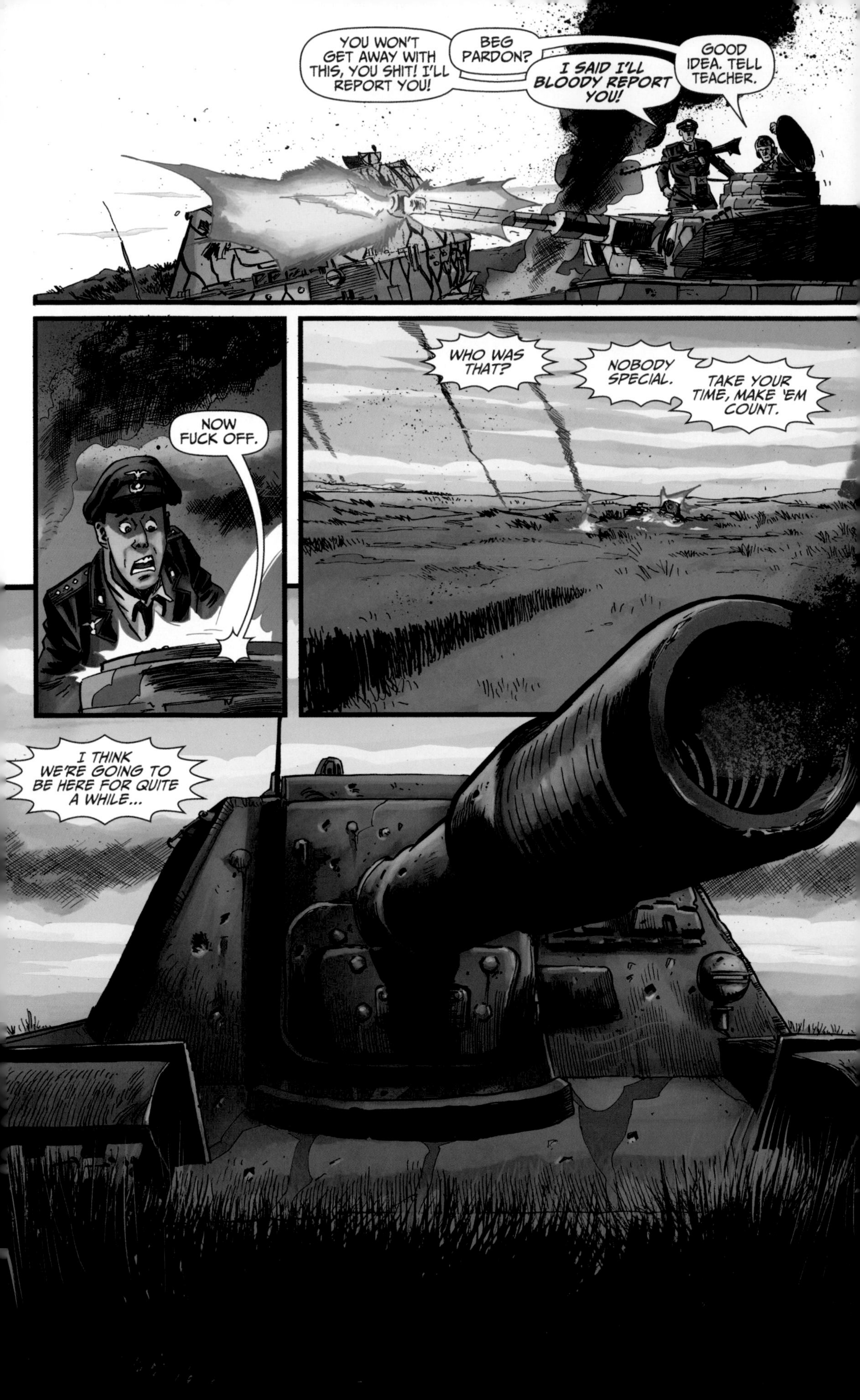
YOU WON'T GET AWAY WITH THIS, YOU SHIT! I'LL REPORT YOU!
BEG PARDON?
I SAID I'LL BLOODY REPORT YOU!
GOOD IDEA. TELL TEACHER.
NOW FUCK OFF.
WHO WAS THAT?
NOBODY SPECIAL.
TAKE YOUR TIME, MAKE 'EM COUNT.
I THINK WE'RE GOING TO BE HERE FOR QUITE A WHILE...

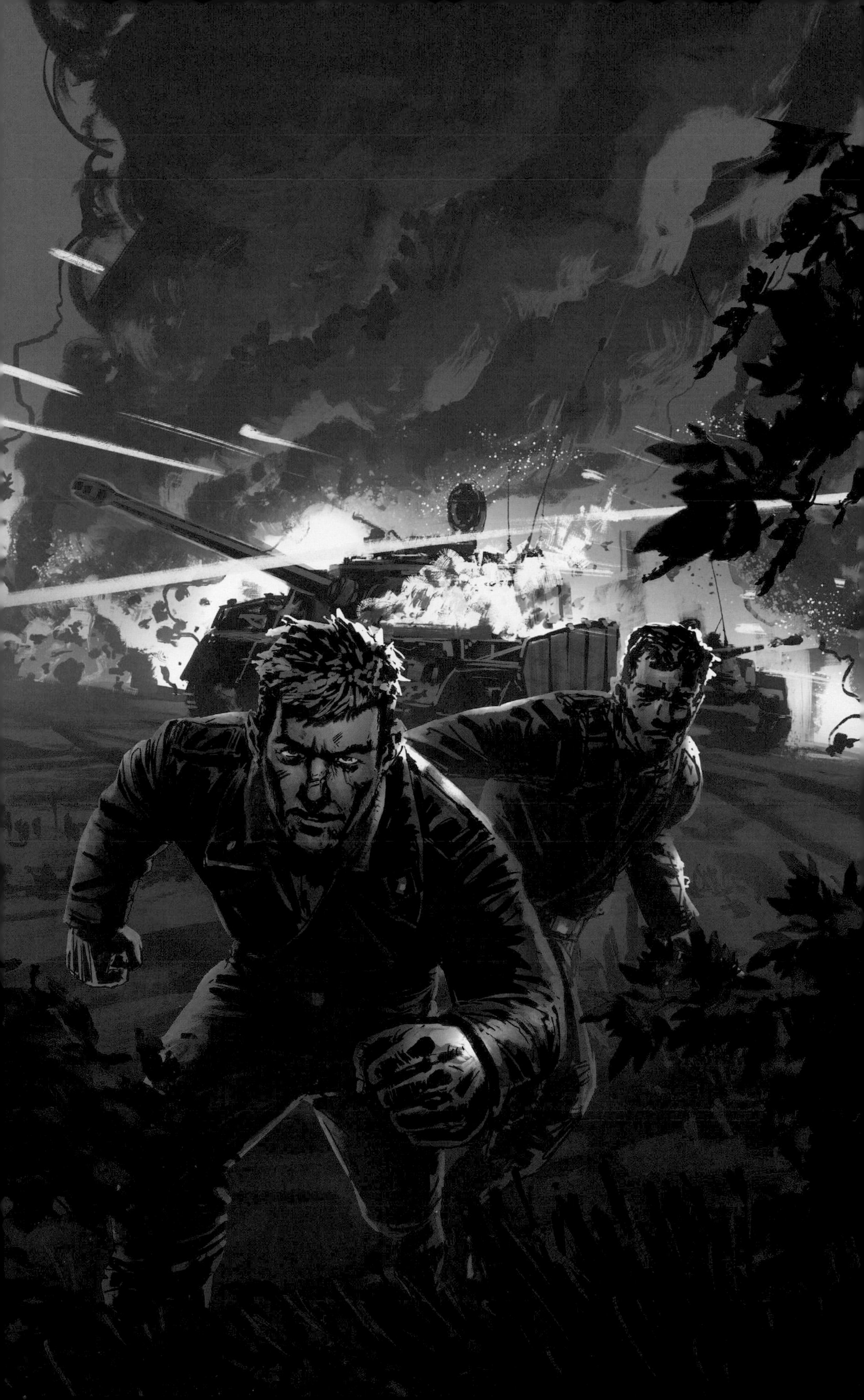

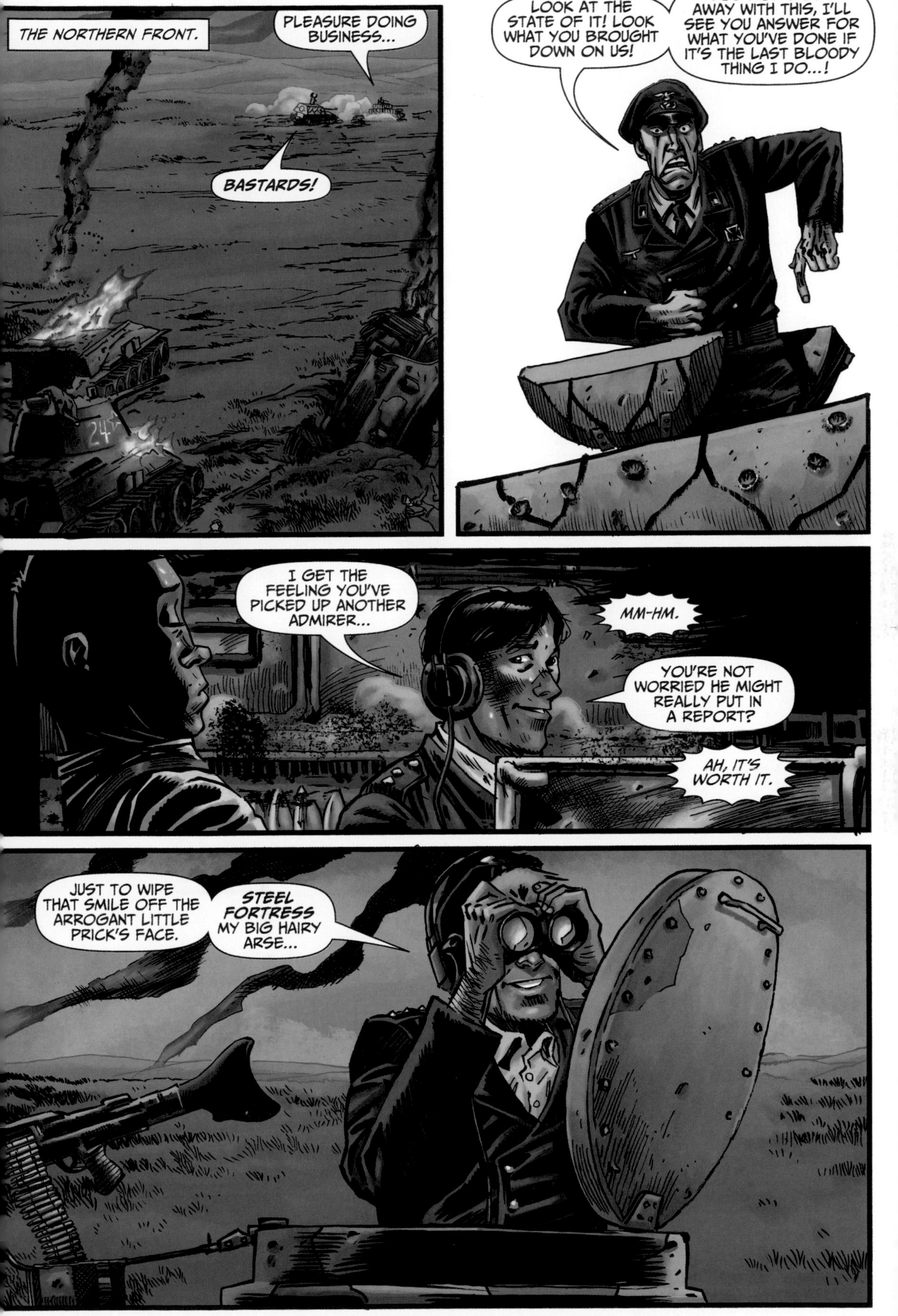
THE NORTHERN FRONT.
PLEASURE DOING BUSINESS...
BASTARDS!
LOOK AT THE STATE OF IT! LOOK WHAT YOU BROUGHT DOWN ON US!
YOU WON'T GET AWAY WITH THIS, I'LL SEE YOU ANSWER FOR WHAT YOU'VE DONE IF IT'S THE LAST BLOODY THING I DO...!
I GET THE FEELING YOU'VE PICKED UP ANOTHER ADMIRER...
MM-HM.
YOU'RE NOT WORRIED HE MIGHT REALLY PUT IN A REPORT?
AH, IT'S WORTH IT.
JUST TO WIPE THAT SMILE OFF THE ARROGANT LITTLE PRICK'S FACE.
STEEL FORTRESS MY BIG HAIRY ARSE...

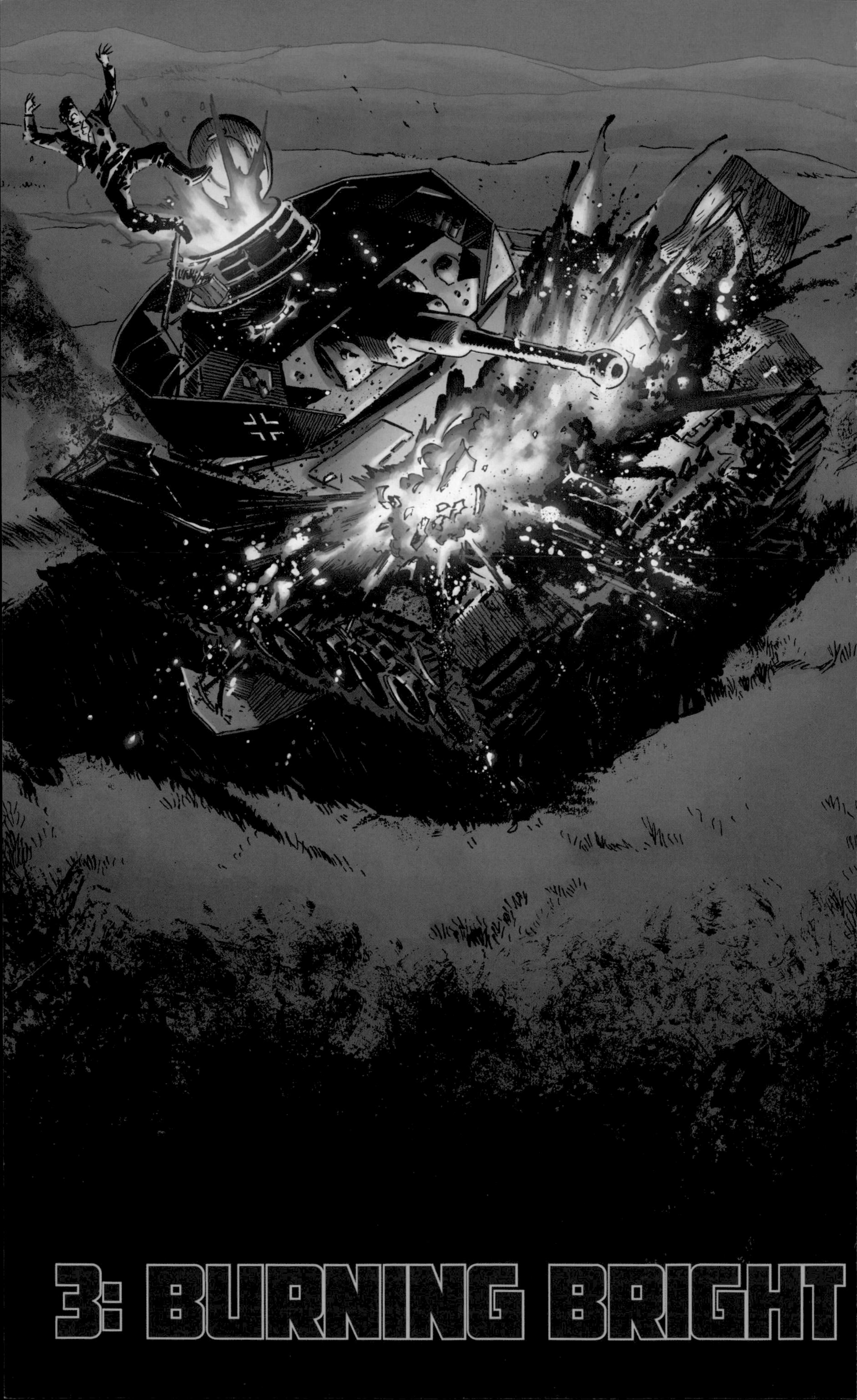

3: BURNING BRIGHT

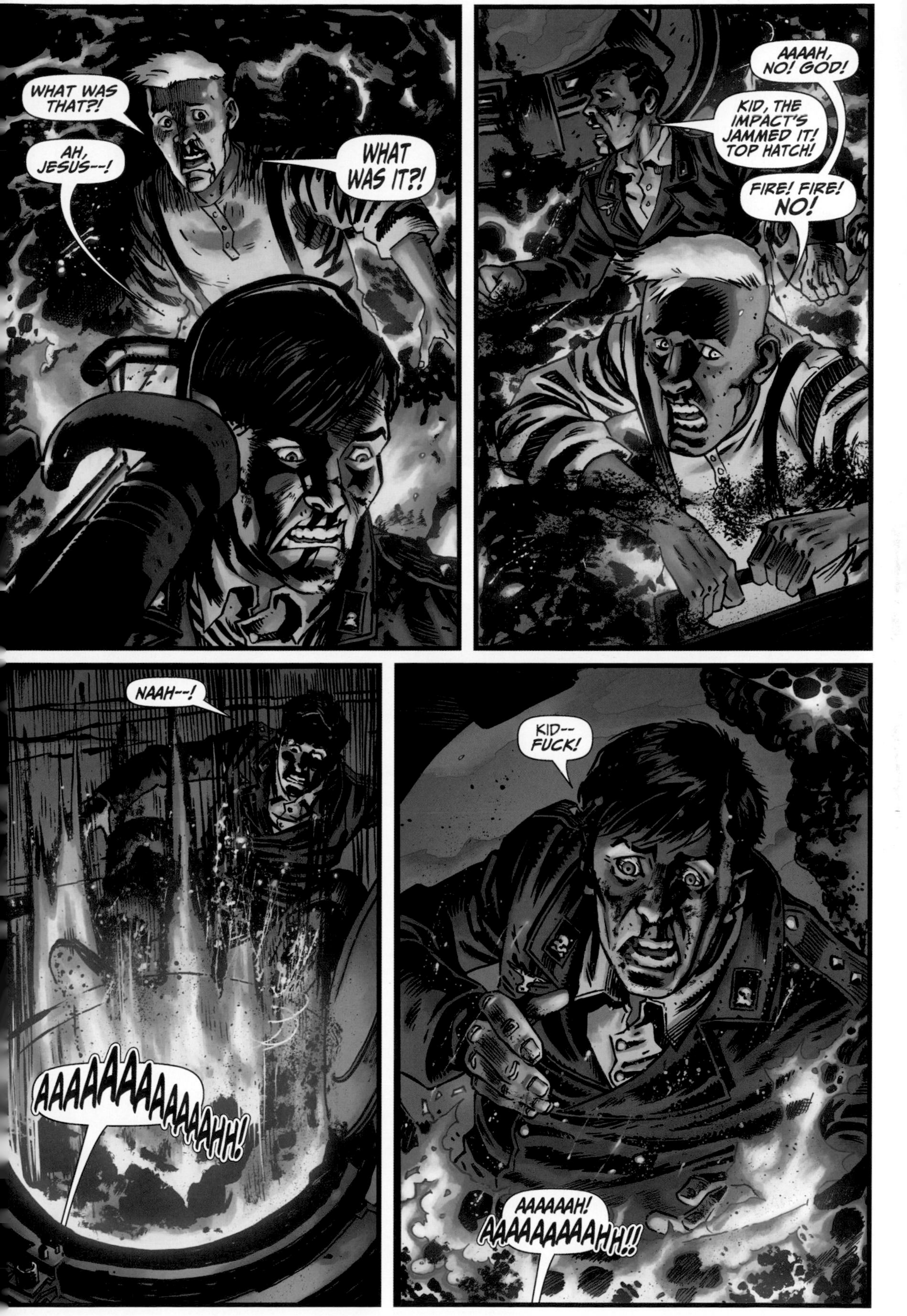
WHAT WAS THAT?!
AH, JESUS--!
WHAT WAS IT?!
AAAAH, NO! GOD!
KID, THE IMPACT'S JAMMED IT! TOP HATCH!
FIRE! FIRE! NO!
NAAH--!
AAAAAAAAAAAAAHH!
KID-- FUCK!
AAAAAAH! AAAAAAAAAHH!!

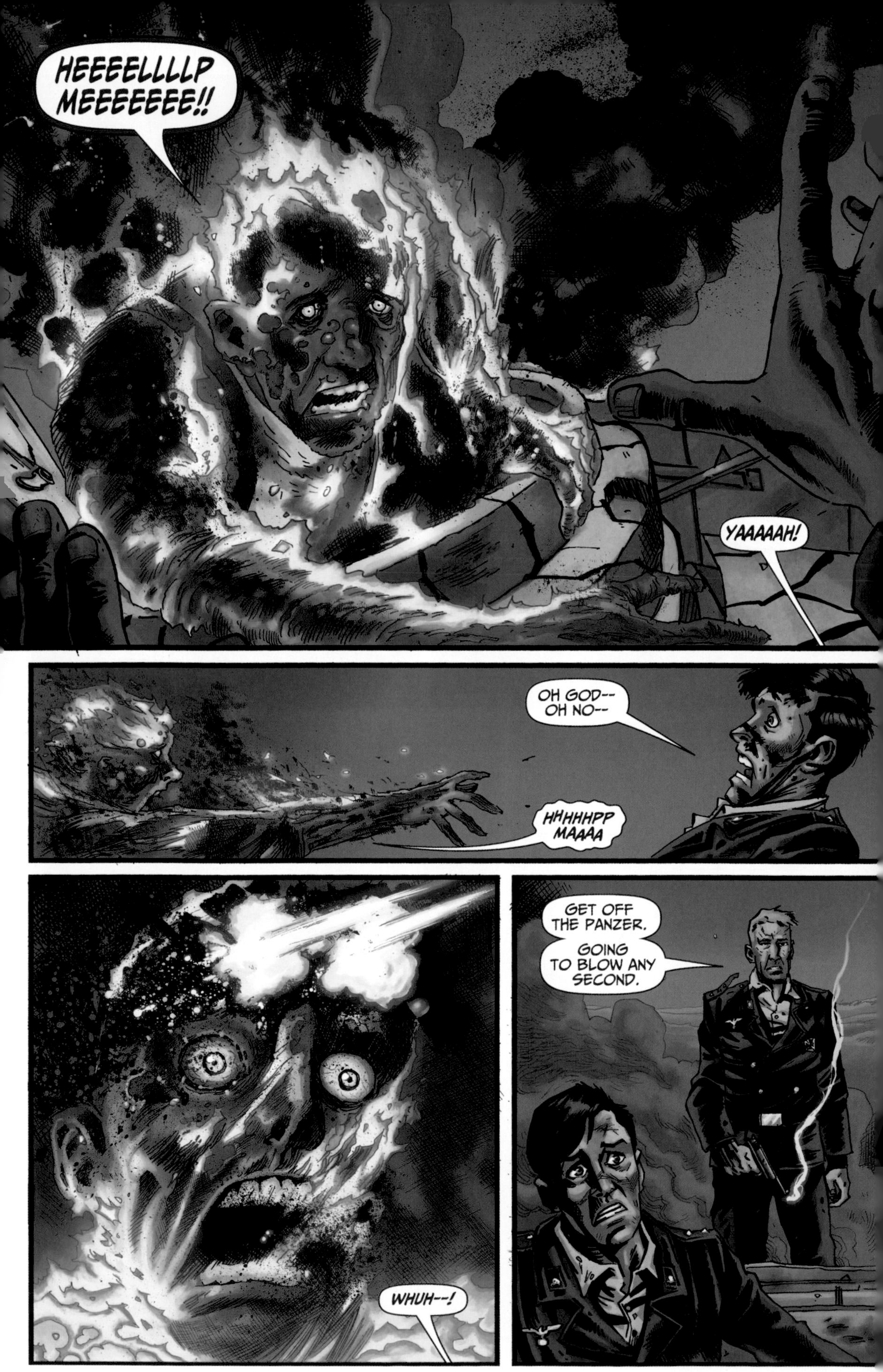
HEEEELLLLP MEEEEEEE!!
YAAAAAH!
OH GOD-- OH NO--
HHHHHPP MAAAA
WHUH--!
GET OFF THE PANZER.
GOING TO BLOW ANY SECOND.

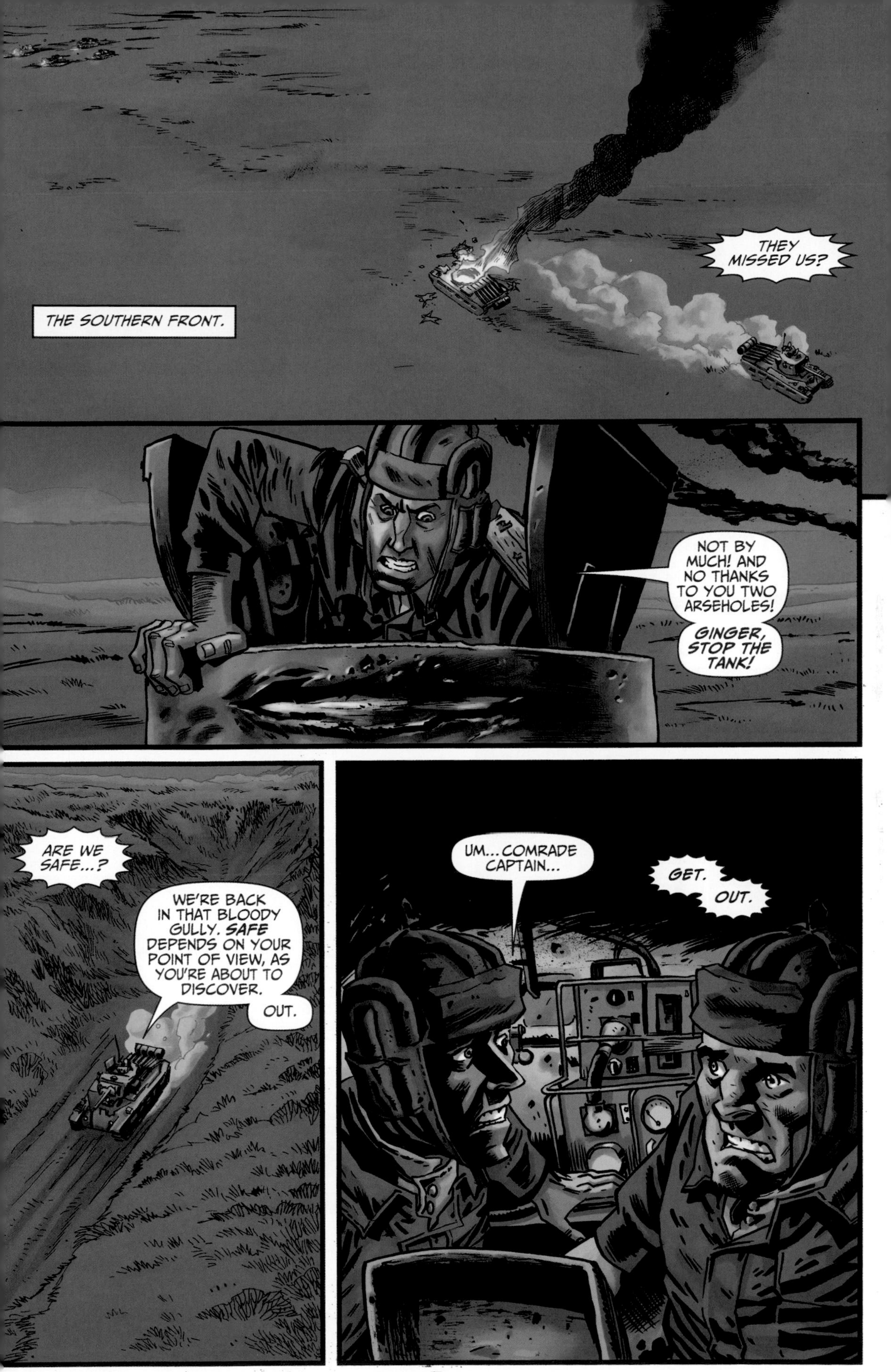
THE SOUTHERN FRONT.
THEY MISSED US?
NOT BY MUCH! AND NO THANKS TO YOU TWO ARSEHOLES!
GINGER, STOP THE TANK!
ARE WE SAFE...?
WE'RE BACK IN THAT BLOODY GULLY. SAFE DEPENDS ON YOUR POINT OF VIEW, AS YOU'RE ABOUT TO DISCOVER.
OUT.
UM...COMRADE CAPTAIN...
GET.
OUT.

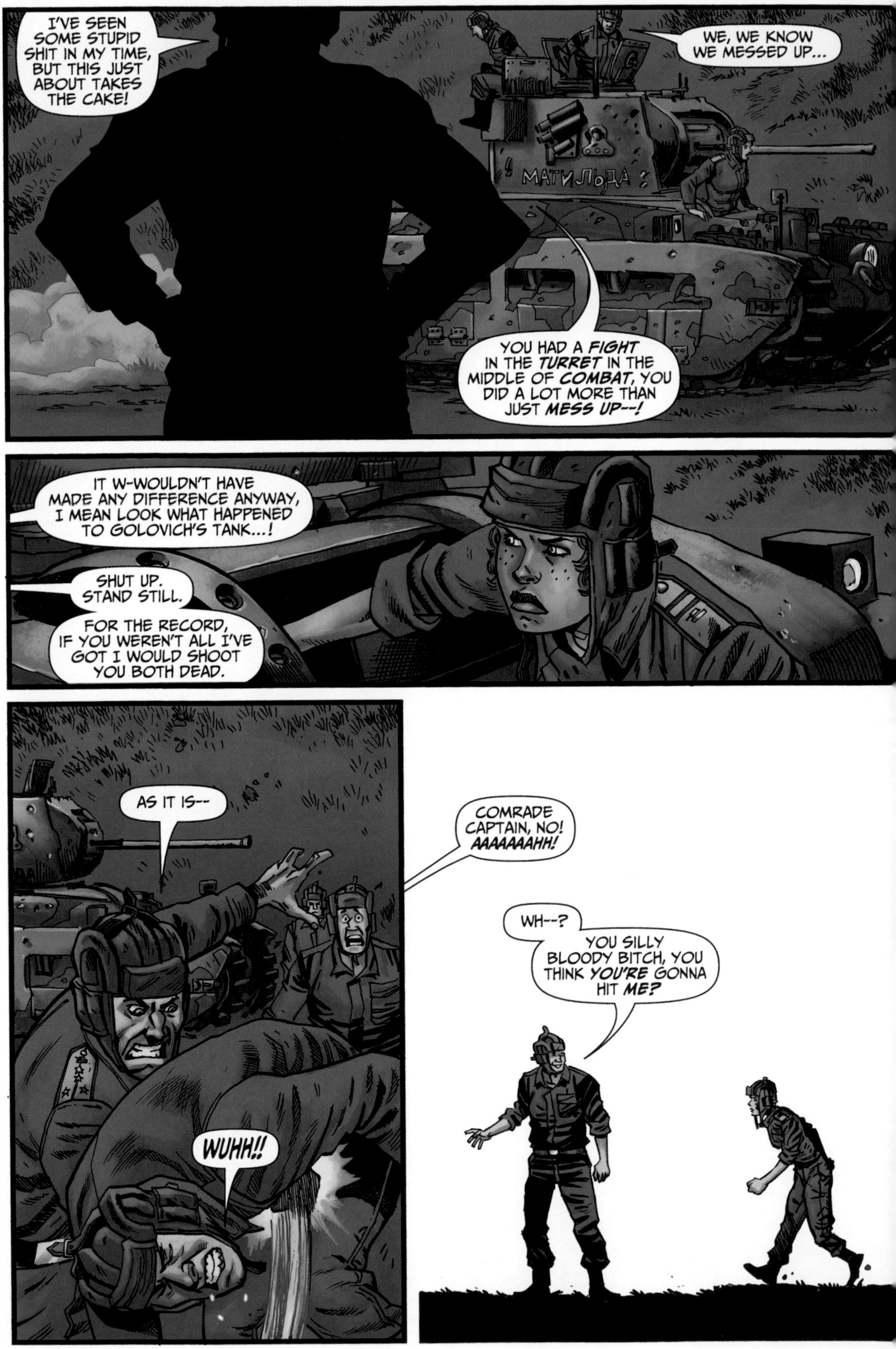
I'VE SEEN SOME STUPID SHIT IN MY TIME, BUT THIS JUST ABOUT TAKES THE CAKE!
WE, WE KNOW WE MESSED UP...
МАТИЛЬДА
YOU HAD A FIGHT IN THE TURRET IN THE MIDDLE OF COMBAT, YOU DID A LOT MORE THAN JUST MESS UP--!
IT W-WOULDN'T HAVE MADE ANY DIFFERENCE ANYWAY, I MEAN LOOK WHAT HAPPENED TO GOLOVICH'S TANK...!
SHUT UP. STAND STILL.
FOR THE RECORD, IF YOU WEREN'T ALL I'VE GOT I WOULD SHOOT YOU BOTH DEAD.
AS IT IS--
COMRADE CAPTAIN, NO! AAAAAAAHH!
WUHH!!
WH--?
YOU SILLY BLOODY BITCH, YOU THINK YOU'RE GONNA HIT ME?

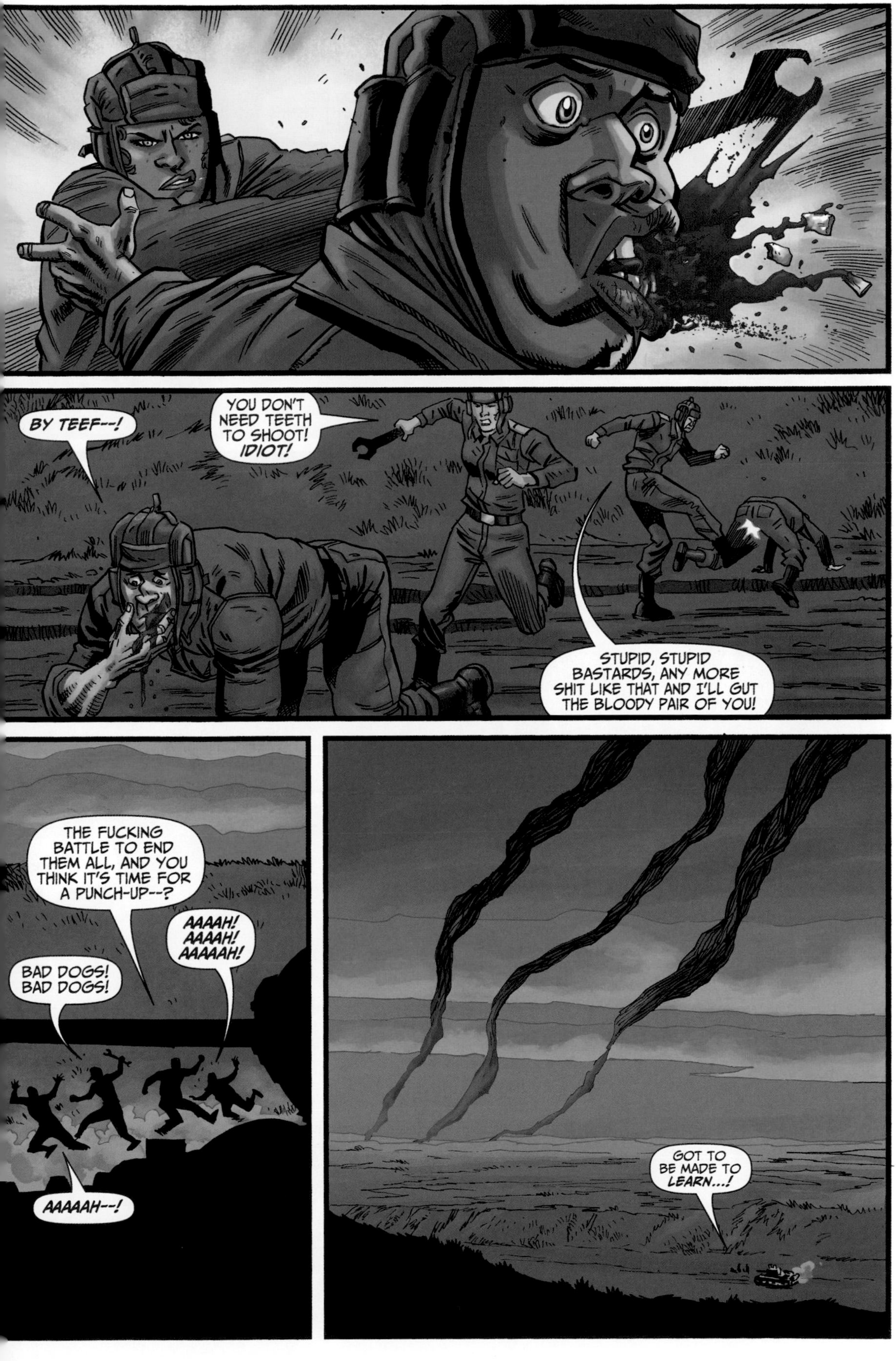
BY TEEF--!
YOU DON'T NEED TEETH TO SHOOT! IDIOT!
STUPID, STUPID BASTARDS, ANY MORE SHIT LIKE THAT AND I'LL GUT THE BLOODY PAIR OF YOU!
THE FUCKING BATTLE TO END THEM ALL, AND YOU THINK IT'S TIME FOR A PUNCH-UP--?
AAAAH! AAAAH! AAAAAH!
BAD DOGS! BAD DOGS!
AAAAAH--!
GOT TO BE MADE TO LEARN...!

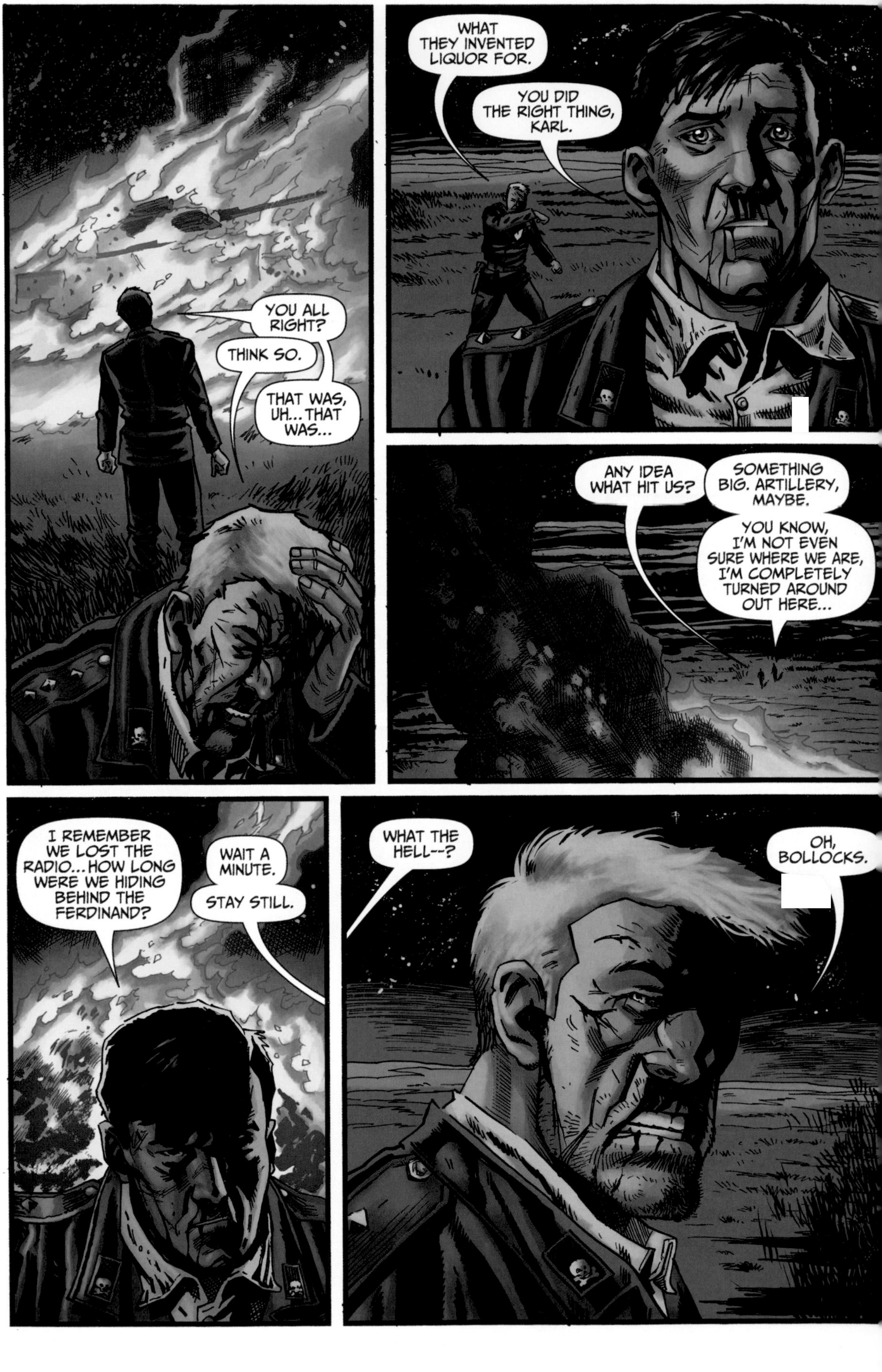
YOU ALL RIGHT?
THINK SO.
THAT WAS, UH...THAT WAS...
WHAT THEY INVENTED LIQUOR FOR.
YOU DID THE RIGHT THING, KARL.
ANY IDEA WHAT HIT US?
SOMETHING BIG. ARTILLERY, MAYBE.
YOU KNOW, I'M NOT EVEN SURE WHERE WE ARE, I'M COMPLETELY TURNED AROUND OUT HERE...
I REMEMBER WE LOST THE RADIO...HOW LONG WERE WE HIDING BEHIND THE FERDINAND?
WAIT A MINUTE.
STAY STILL.
WHAT THE HELL--?
OH, BOLLOCKS.

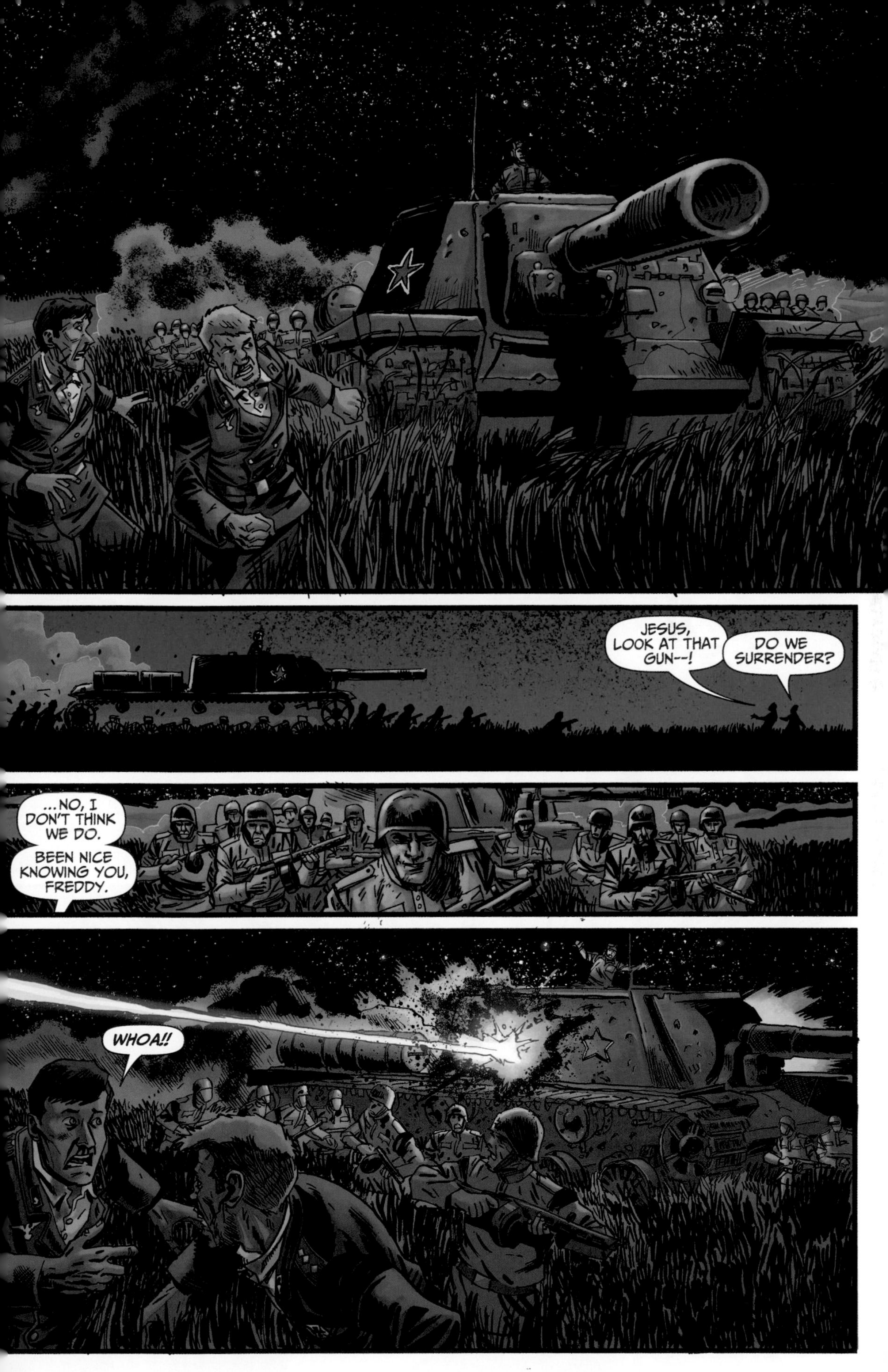
JESUS, LOOK AT THAT GUN--!
DO WE SURRENDER?
...NO, I DON'T THINK WE DO.
BEEN NICE KNOWING YOU, FREDDY.
WHOA!!

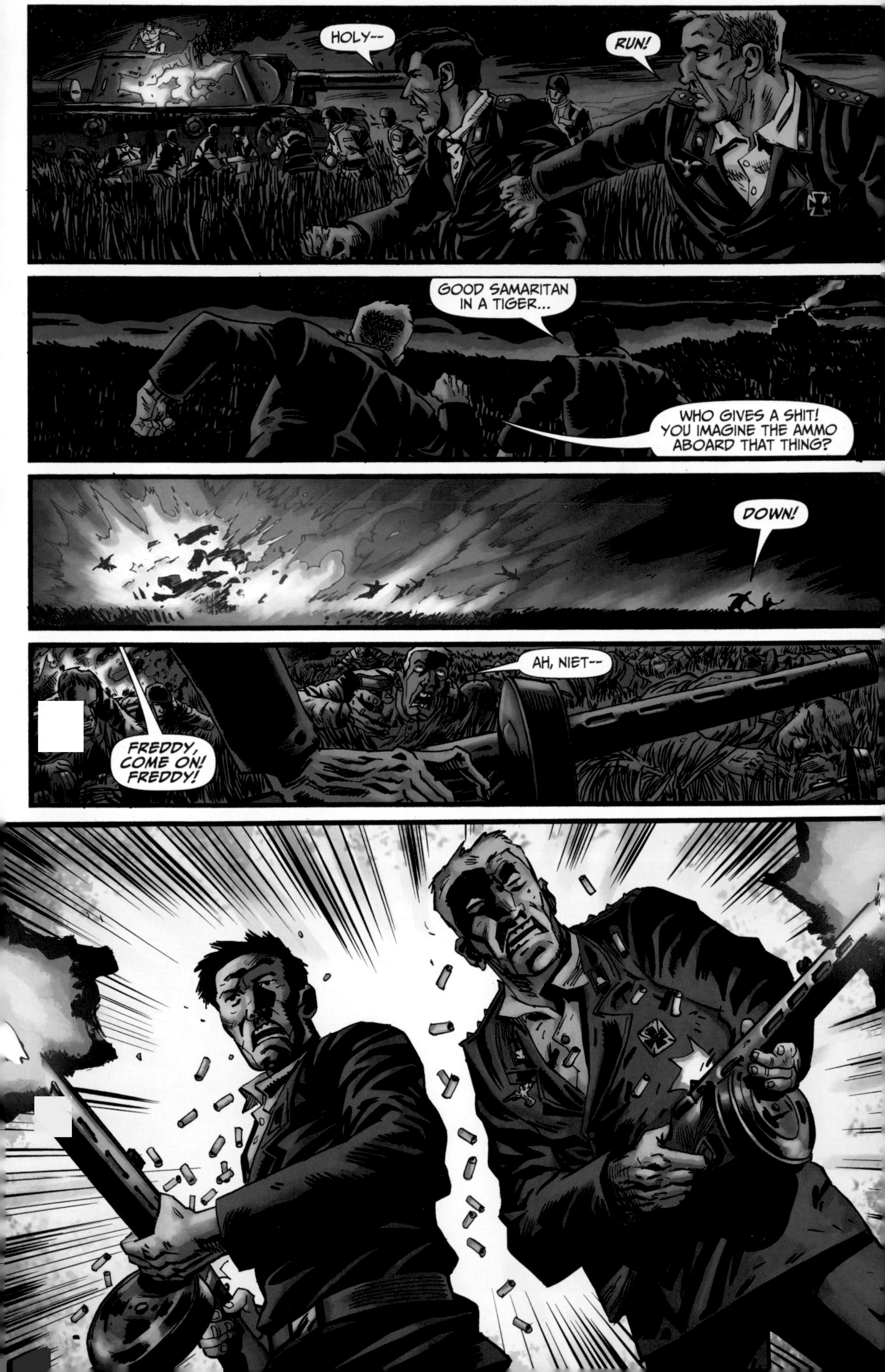
HOLY--
RUN!
GOOD SAMARITAN IN A TIGER...
WHO GIVES A SHIT! YOU IMAGINE THE AMMO ABOARD THAT THING?
DOWN!
AH, NIET--
FREDDY, COME ON! FREDDY!

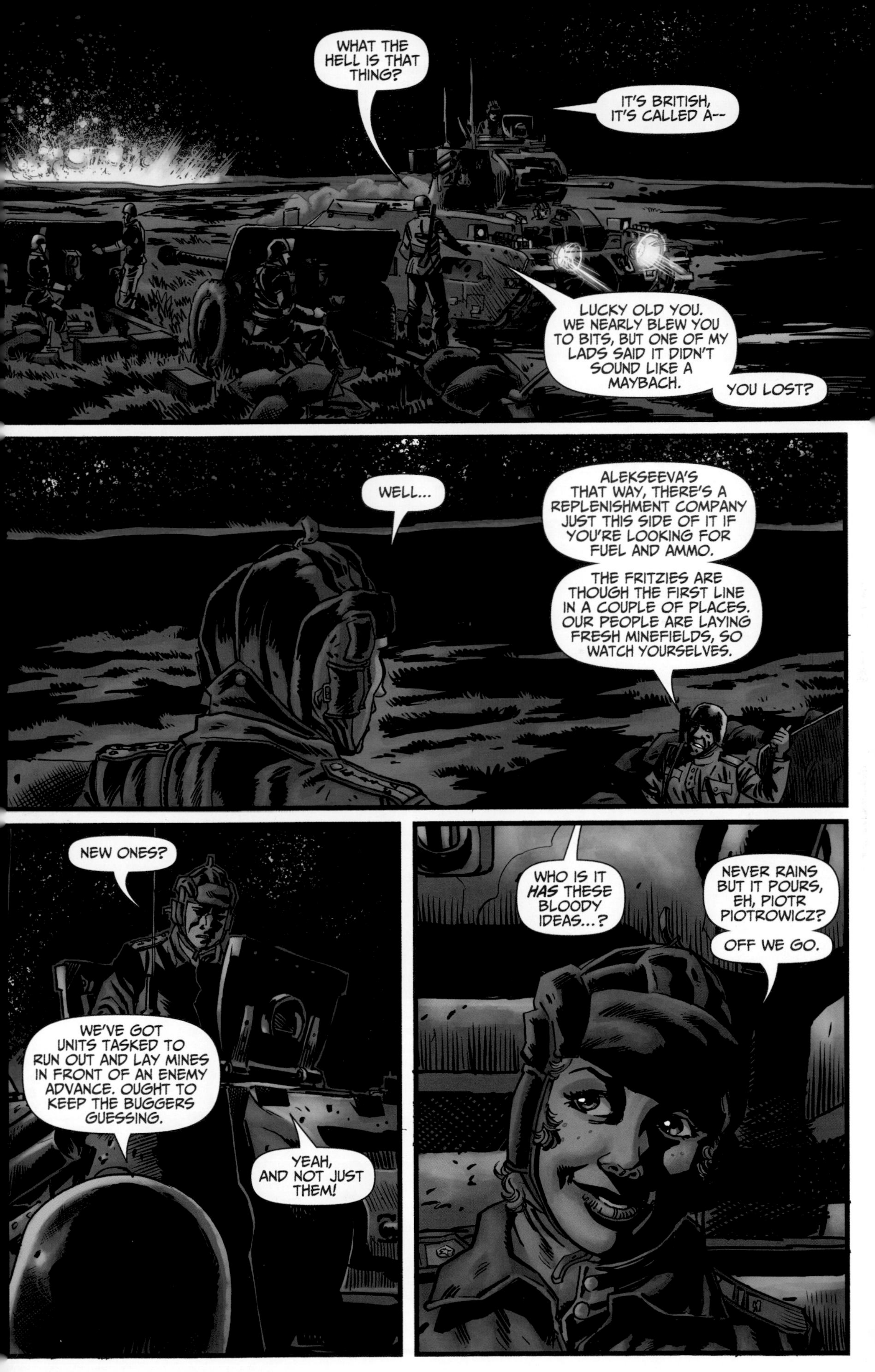
WHAT THE HELL IS THAT THING?
IT'S BRITISH, IT'S CALLED A--
LUCKY OLD YOU. WE NEARLY BLEW YOU TO BITS, BUT ONE OF MY LADS SAID IT DIDN'T SOUND LIKE A MAYBACH.
YOU LOST?
WELL...
ALEKSEEVA'S THAT WAY, THERE'S A REPLENISHMENT COMPANY JUST THIS SIDE OF IT IF YOU'RE LOOKING FOR FUEL AND AMMO.
THE FRITZIES ARE THOUGH THE FIRST LINE IN A COUPLE OF PLACES. OUR PEOPLE ARE LAYING FRESH MINEFIELDS, SO WATCH YOURSELVES.
NEW ONES?
WE'VE GOT UNITS TASKED TO RUN OUT AND LAY MINES IN FRONT OF AN ENEMY ADVANCE. OUGHT TO KEEP THE BUGGERS GUESSING.
YEAH, AND NOT JUST THEM!
WHO IS IT *HAS* THESE BLOODY IDEAS...?
NEVER RAINS BUT IT POURS, EH, PIOTR PIOTROWICZ?
OFF WE GO.

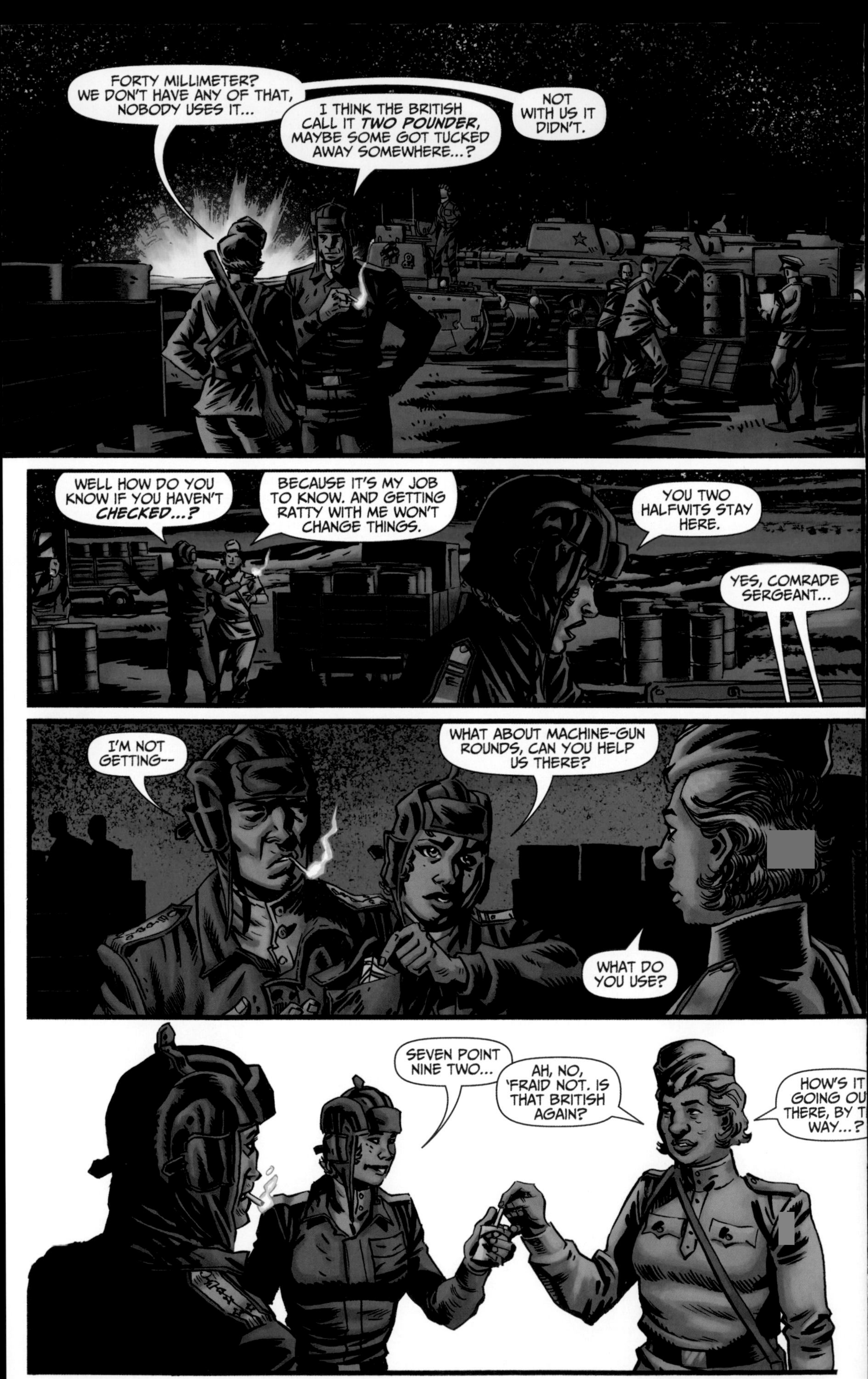
FORTY MILLIMETER? WE DON'T HAVE ANY OF THAT, NOBODY USES IT...
I THINK THE BRITISH CALL IT *TWO POUNDER*, MAYBE SOME GOT TUCKED AWAY SOMEWHERE...?
NOT WITH US IT DIDN'T.
WELL HOW DO YOU KNOW IF YOU HAVEN'T *CHECKED...?*
BECAUSE IT'S MY JOB TO KNOW. AND GETTING RATTY WITH ME WON'T CHANGE THINGS.
YOU TWO HALFWITS STAY HERE.
YES, COMRADE SERGEANT...
I'M NOT GETTING--
WHAT ABOUT MACHINE-GUN ROUNDS, CAN YOU HELP US THERE?
WHAT DO YOU USE?
SEVEN POINT NINE TWO...
AH, NO, 'FRAID NOT. IS THAT BRITISH AGAIN?
HOW'S IT GOING OU THERE, BY T WAY...?

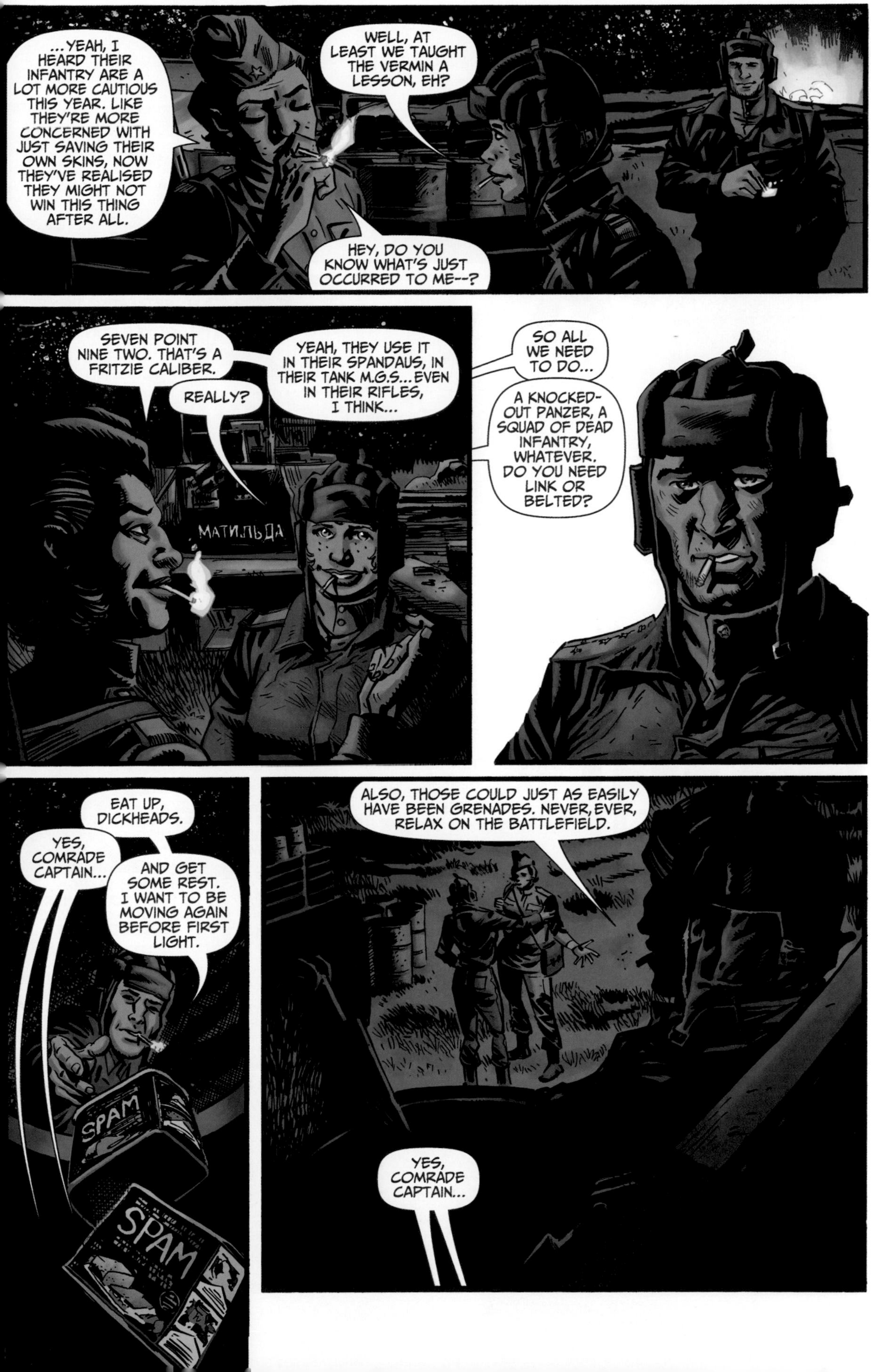
...YEAH, I HEARD THEIR INFANTRY ARE A LOT MORE CAUTIOUS THIS YEAR. LIKE THEY'RE MORE CONCERNED WITH JUST SAVING THEIR OWN SKINS, NOW THEY'VE REALISED THEY MIGHT NOT WIN THIS THING AFTER ALL.
WELL, AT LEAST WE TAUGHT THE VERMIN A LESSON, EH?
HEY, DO YOU KNOW WHAT'S JUST OCCURRED TO ME--?
SEVEN POINT NINE TWO. THAT'S A FRITZIE CALIBER.
REALLY?
YEAH, THEY USE IT IN THEIR SPANDAUS, IN THEIR TANK M.G.S...EVEN IN THEIR RIFLES, I THINK...
МАТИЛЬДА
SO ALL WE NEED TO DO...
A KNOCKED-OUT PANZER, A SQUAD OF DEAD INFANTRY, WHATEVER. DO YOU NEED LINK OR BELTED?
EAT UP, DICKHEADS.
YES, COMRADE CAPTAIN...
AND GET SOME REST. I WANT TO BE MOVING AGAIN BEFORE FIRST LIGHT.
SPAM
SPAM
ALSO, THOSE COULD JUST AS EASILY HAVE BEEN GRENADES. NEVER, EVER, RELAX ON THE BATTLEFIELD.
YES, COMRADE CAPTAIN...

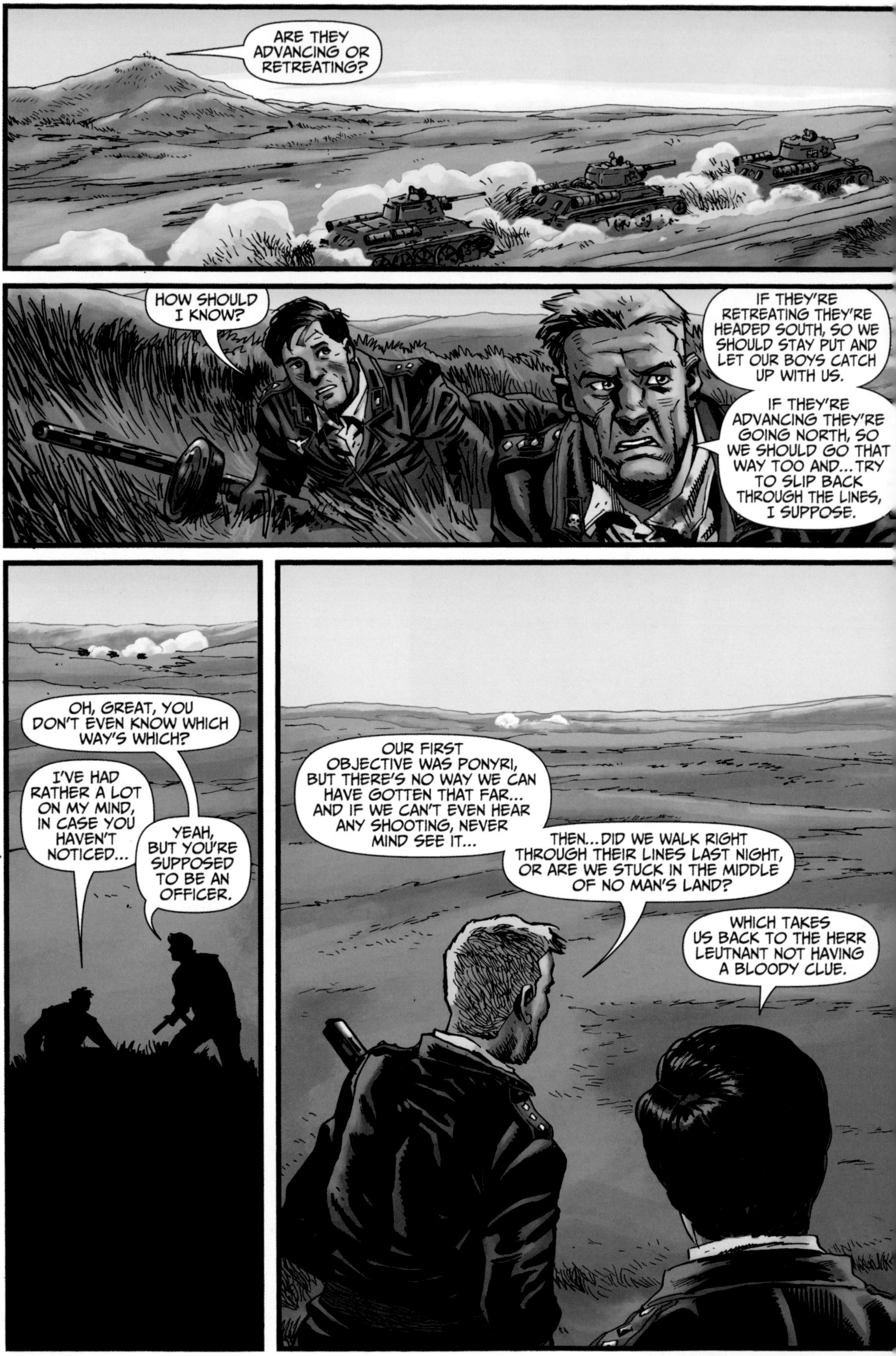
ARE THEY ADVANCING OR RETREATING?
HOW SHOULD I KNOW?
IF THEY'RE RETREATING THEY'RE HEADED SOUTH, SO WE SHOULD STAY PUT AND LET OUR BOYS CATCH UP WITH US.
IF THEY'RE ADVANCING THEY'RE GOING NORTH, SO WE SHOULD GO THAT WAY TOO AND...TRY TO SLIP BACK THROUGH THE LINES, I SUPPOSE.
OH, GREAT, YOU DON'T EVEN KNOW WHICH WAY'S WHICH?
I'VE HAD RATHER A LOT ON MY MIND, IN CASE YOU HAVEN'T NOTICED...
YEAH, BUT YOU'RE SUPPOSED TO BE AN OFFICER.
OUR FIRST OBJECTIVE WAS PONYRI, BUT THERE'S NO WAY WE CAN HAVE GOTTEN THAT FAR... AND IF WE CAN'T EVEN HEAR ANY SHOOTING, NEVER MIND SEE IT...
THEN...DID WE WALK RIGHT THROUGH THEIR LINES LAST NIGHT, OR ARE WE STUCK IN THE MIDDLE OF NO MAN'S LAND?
WHICH TAKES US BACK TO THE HERR LEUTNANT NOT HAVING A BLOODY CLUE.

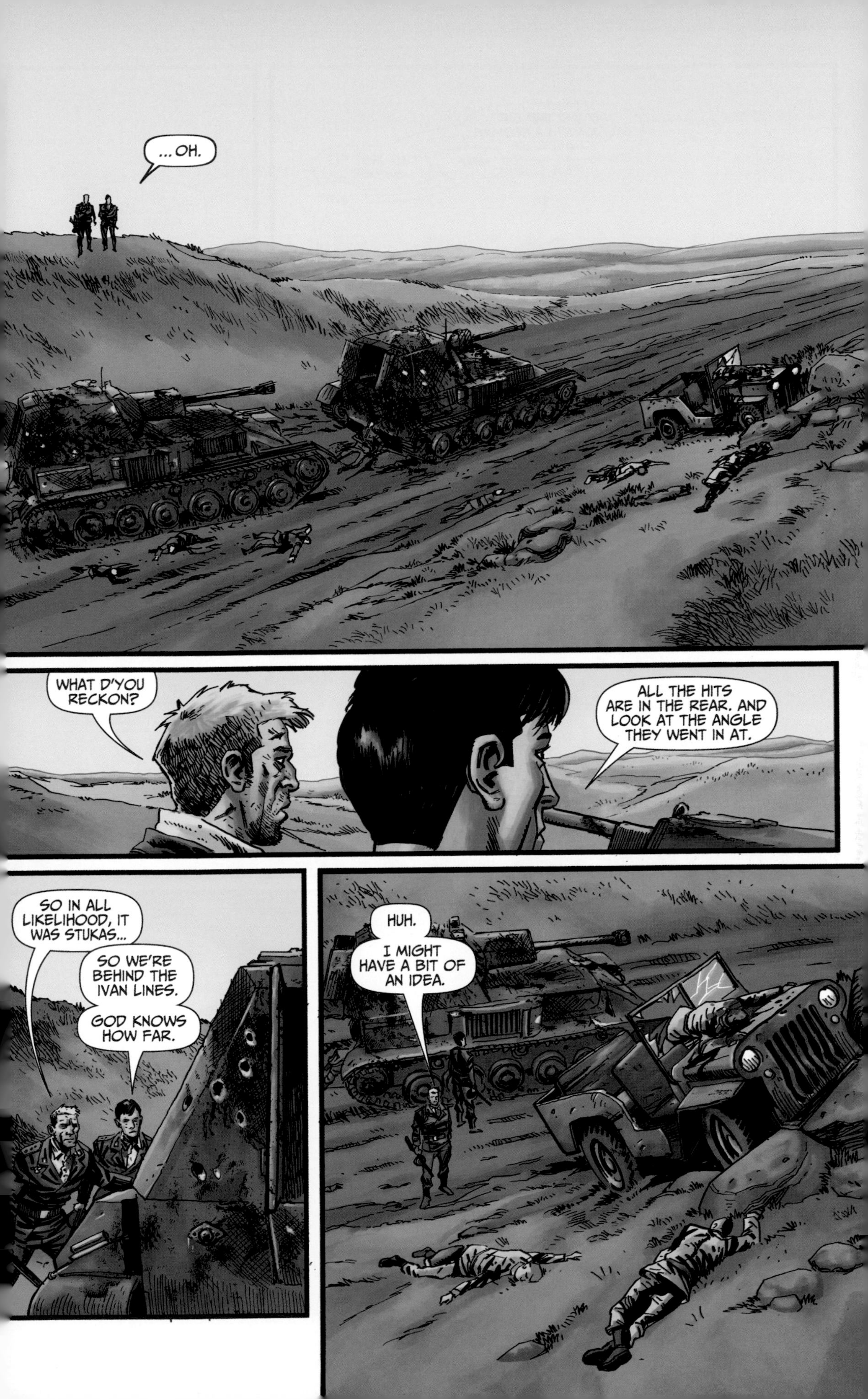
...OH.
WHAT D'YOU RECKON?
ALL THE HITS ARE IN THE REAR. AND LOOK AT THE ANGLE THEY WENT IN AT.
SO IN ALL LIKELIHOOD, IT WAS STUKAS...
SO WE'RE BEHIND THE IVAN LINES.
GOD KNOWS HOW FAR.
HUH.
I MIGHT HAVE A BIT OF AN IDEA.

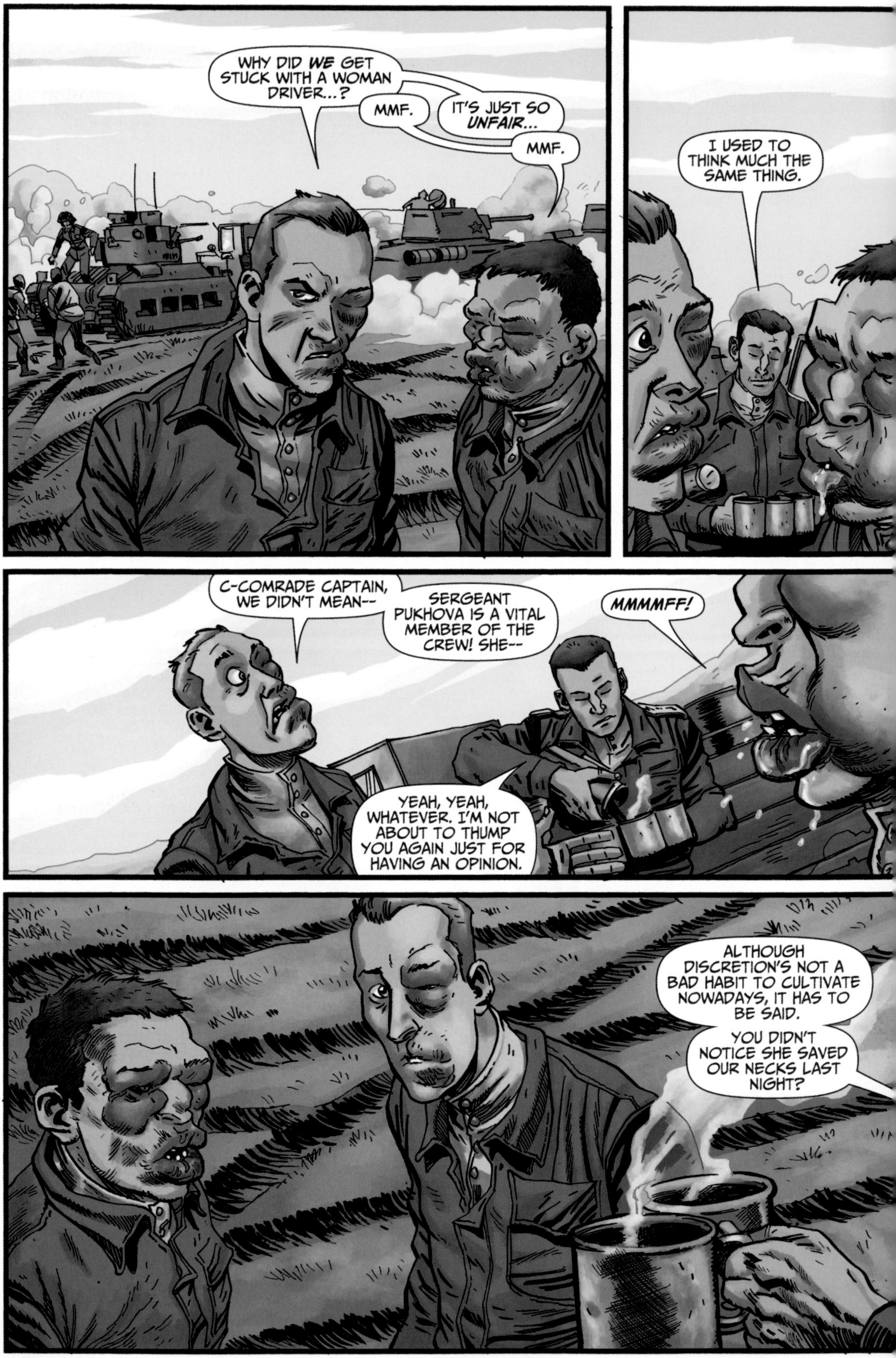
WHY DID WE GET STUCK WITH A WOMAN DRIVER...?
MMF.
IT'S JUST SO UNFAIR...
MMF.
I USED TO THINK MUCH THE SAME THING.
C-COMRADE CAPTAIN, WE DIDN'T MEAN--
SERGEANT PUKHOVA IS A VITAL MEMBER OF THE CREW! SHE--
MMMMFF!
YEAH, YEAH, WHATEVER. I'M NOT ABOUT TO THUMP YOU AGAIN JUST FOR HAVING AN OPINION.
ALTHOUGH DISCRETION'S NOT A BAD HABIT TO CULTIVATE NOWADAYS, IT HAS TO BE SAID.
YOU DIDN'T NOTICE SHE SAVED OUR NECKS LAST NIGHT?

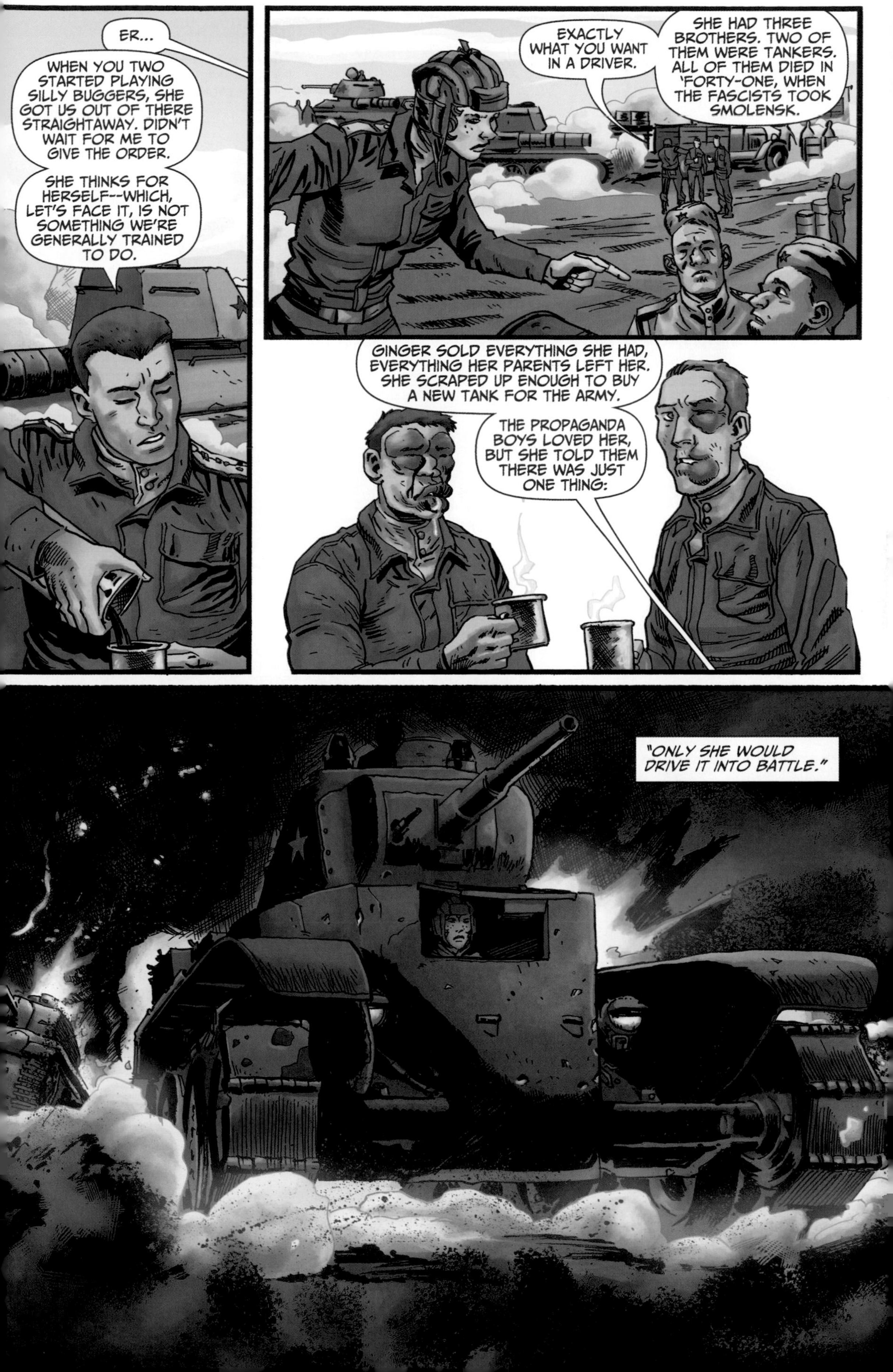
ER...
WHEN YOU TWO STARTED PLAYING SILLY BUGGERS, SHE GOT US OUT OF THERE STRAIGHTAWAY. DIDN'T WAIT FOR ME TO GIVE THE ORDER.
SHE THINKS FOR HERSELF--WHICH, LET'S FACE IT, IS NOT SOMETHING WE'RE GENERALLY TRAINED TO DO.
EXACTLY WHAT YOU WANT IN A DRIVER.
SHE HAD THREE BROTHERS. TWO OF THEM WERE TANKERS. ALL OF THEM DIED IN 'FORTY-ONE, WHEN THE FASCISTS TOOK SMOLENSK.
GINGER SOLD EVERYTHING SHE HAD, EVERYTHING HER PARENTS LEFT HER. SHE SCRAPED UP ENOUGH TO BUY A NEW TANK FOR THE ARMY.
THE PROPAGANDA BOYS LOVED HER, BUT SHE TOLD THEM THERE WAS JUST ONE THING:
"ONLY SHE WOULD DRIVE IT INTO BATTLE."

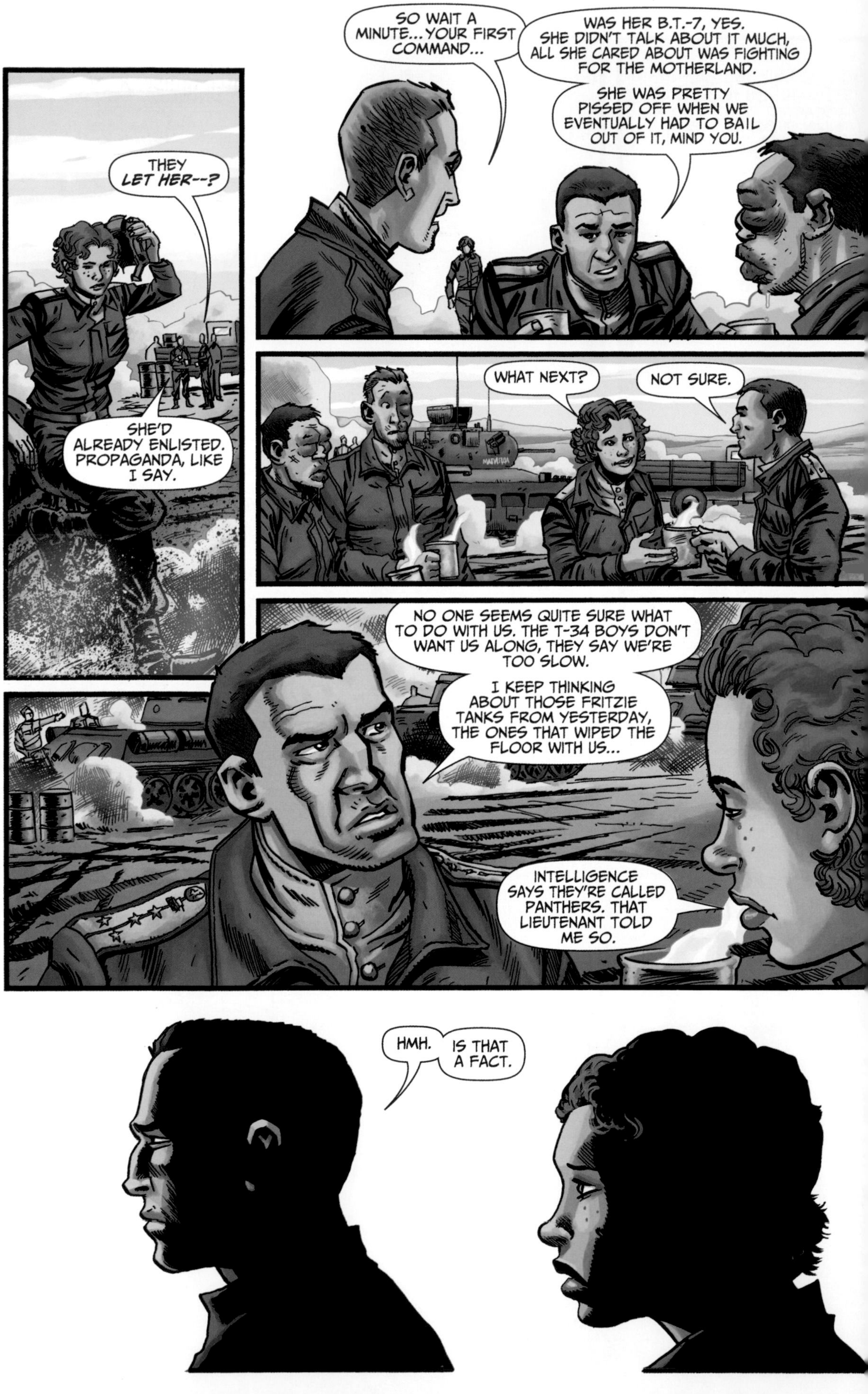
SO WAIT A MINUTE... YOUR FIRST COMMAND...
WAS HER B.T.-7, YES. SHE DIDN'T TALK ABOUT IT MUCH, ALL SHE CARED ABOUT WAS FIGHTING FOR THE MOTHERLAND.
SHE WAS PRETTY PISSED OFF WHEN WE EVENTUALLY HAD TO BAIL OUT OF IT, MIND YOU.
THEY LET HER--?
SHE'D ALREADY ENLISTED. PROPAGANDA, LIKE I SAY.
WHAT NEXT?
NOT SURE.
NO ONE SEEMS QUITE SURE WHAT TO DO WITH US. THE T-34 BOYS DON'T WANT US ALONG, THEY SAY WE'RE TOO SLOW.
I KEEP THINKING ABOUT THOSE FRITZIE TANKS FROM YESTERDAY, THE ONES THAT WIPED THE FLOOR WITH US...
INTELLIGENCE SAYS THEY'RE CALLED PANTHERS. THAT LIEUTENANT TOLD ME SO.
HMH.
IS THAT A FACT.

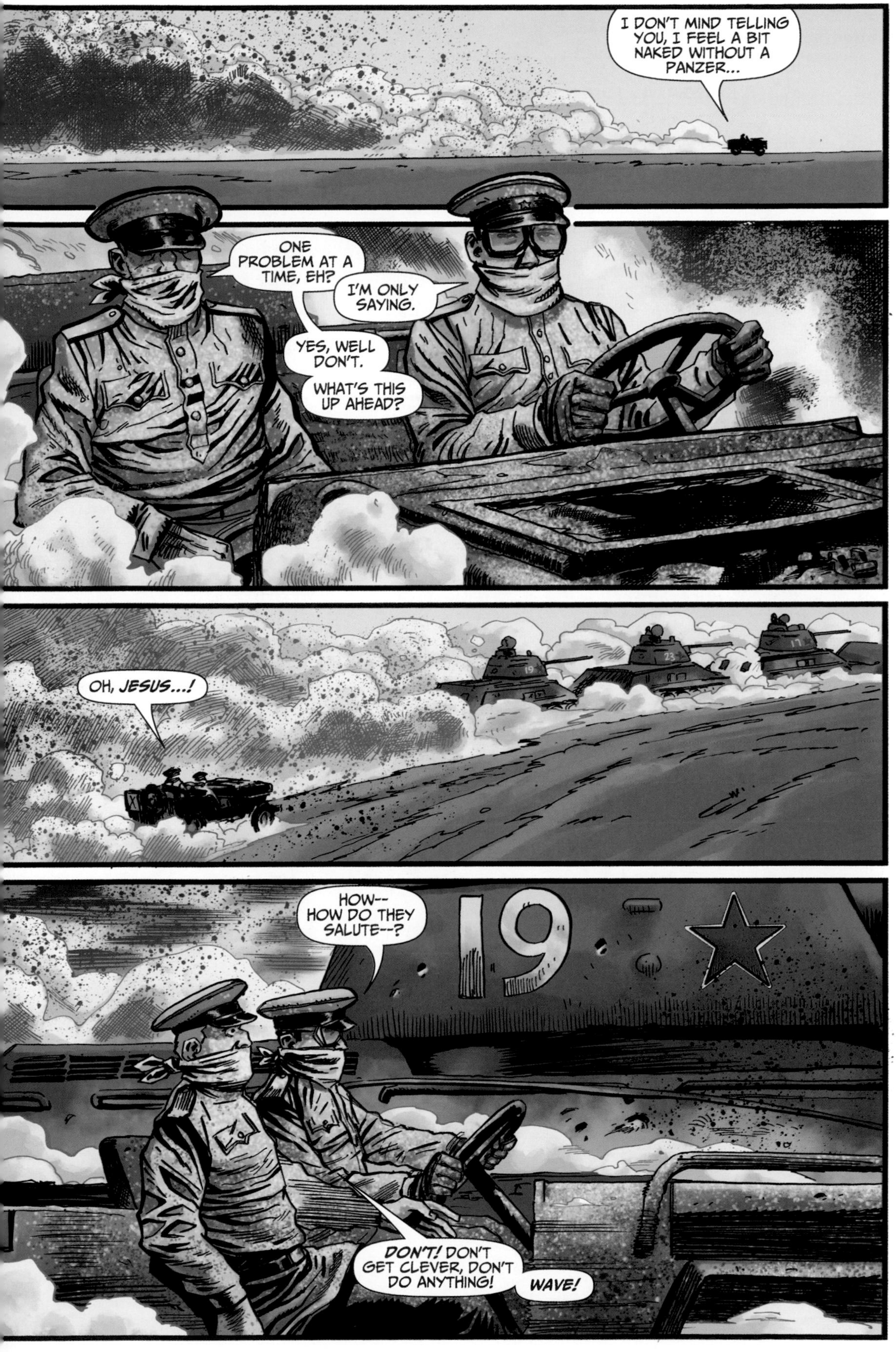
I DON'T MIND TELLING YOU, I FEEL A BIT NAKED WITHOUT A PANZER...
ONE PROBLEM AT A TIME, EH?
I'M ONLY SAYING.
YES, WELL DON'T.
WHAT'S THIS UP AHEAD?
19
23
17
OH, *JESUS...!*
HOW-- HOW DO THEY SALUTE--?
19
DON'T! DON'T GET CLEVER, DON'T DO ANYTHING!
WAVE!

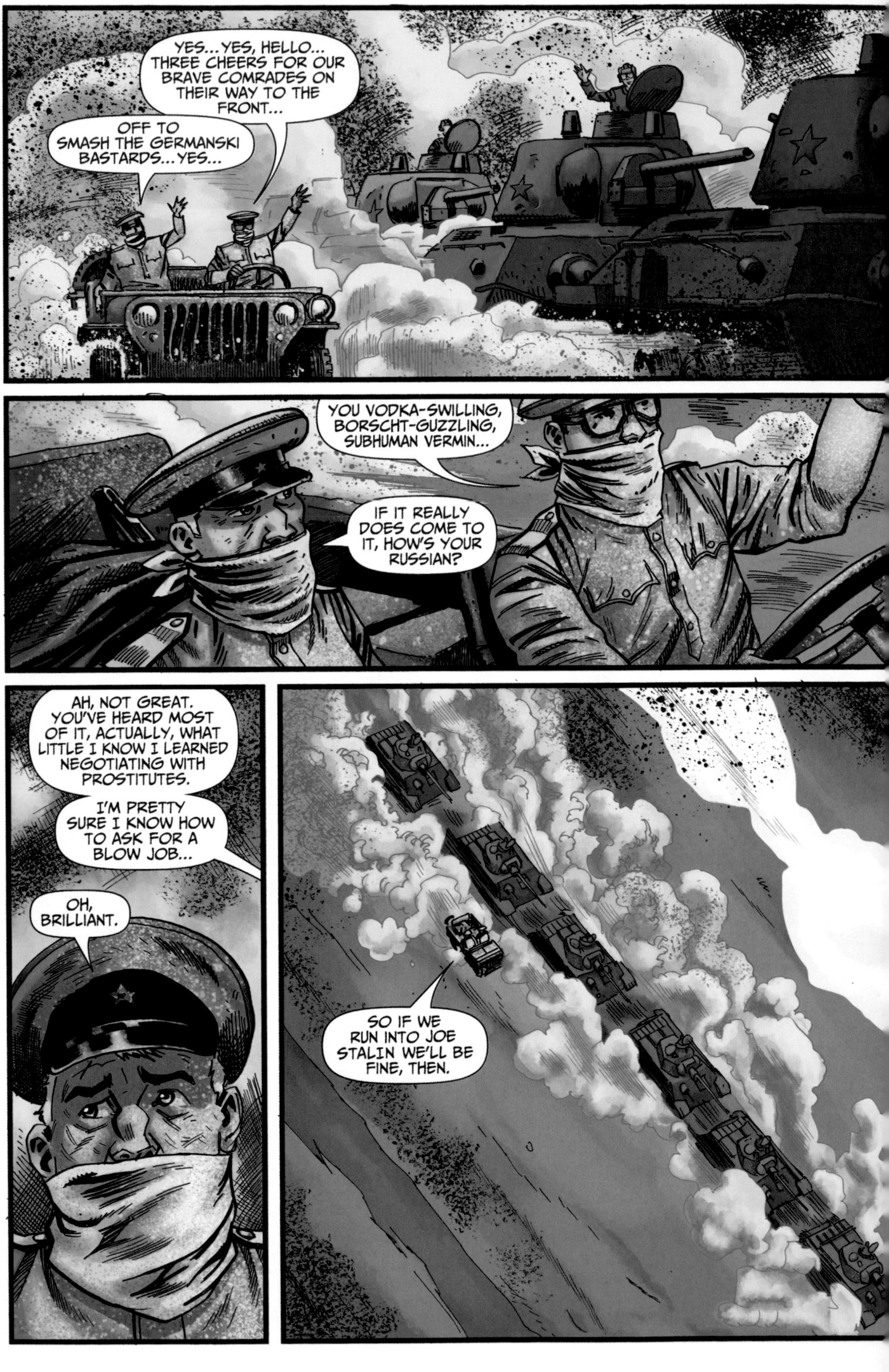
YES...YES, HELLO... THREE CHEERS FOR OUR BRAVE COMRADES ON THEIR WAY TO THE FRONT...
OFF TO SMASH THE GERMANSKI BASTARDS...YES...
YOU VODKA-SWILLING, BORSCHT-GUZZLING, SUBHUMAN VERMIN...
IF IT REALLY DOES COME TO IT, HOW'S YOUR RUSSIAN?
AH, NOT GREAT. YOU'VE HEARD MOST OF IT, ACTUALLY, WHAT LITTLE I KNOW I LEARNED NEGOTIATING WITH PROSTITUTES.
I'M PRETTY SURE I KNOW HOW TO ASK FOR A BLOW JOB...
OH, BRILLIANT.
SO IF WE RUN INTO JOE STALIN WE'LL BE FINE, THEN.

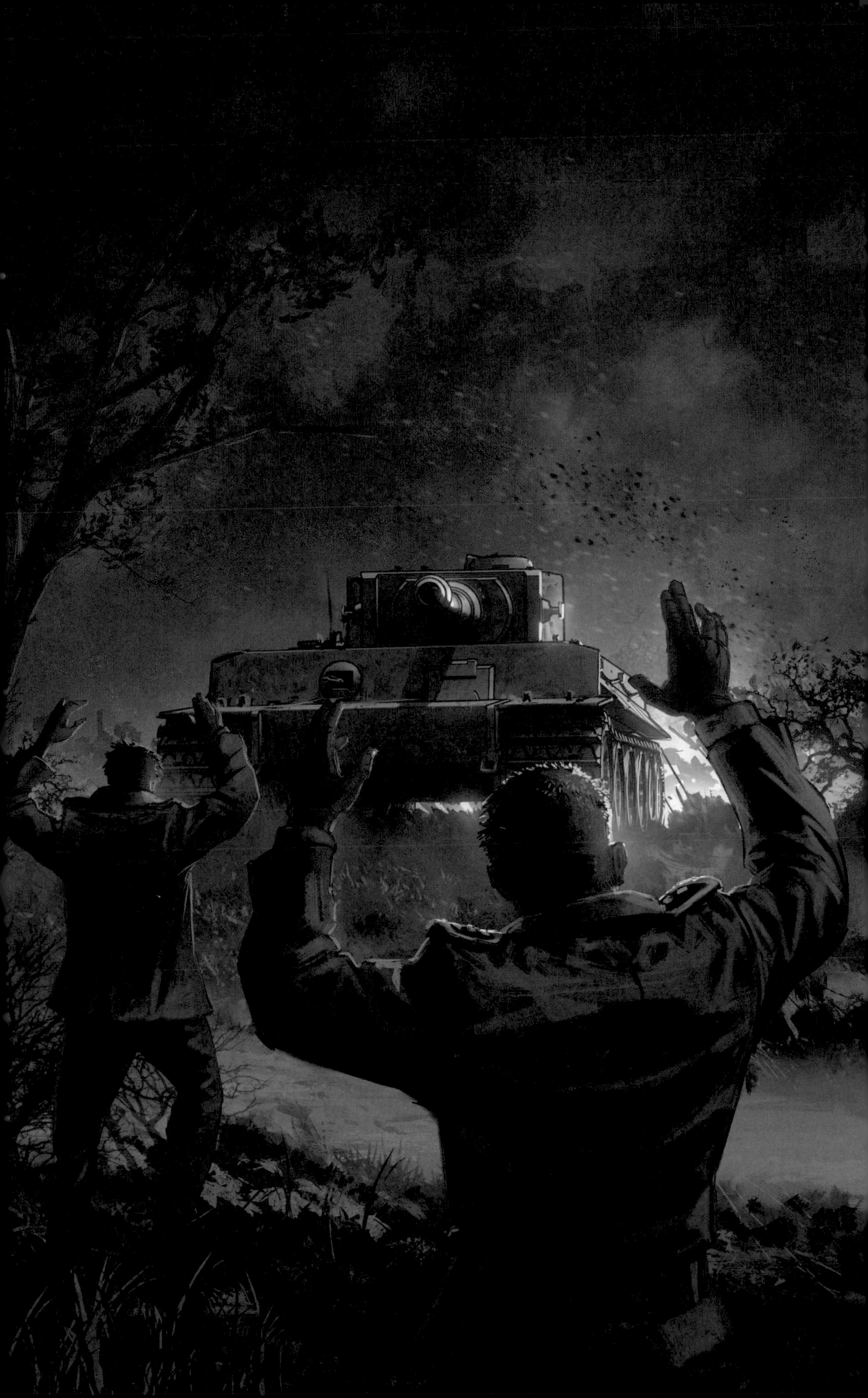

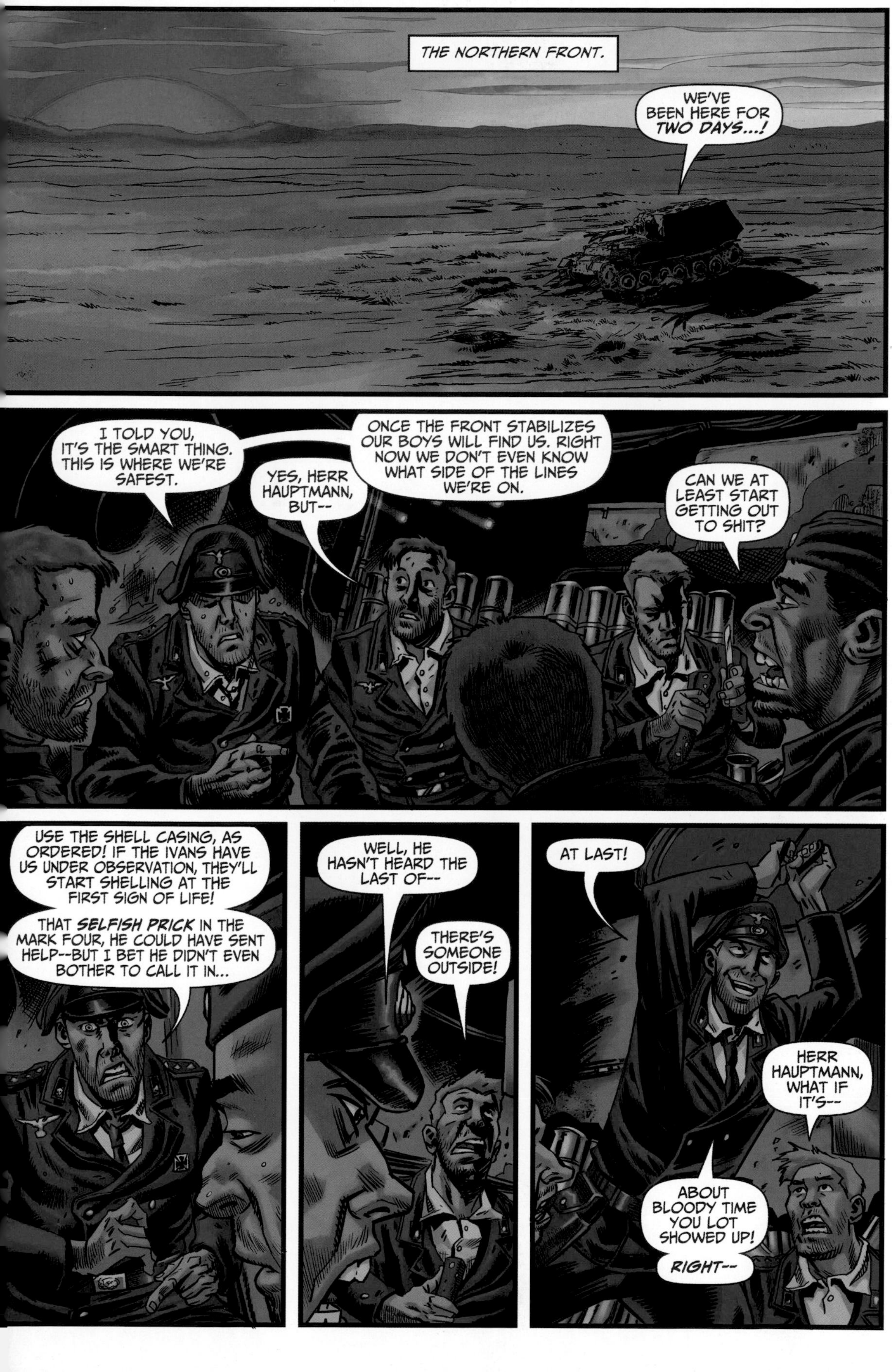
THE NORTHERN FRONT.
WE'VE BEEN HERE FOR TWO DAYS...!
I TOLD YOU, IT'S THE SMART THING. THIS IS WHERE WE'RE SAFEST.
YES, HERR HAUPTMANN, BUT--
ONCE THE FRONT STABILIZES OUR BOYS WILL FIND US. RIGHT NOW WE DON'T EVEN KNOW WHAT SIDE OF THE LINES WE'RE ON.
CAN WE AT LEAST START GETTING OUT TO SHIT?
USE THE SHELL CASING, AS ORDERED! IF THE IVANS HAVE US UNDER OBSERVATION, THEY'LL START SHELLING AT THE FIRST SIGN OF LIFE!
THAT SELFISH PRICK IN THE MARK FOUR, HE COULD HAVE SENT HELP--BUT I BET HE DIDN'T EVEN BOTHER TO CALL IT IN...
WELL, HE HASN'T HEARD THE LAST OF--
THERE'S SOMEONE OUTSIDE!
AT LAST!
HERR HAUPTMANN, WHAT IF IT'S--
ABOUT BLOODY TIME YOU LOT SHOWED UP!
RIGHT--

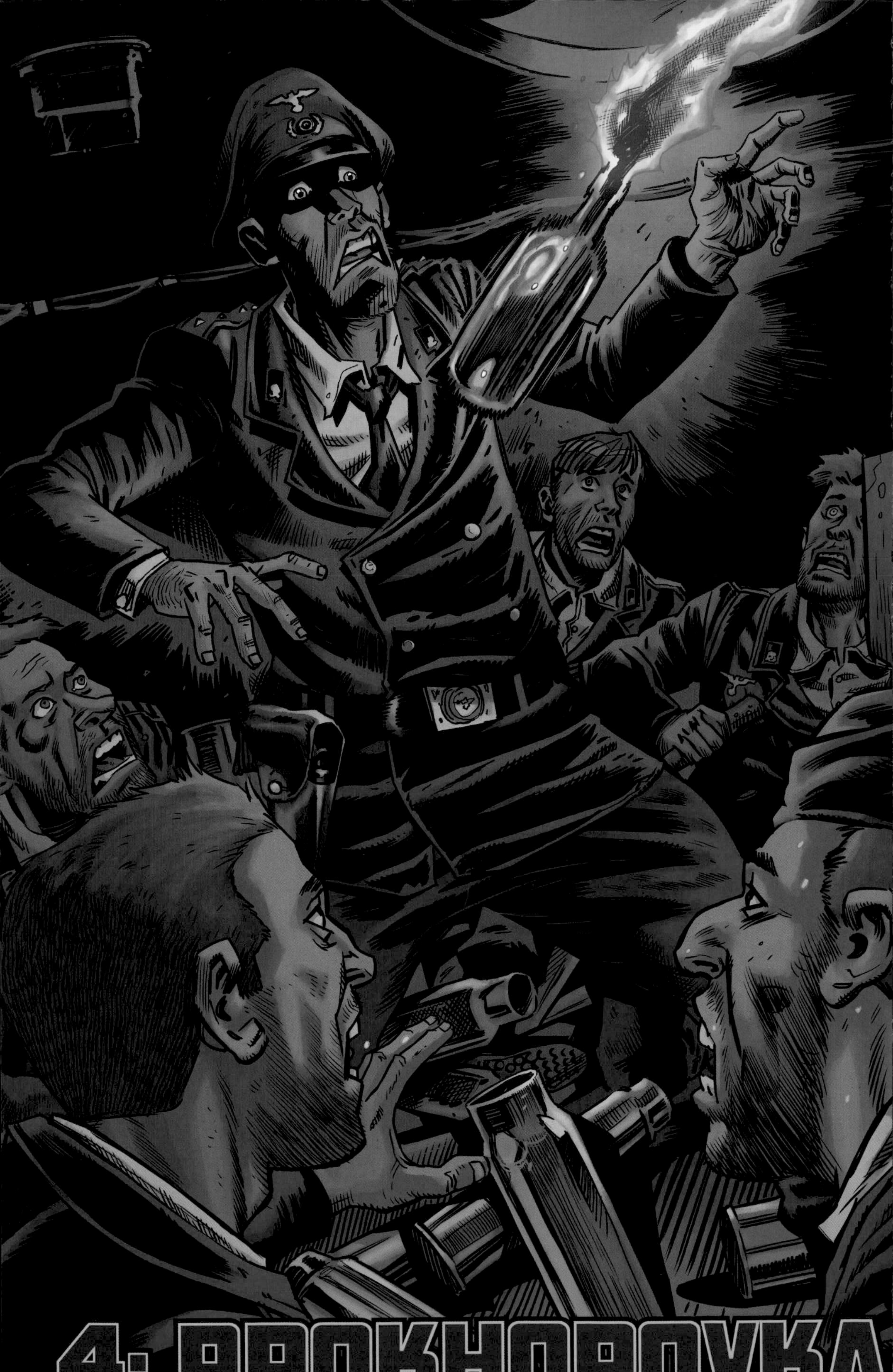

4: PROKHOROVKA

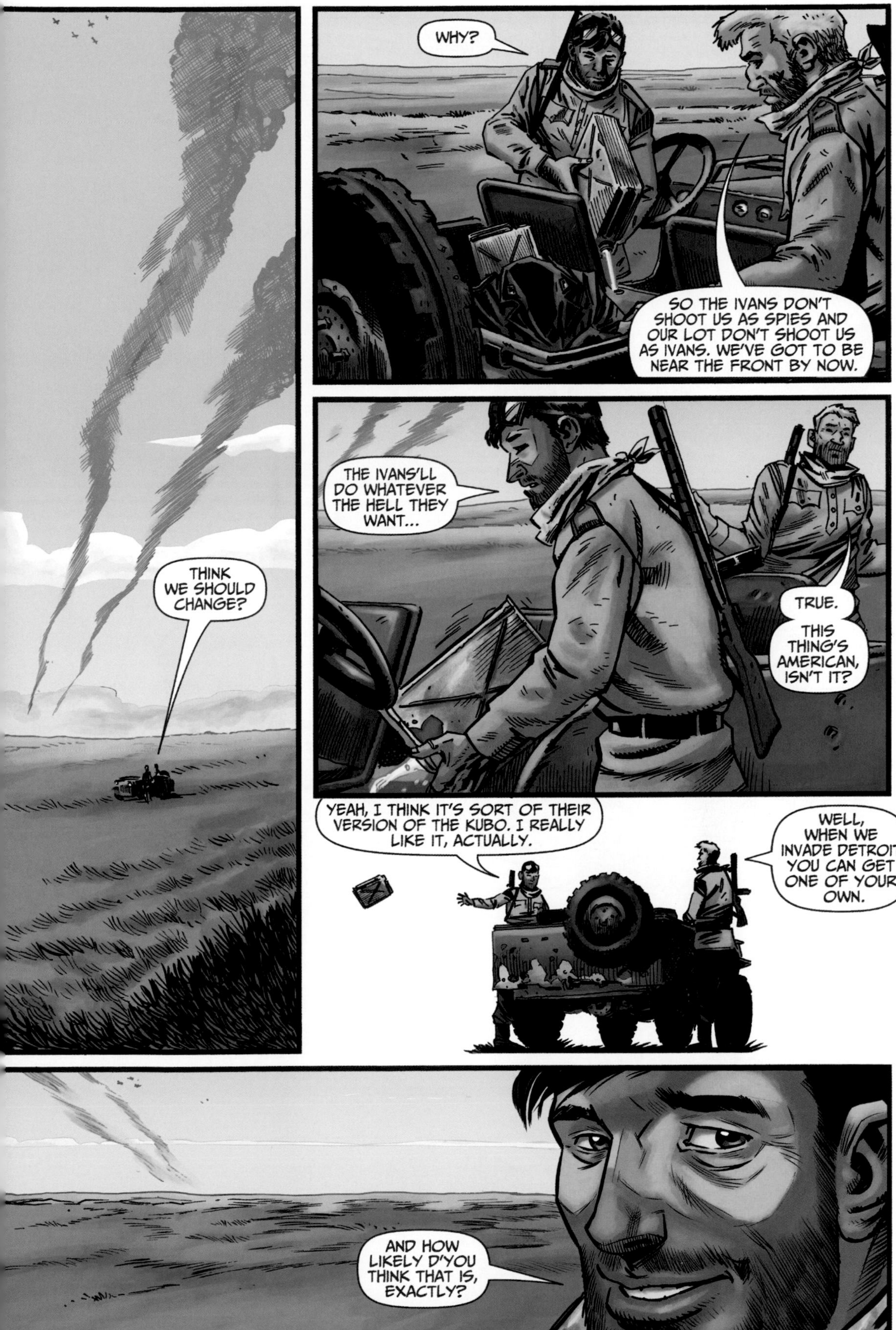
THINK WE SHOULD CHANGE?
WHY?
SO THE IVANS DON'T SHOOT US AS SPIES AND OUR LOT DON'T SHOOT US AS IVANS. WE'VE GOT TO BE NEAR THE FRONT BY NOW.
THE IVANS'LL DO WHATEVER THE HELL THEY WANT...
TRUE.
THIS THING'S AMERICAN, ISN'T IT?
YEAH, I THINK IT'S SORT OF THEIR VERSION OF THE KUBO. I REALLY LIKE IT, ACTUALLY.
WELL, WHEN WE INVADE DETROIT YOU CAN GET ONE OF YOUR OWN.
AND HOW LIKELY D'YOU THINK THAT IS, EXACTLY?

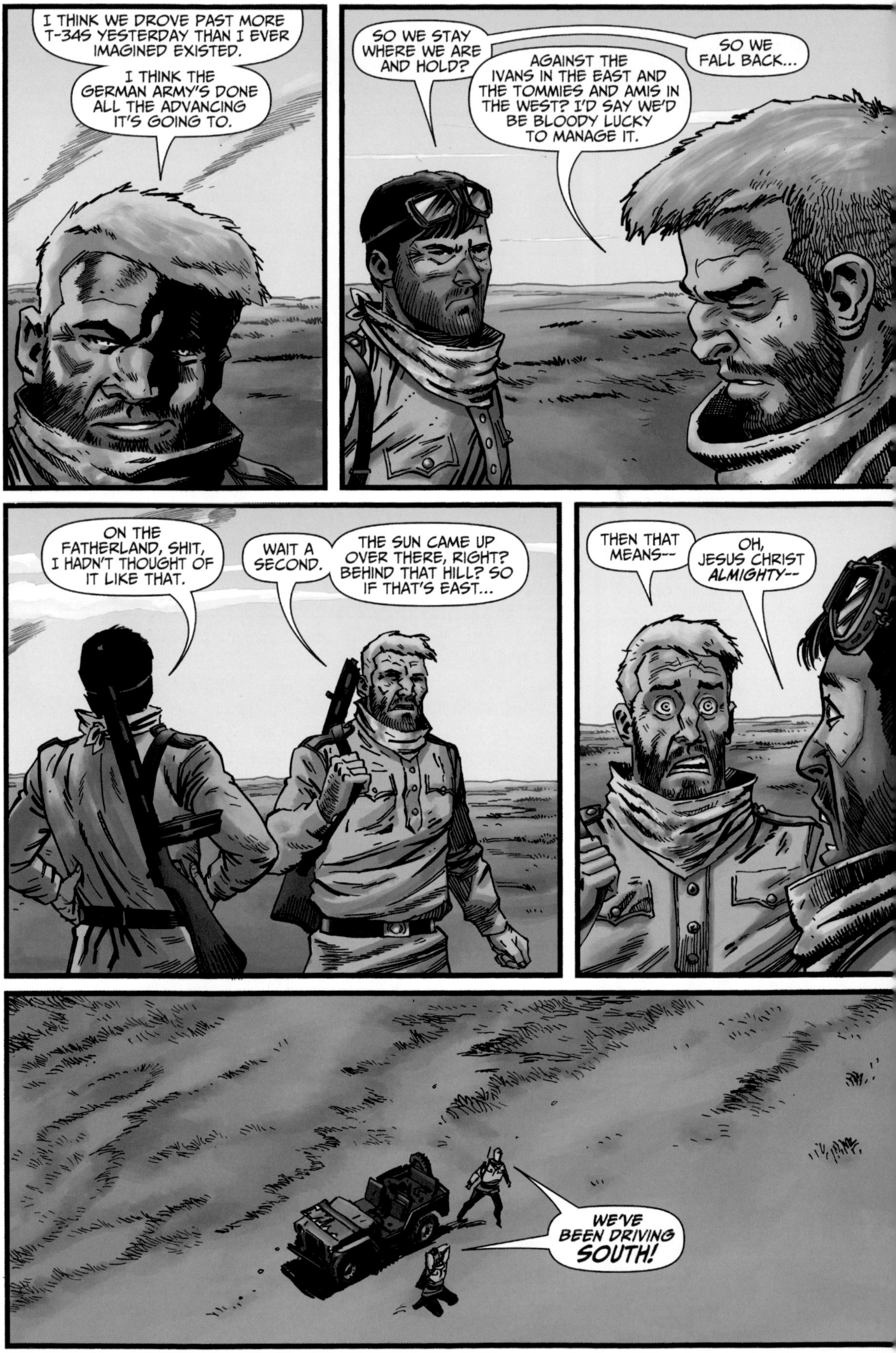

I THINK WE DROVE PAST MORE T-34S YESTERDAY THAN I EVER IMAGINED EXISTED.
I THINK THE GERMAN ARMY'S DONE ALL THE ADVANCING IT'S GOING TO.
SO WE STAY WHERE WE ARE AND HOLD?
SO WE FALL BACK...
AGAINST THE IVANS IN THE EAST AND THE TOMMIES AND AMIS IN THE WEST? I'D SAY WE'D BE BLOODY LUCKY TO MANAGE IT.
ON THE FATHERLAND, SHIT, I HADN'T THOUGHT OF IT LIKE THAT.
WAIT A SECOND.
THE SUN CAME UP OVER THERE, RIGHT? BEHIND THAT HILL? SO IF THAT'S EAST...
THEN THAT MEANS--
OH, JESUS CHRIST *ALMIGHTY*--
WE'VE BEEN DRIVING ***SOUTH!***

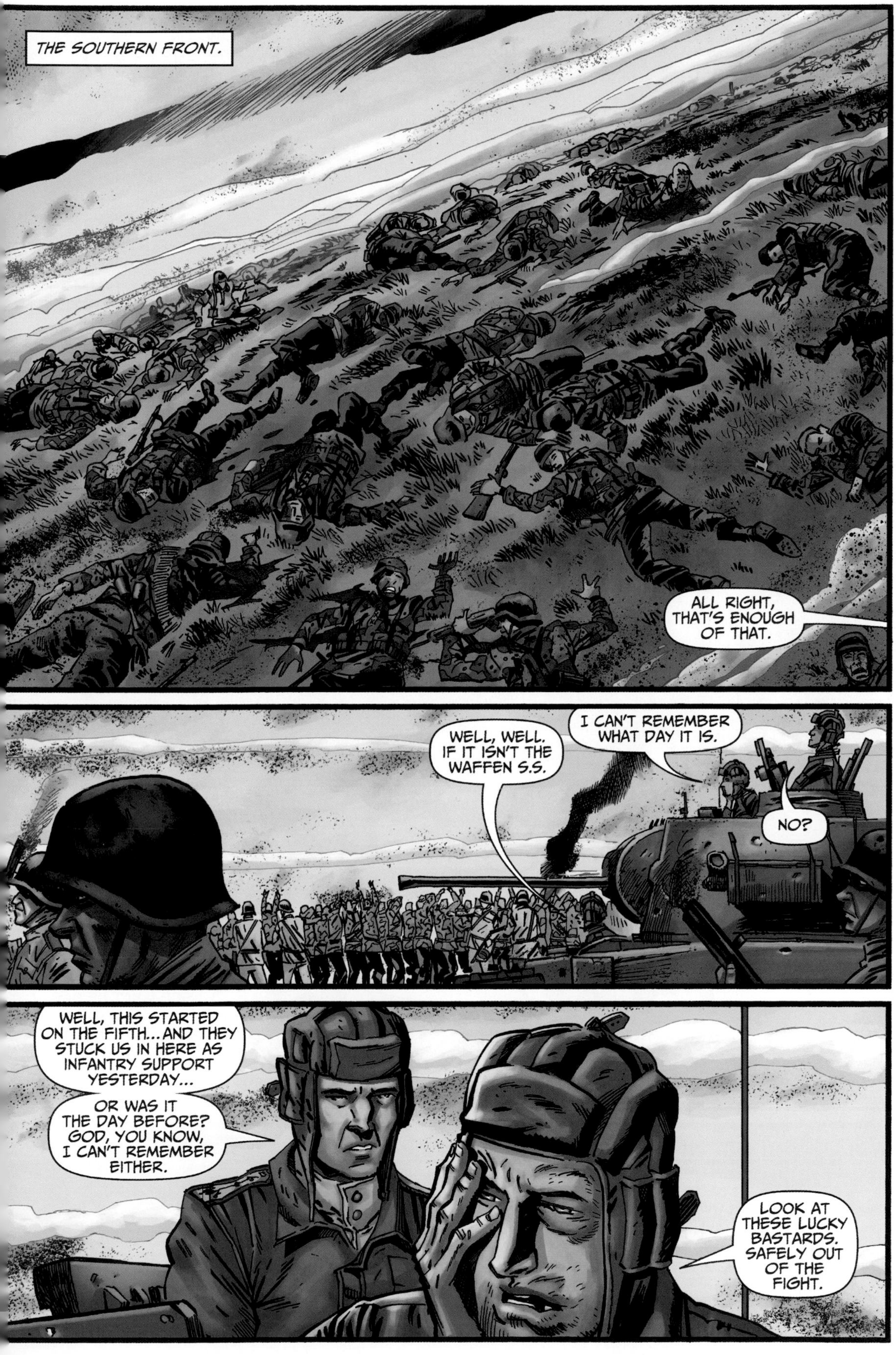
THE SOUTHERN FRONT.
ALL RIGHT, THAT'S ENOUGH OF THAT.
WELL, WELL. IF IT ISN'T THE WAFFEN S.S.
I CAN'T REMEMBER WHAT DAY IT IS.
NO?
WELL, THIS STARTED ON THE FIFTH... AND THEY STUCK US IN HERE AS INFANTRY SUPPORT YESTERDAY...
OR WAS IT THE DAY BEFORE? GOD, YOU KNOW, I CAN'T REMEMBER EITHER.
LOOK AT THESE LUCKY BASTARDS. SAFELY OUT OF THE FIGHT.

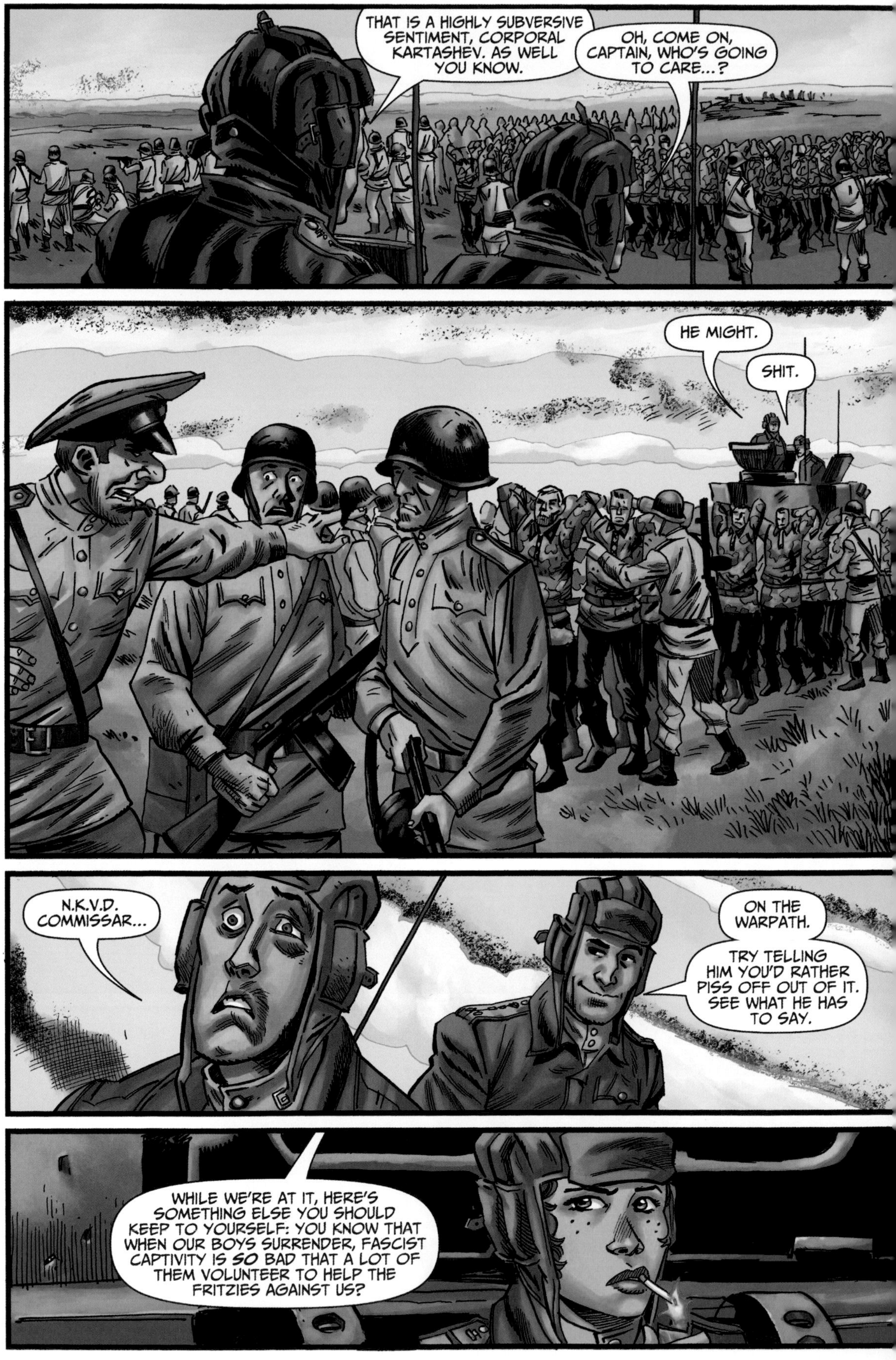
THAT IS A HIGHLY SUBVERSIVE SENTIMENT, CORPORAL KARTASHEV. AS WELL YOU KNOW.
OH, COME ON, CAPTAIN, WHO'S GOING TO CARE...?
HE MIGHT.
SHIT.
N.K.V.D. COMMISSAR...
ON THE WARPATH.
TRY TELLING HIM YOU'D RATHER PISS OFF OUT OF IT. SEE WHAT HE HAS TO SAY.
WHILE WE'RE AT IT, HERE'S SOMETHING ELSE YOU SHOULD KEEP TO YOURSELF: YOU KNOW THAT WHEN OUR BOYS SURRENDER, FASCIST CAPTIVITY IS SO BAD THAT A LOT OF THEM VOLUNTEER TO HELP THE FRITZIES AGAINST US?

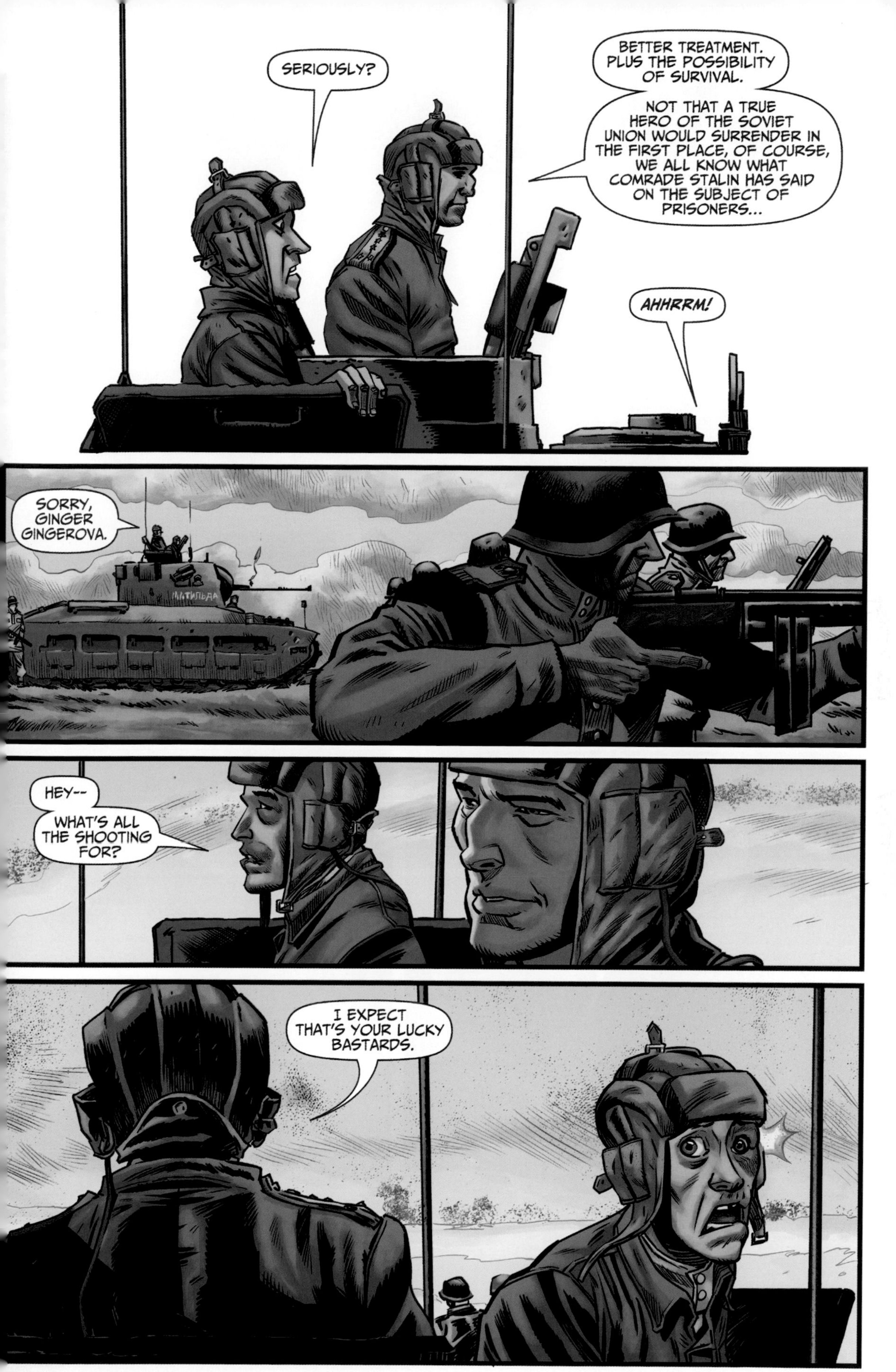
SERIOUSLY?
BETTER TREATMENT. PLUS THE POSSIBILITY OF SURVIVAL.
NOT THAT A TRUE HERO OF THE SOVIET UNION WOULD SURRENDER IN THE FIRST PLACE, OF COURSE, WE ALL KNOW WHAT COMRADE STALIN HAS SAID ON THE SUBJECT OF PRISONERS...
AHHRRM!
SORRY, GINGER GINGEROVA.
HEY--
WHAT'S ALL THE SHOOTING FOR?
I EXPECT THAT'S YOUR LUCKY BASTARDS.

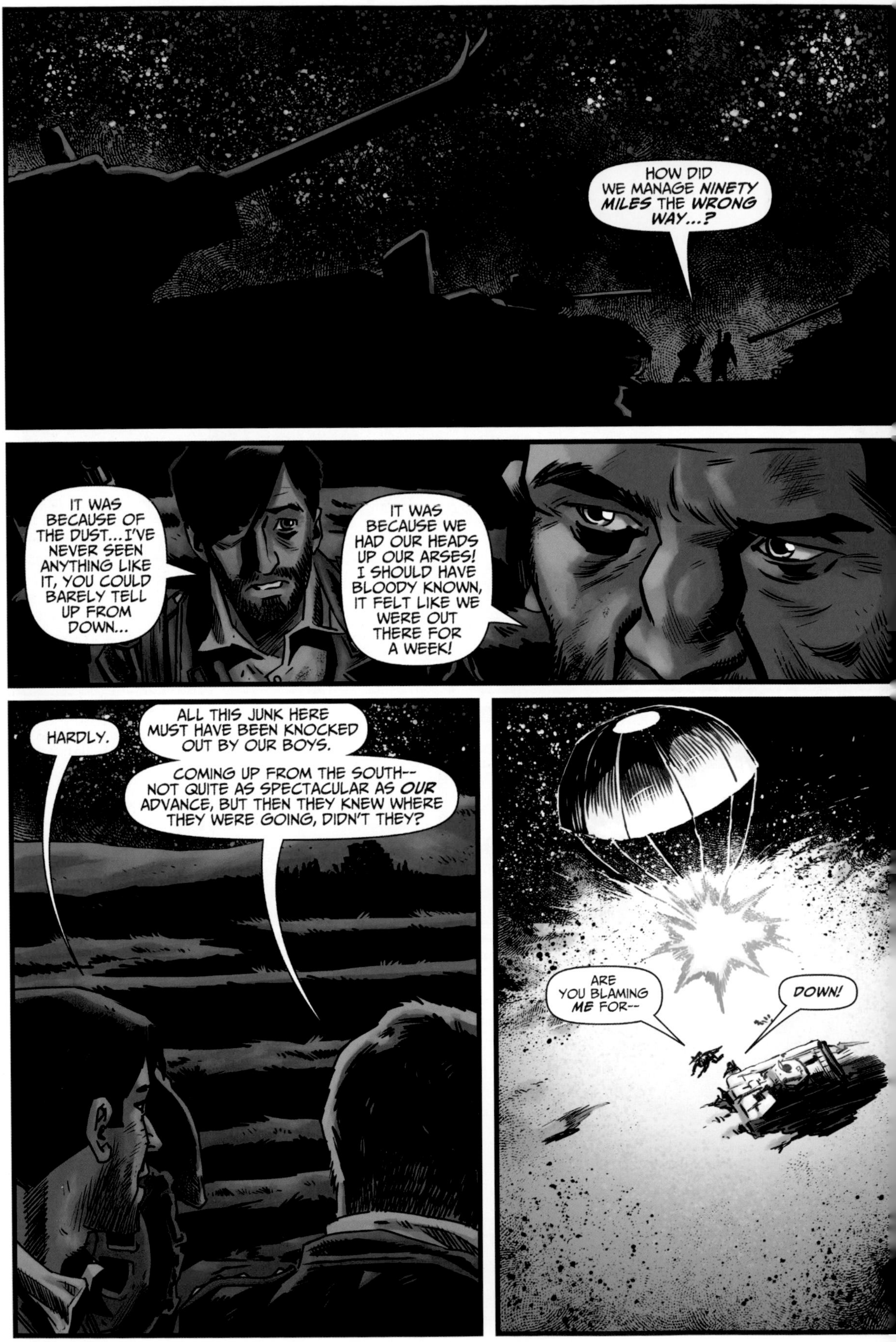
HOW DID WE MANAGE *NINETY MILES* THE *WRONG* WAY...?
IT WAS BECAUSE OF THE DUST...I'VE NEVER SEEN ANYTHING LIKE IT, YOU COULD BARELY TELL UP FROM DOWN...
IT WAS BECAUSE WE HAD OUR HEADS UP OUR ARSES! I SHOULD HAVE BLOODY KNOWN, IT FELT LIKE WE WERE OUT THERE FOR A WEEK!
HARDLY.
ALL THIS JUNK HERE MUST HAVE BEEN KNOCKED OUT BY OUR BOYS.
COMING UP FROM THE SOUTH-- NOT QUITE AS SPECTACULAR AS *OUR* ADVANCE, BUT THEN THEY KNEW WHERE THEY WERE GOING, DIDN'T THEY?
ARE YOU BLAMING *ME* FOR--
DOWN!

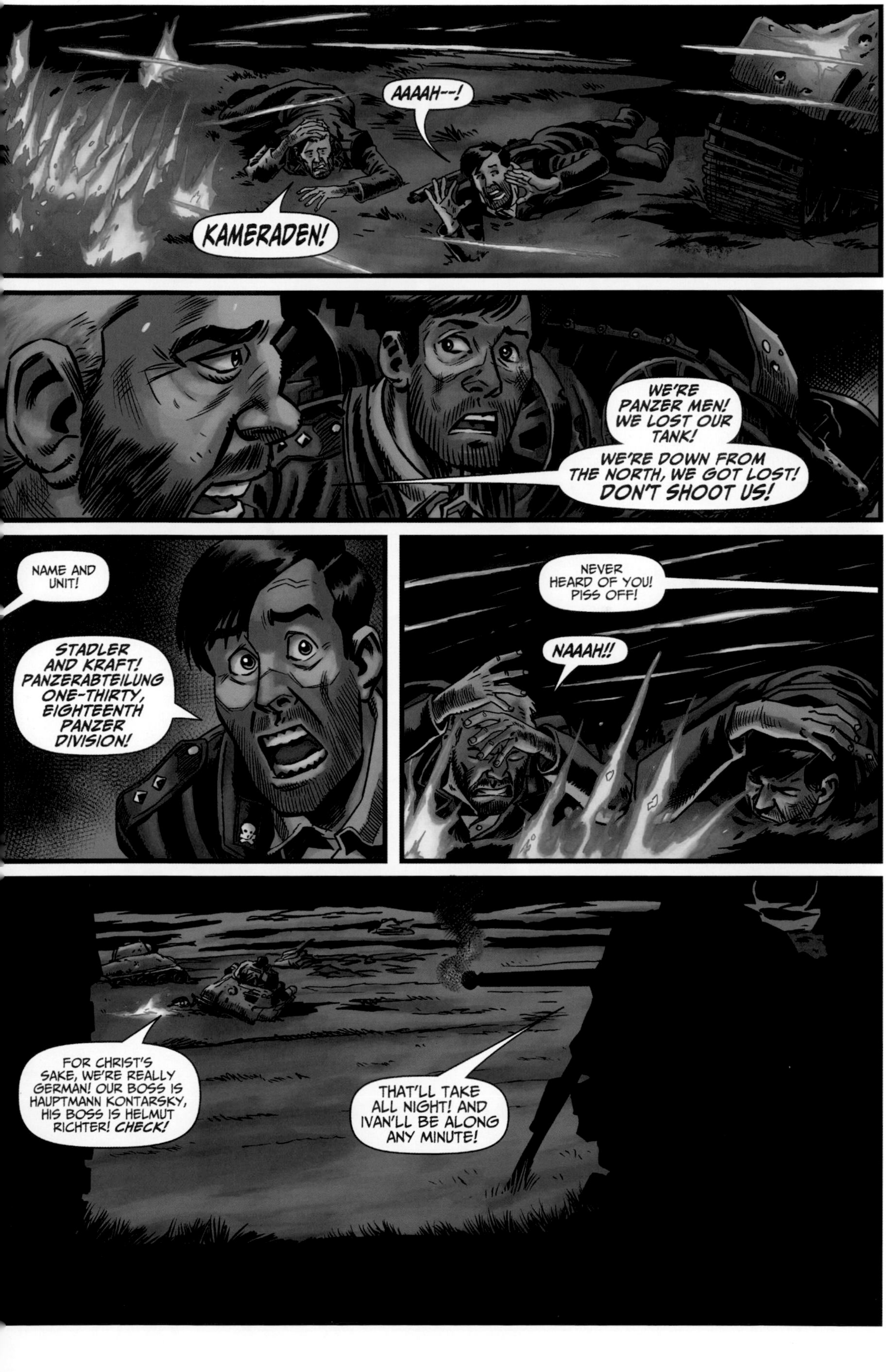
AAAAH--!
KAMERADEN!
WE'RE PANZER MEN! WE LOST OUR TANK!
WE'RE DOWN FROM THE NORTH, WE GOT LOST! DON'T SHOOT US!
NAME AND UNIT!
STADLER AND KRAFT! PANZERABTEILUNG ONE-THIRTY, EIGHTEENTH PANZER DIVISION!
NEVER HEARD OF YOU! PISS OFF!
NAAAH!!
FOR CHRIST'S SAKE, WE'RE REALLY GERMAN! OUR BOSS IS HAUPTMANN KONTARSKY, HIS BOSS IS HELMUT RICHTER! CHECK!
THAT'LL TAKE ALL NIGHT! AND IVAN'LL BE ALONG ANY MINUTE!

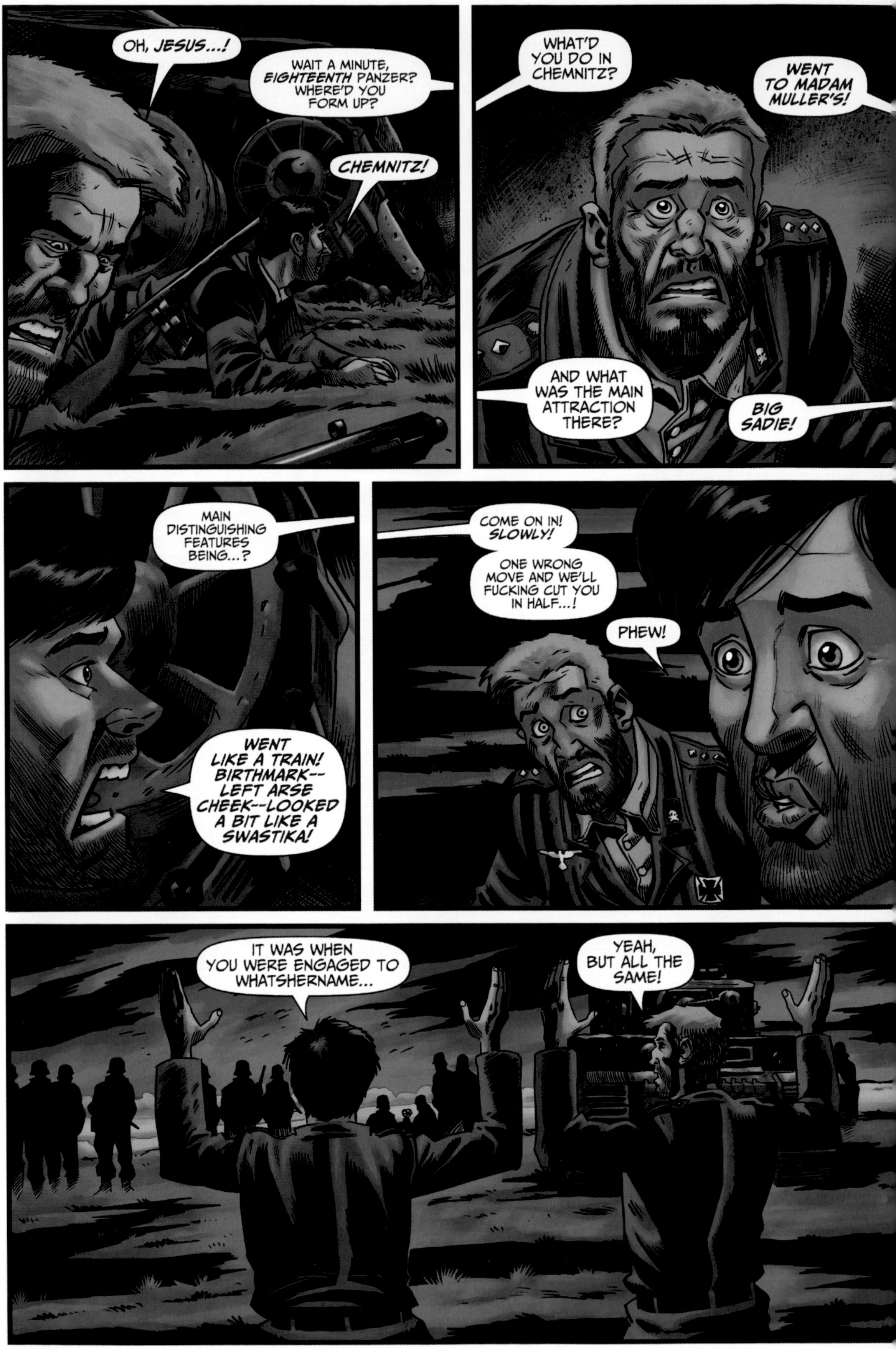
OH, JESUS...!
WAIT A MINUTE, EIGHTEENTH PANZER? WHERE'D YOU FORM UP?
CHEMNITZ!
WHAT'D YOU DO IN CHEMNITZ?
WENT TO MADAM MULLER'S!
AND WHAT WAS THE MAIN ATTRACTION THERE?
BIG SADIE!
MAIN DISTINGUISHING FEATURES BEING...?
WENT LIKE A TRAIN! BIRTHMARK--LEFT ARSE CHEEK--LOOKED A BIT LIKE A SWASTIKA!
COME ON IN! SLOWLY!
ONE WRONG MOVE AND WE'LL FUCKING CUT YOU IN HALF...!
PHEW!
IT WAS WHEN YOU WERE ENGAGED TO WHATSHERNAME...
YEAH, BUT ALL THE SAME!

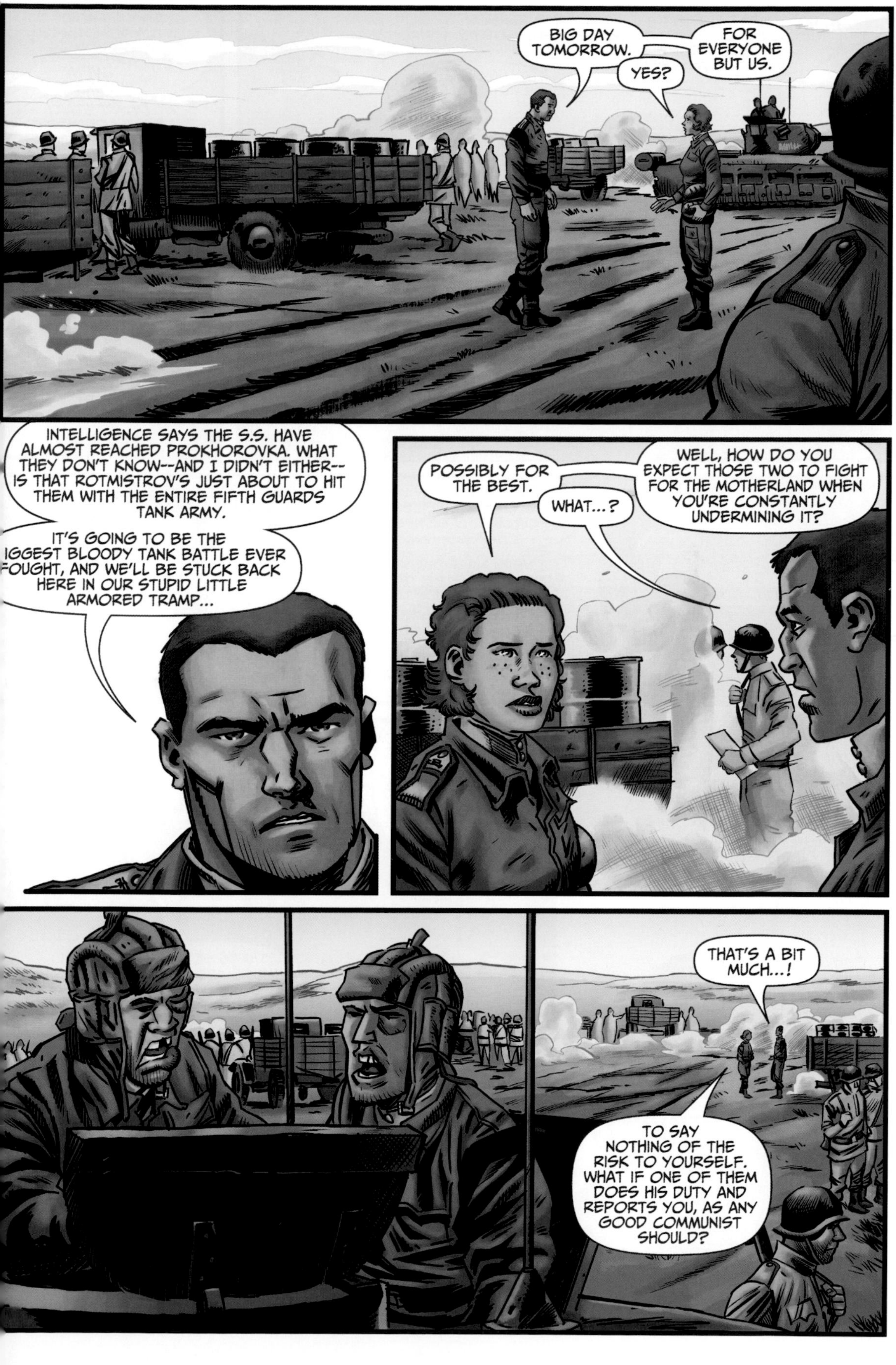
BIG DAY TOMORROW.
YES?
FOR EVERYONE BUT US.
INTELLIGENCE SAYS THE S.S. HAVE ALMOST REACHED PROKHOROVKA. WHAT THEY DON'T KNOW--AND I DIDN'T EITHER--IS THAT ROTMISTROV'S JUST ABOUT TO HIT THEM WITH THE ENTIRE FIFTH GUARDS TANK ARMY.
IT'S GOING TO BE THE IGGEST BLOODY TANK BATTLE EVER OUGHT, AND WE'LL BE STUCK BACK HERE IN OUR STUPID LITTLE ARMORED TRAMP...
POSSIBLY FOR THE BEST.
WHAT...?
WELL, HOW DO YOU EXPECT THOSE TWO TO FIGHT FOR THE MOTHERLAND WHEN YOU'RE CONSTANTLY UNDERMINING IT?
THAT'S A BIT MUCH...!
TO SAY NOTHING OF THE RISK TO YOURSELF. WHAT IF ONE OF THEM DOES HIS DUTY AND REPORTS YOU, AS ANY GOOD COMMUNIST SHOULD?

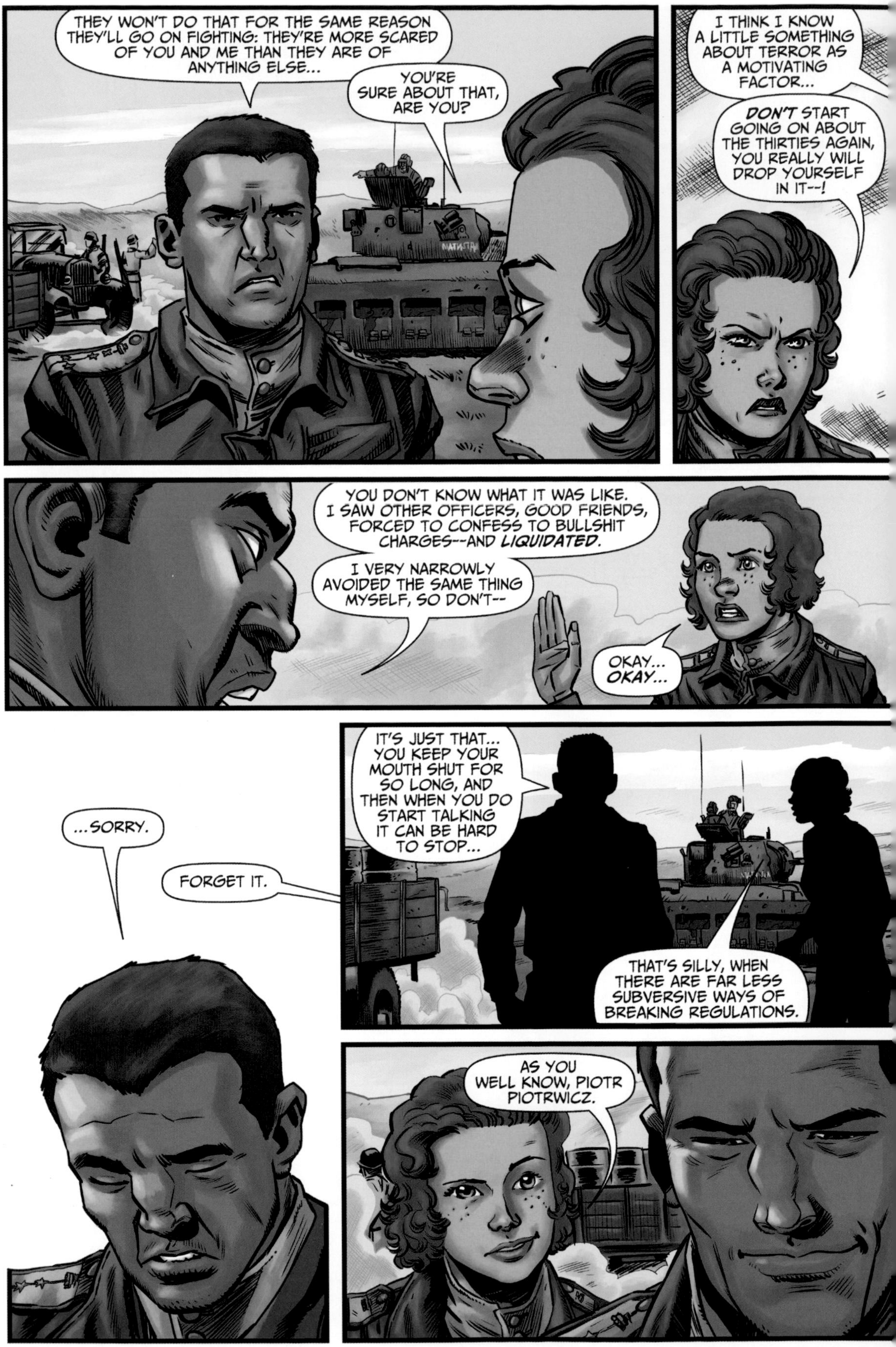
THEY WON'T DO THAT FOR THE SAME REASON THEY'LL GO ON FIGHTING: THEY'RE MORE SCARED OF YOU AND ME THAN THEY ARE OF ANYTHING ELSE...
YOU'RE SURE ABOUT THAT, ARE YOU?
I THINK I KNOW A LITTLE SOMETHING ABOUT TERROR AS A MOTIVATING FACTOR...
DON'T START GOING ON ABOUT THE THIRTIES AGAIN, YOU REALLY WILL DROP YOURSELF IN IT--!
YOU DON'T KNOW WHAT IT WAS LIKE. I SAW OTHER OFFICERS, GOOD FRIENDS, FORCED TO CONFESS TO BULLSHIT CHARGES--AND *LIQUIDATED*.
I VERY NARROWLY AVOIDED THE SAME THING MYSELF, SO DON'T--
OKAY... **OKAY...**
IT'S JUST THAT... YOU KEEP YOUR MOUTH SHUT FOR SO LONG, AND THEN WHEN YOU DO START TALKING IT CAN BE HARD TO STOP...
...SORRY.
FORGET IT.
THAT'S SILLY, WHEN THERE ARE FAR LESS SUBVERSIVE WAYS OF BREAKING REGULATIONS.
AS YOU WELL KNOW, PIOTR PIOTRWICZ.

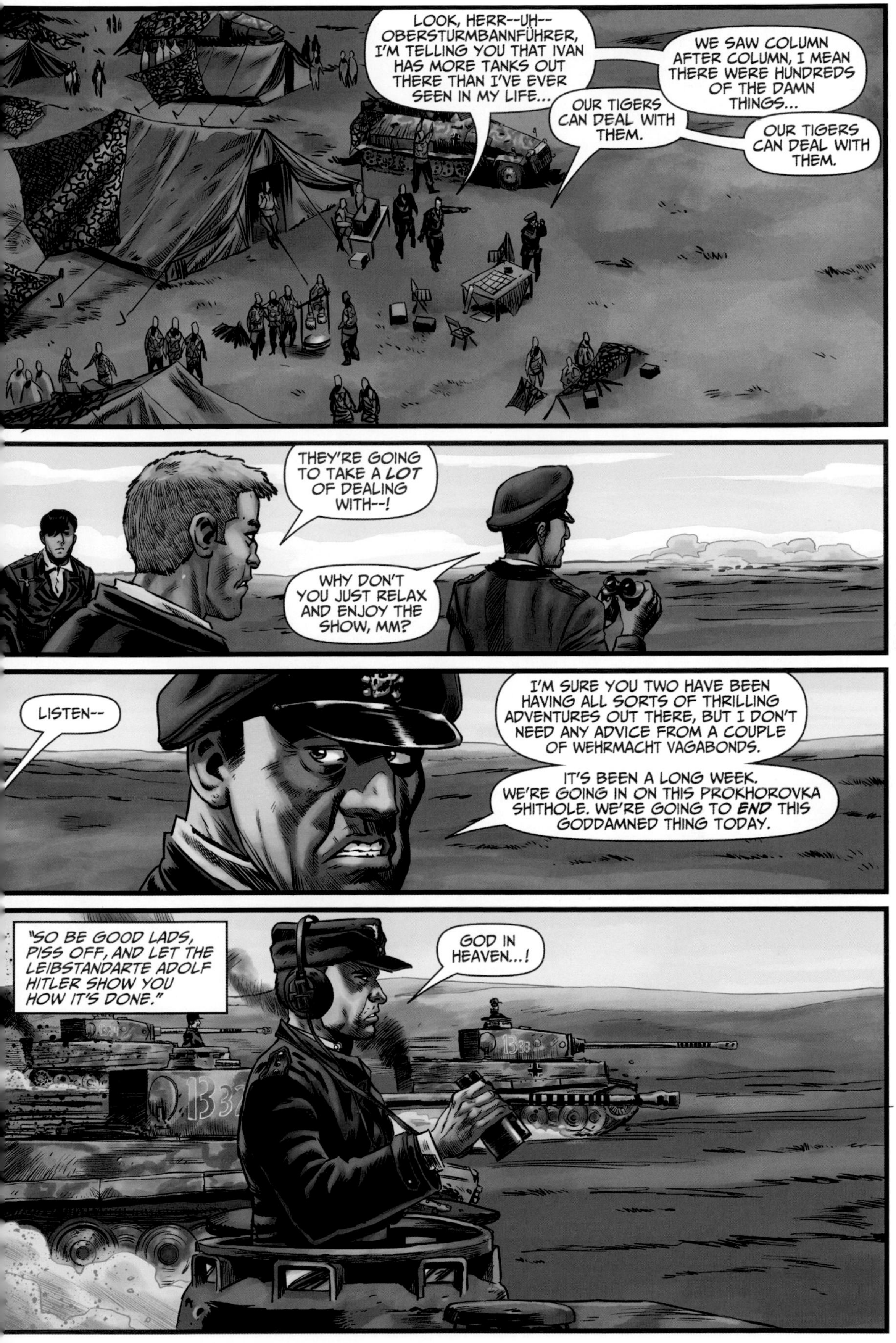
LOOK, HERR--UH--
OBERSTURMBANNFÜHRER,
I'M TELLING YOU THAT IVAN
HAS MORE TANKS OUT
THERE THAN I'VE EVER
SEEN IN MY LIFE...
WE SAW COLUMN
AFTER COLUMN, I MEAN
THERE WERE HUNDREDS
OF THE DAMN
THINGS...
OUR TIGERS
CAN DEAL WITH
THEM.
OUR TIGERS
CAN DEAL WITH
THEM.
THEY'RE GOING
TO TAKE A *LOT*
OF DEALING
WITH--!
WHY DON'T
YOU JUST RELAX
AND ENJOY THE
SHOW, MM?
LISTEN--
I'M SURE YOU TWO HAVE BEEN
HAVING ALL SORTS OF THRILLING
ADVENTURES OUT THERE, BUT I DON'T
NEED ANY ADVICE FROM A COUPLE
OF WEHRMACHT VAGABONDS.
IT'S BEEN A LONG WEEK.
WE'RE GOING IN ON THIS PROKHOROVKA
SHITHOLE. WE'RE GOING TO ***END*** THIS
GODDAMNED THING TODAY.
"SO BE GOOD LADS,
PISS OFF, AND LET THE
LEIBSTANDARTE ADOLF
HITLER SHOW YOU
HOW IT'S DONE."
GOD IN
HEAVEN...!

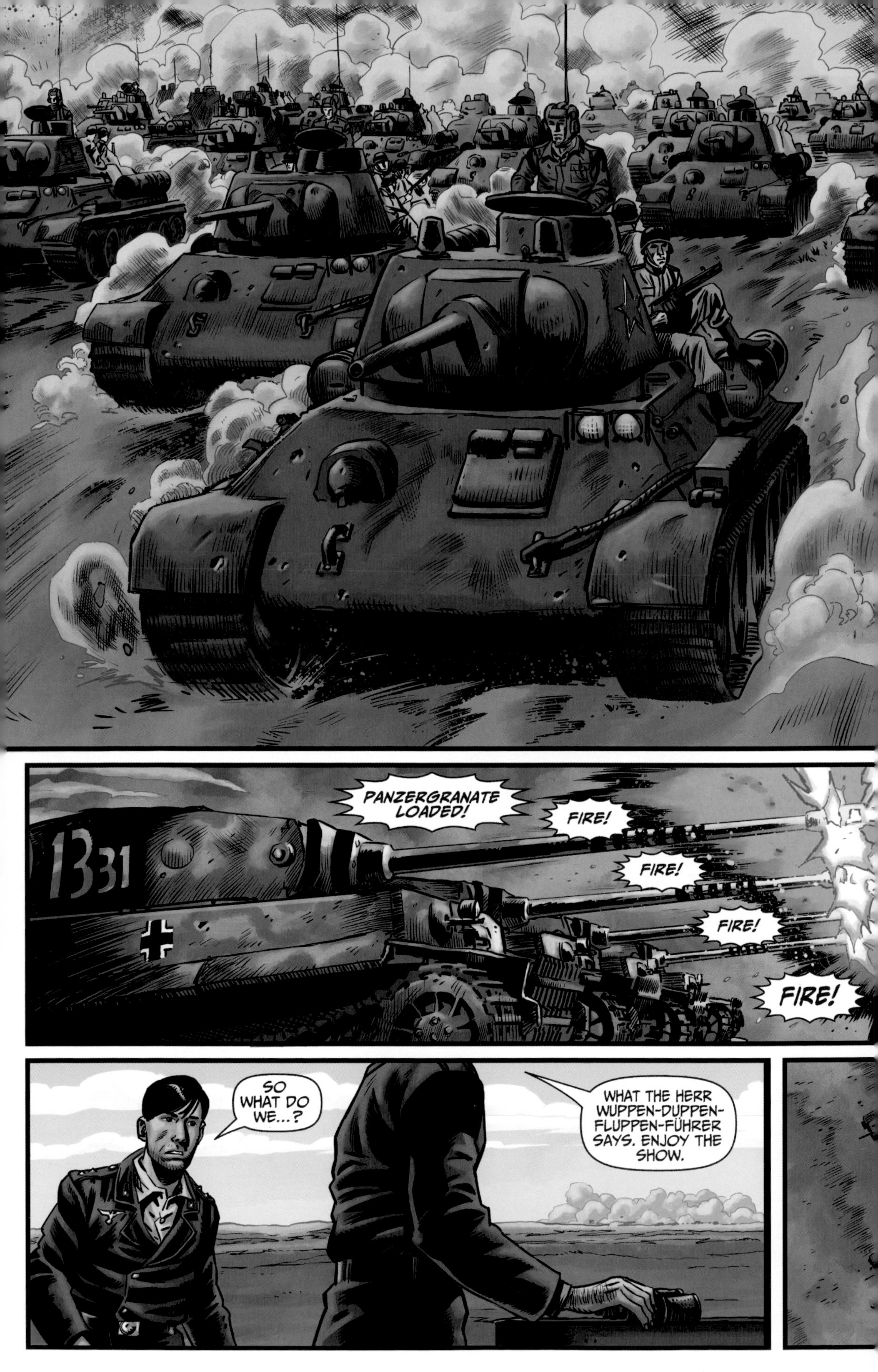
PANZERGRANATE LOADED!
FIRE!
FIRE!
FIRE!
FIRE!
SO WHAT DO WE...?
WHAT THE HERR WUPPEN-DUPPEN-FLUPPEN-FÜHRER SAYS. ENJOY THE SHOW.
13 31

OH, SHIT!

CALL THE GUNS! DROP EVERYTHING WE'VE GOT ON THE BASTARDS!

SIR, IT'S HAPPENING ALL ALONG THE LINE! IVAN TANKS ALL OVER THE PLACE!

AND WHERE THE HELL ARE THE LUFTWAFFE?!

DAS REICH-- TOTENKOPF--AND PEIPER SAYS HE'S ABOUT TO BE OVERRUN!

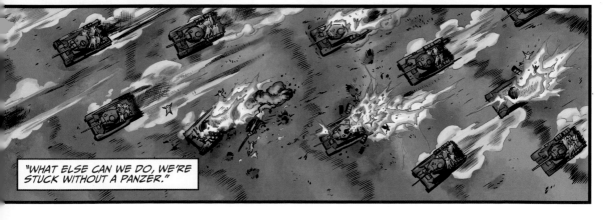

"WHAT ELSE CAN WE DO, WE'RE STUCK WITHOUT A PANZER."

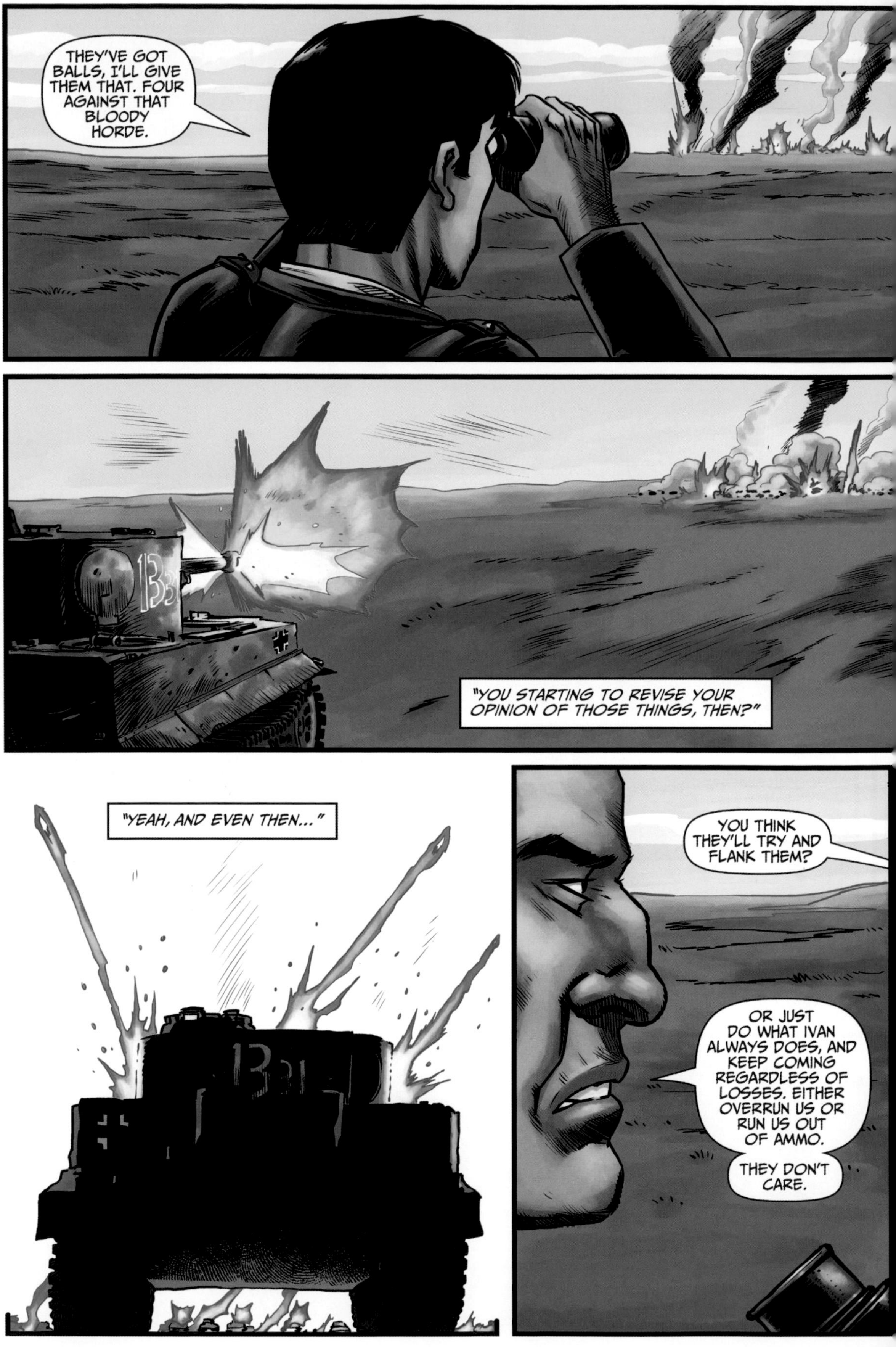
THEY'VE GOT BALLS, I'LL GIVE THEM THAT. FOUR AGAINST THAT BLOODY HORDE.
"YOU STARTING TO REVISE YOUR OPINION OF THOSE THINGS, THEN?"
"YEAH, AND EVEN THEN..."
YOU THINK THEY'LL TRY AND FLANK THEM?
OR JUST DO WHAT IVAN ALWAYS DOES, AND KEEP COMING REGARDLESS OF LOSSES. EITHER OVERRUN US OR RUN US OUT OF AMMO.
THEY DON'T CARE.

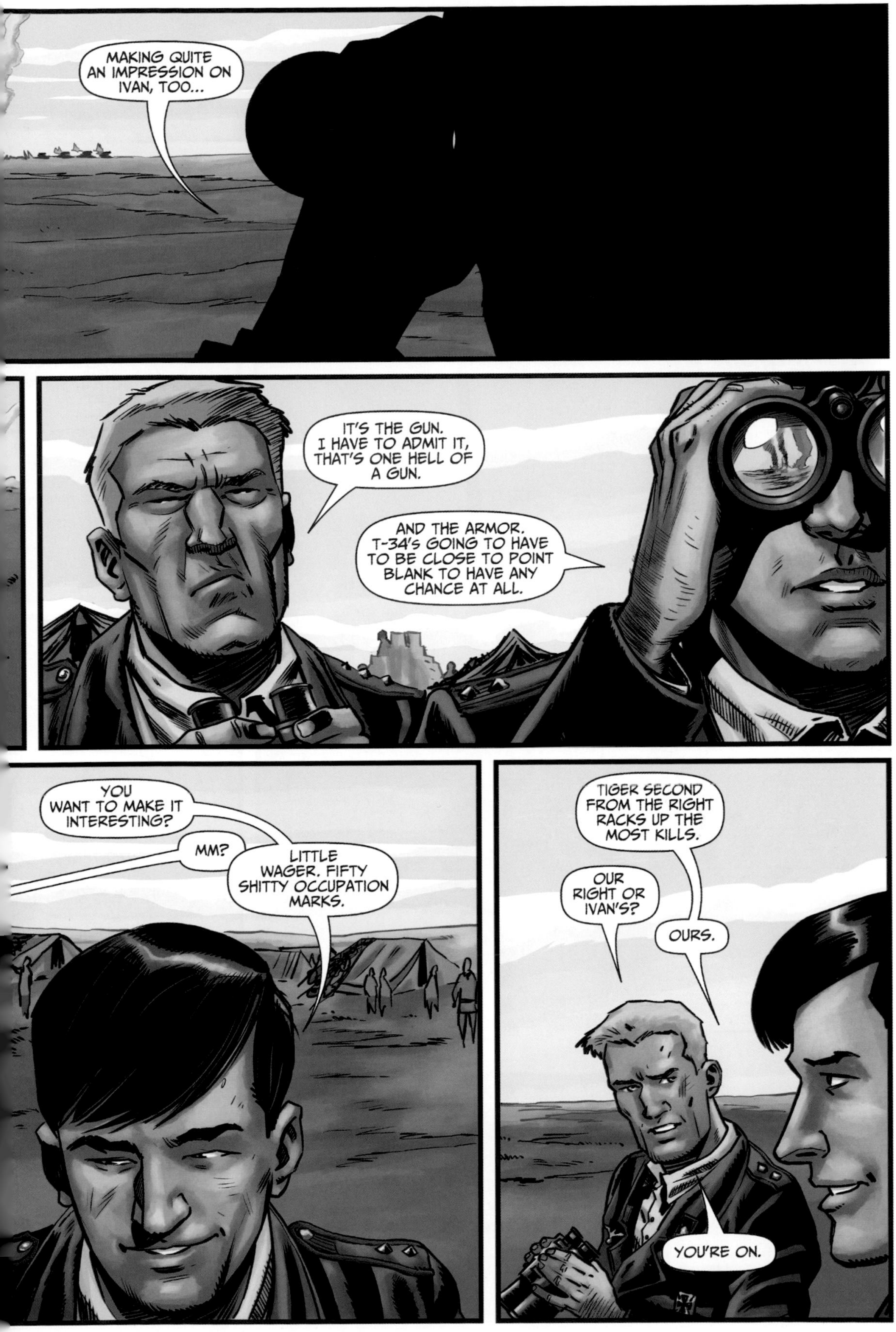
MAKING QUITE AN IMPRESSION ON IVAN, TOO...
IT'S THE GUN. I HAVE TO ADMIT IT, THAT'S ONE HELL OF A GUN.
AND THE ARMOR. T-34'S GOING TO HAVE TO BE CLOSE TO POINT BLANK TO HAVE ANY CHANCE AT ALL.
YOU WANT TO MAKE IT INTERESTING?
MM?
LITTLE WAGER. FIFTY SHITTY OCCUPATION MARKS.
TIGER SECOND FROM THE RIGHT RACKS UP THE MOST KILLS.
OUR RIGHT OR IVAN'S?
OURS.
YOU'RE ON.

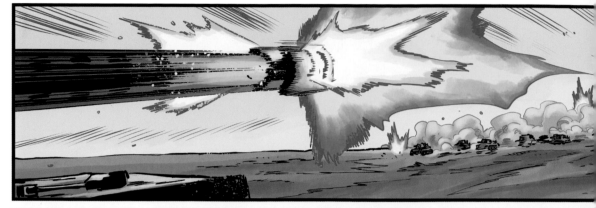

"JESUS!"

OH, THAT HAD TO HURT...!

I WONDER WHO THAT IS OUT THERE, ANYWAY...?

DON'T KNOW ABOUT THE GUNNER--BUT THEN NO ONE EVER CARES ABOUT THE GUNNER ANYWAY, DO THEY?

THE UNSUNG HERO...

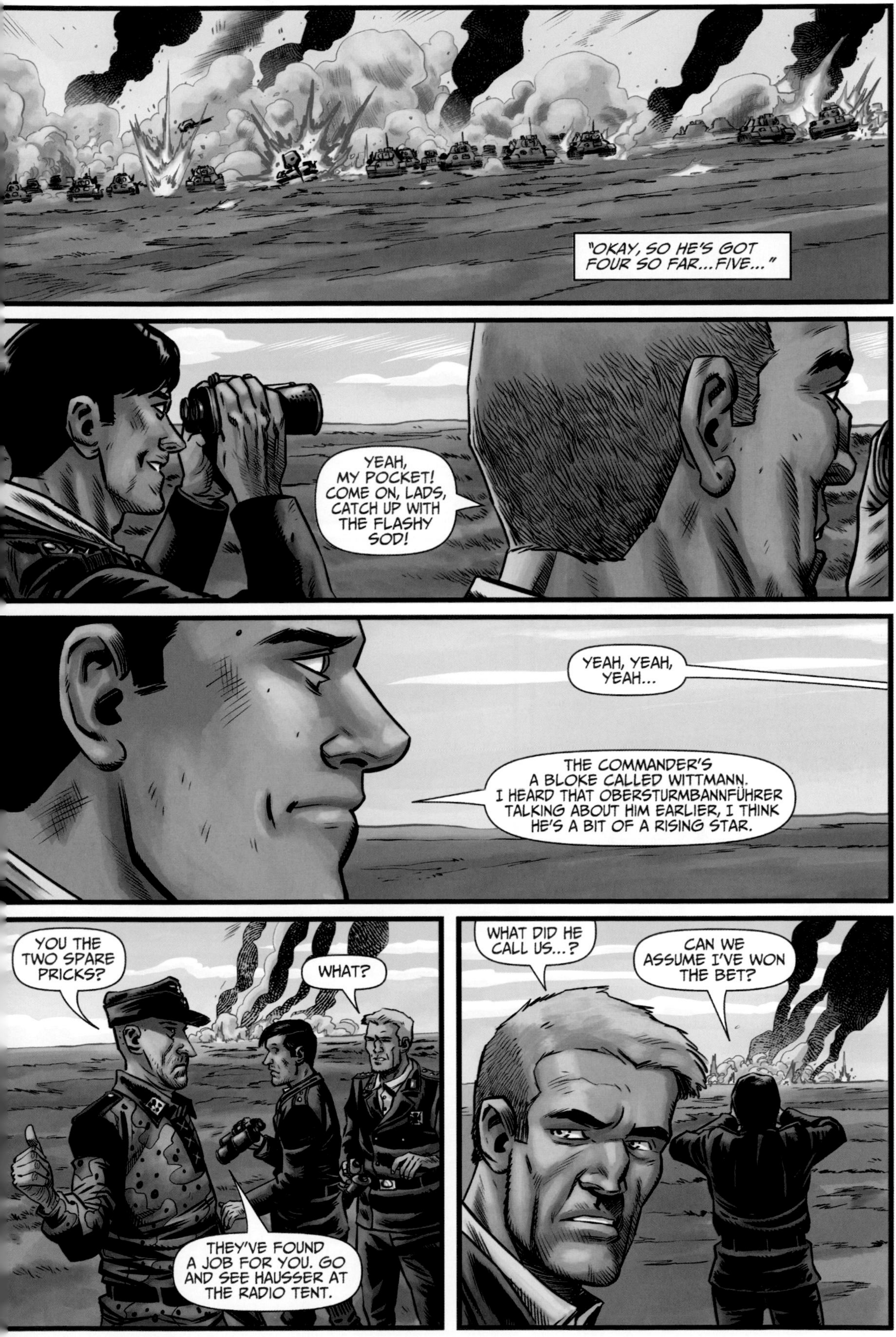
"OKAY, SO HE'S GOT FOUR SO FAR...FIVE..."
YEAH, MY POCKET! COME ON, LADS, CATCH UP WITH THE FLASHY SOD!
YEAH, YEAH, YEAH...
THE COMMANDER'S A BLOKE CALLED WITTMANN. I HEARD THAT OBERSTURMBANNFÜHRER TALKING ABOUT HIM EARLIER, I THINK HE'S A BIT OF A RISING STAR.
YOU THE TWO SPARE PRICKS?
WHAT?
THEY'VE FOUND A JOB FOR YOU. GO AND SEE HAUSSER AT THE RADIO TENT.
WHAT DID HE CALL US...?
CAN WE ASSUME I'VE WON THE BET?

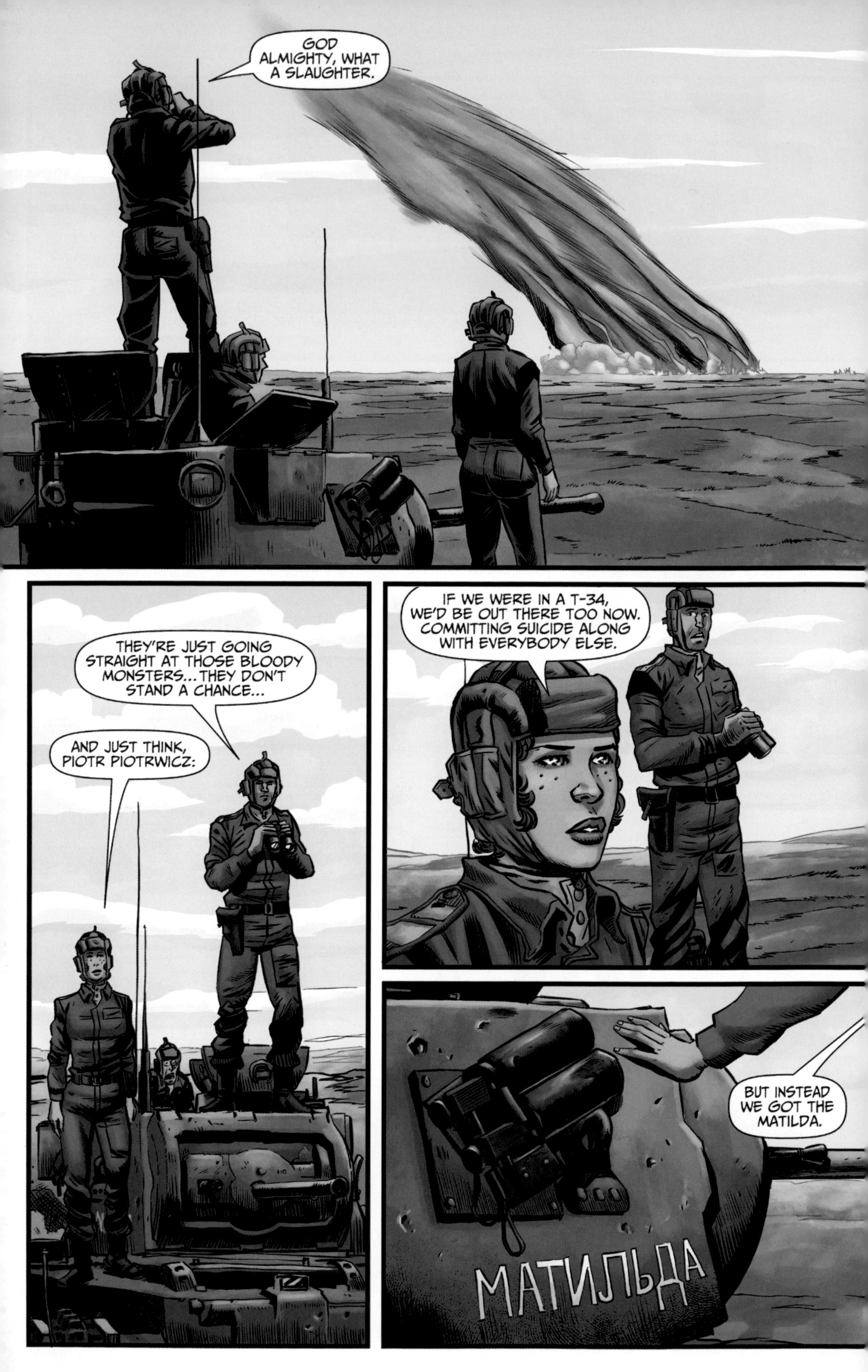
GOD ALMIGHTY, WHAT A SLAUGHTER.
THEY'RE JUST GOING STRAIGHT AT THOSE BLOODY MONSTERS...THEY DON'T STAND A CHANCE...
AND JUST THINK, PIOTR PIOTRWICZ:
IF WE WERE IN A T-34, WE'D BE OUT THERE TOO NOW. COMMITTING SUICIDE ALONG WITH EVERYBODY ELSE.
BUT INSTEAD WE GOT THE MATILDA.
МАТИЛЬДА

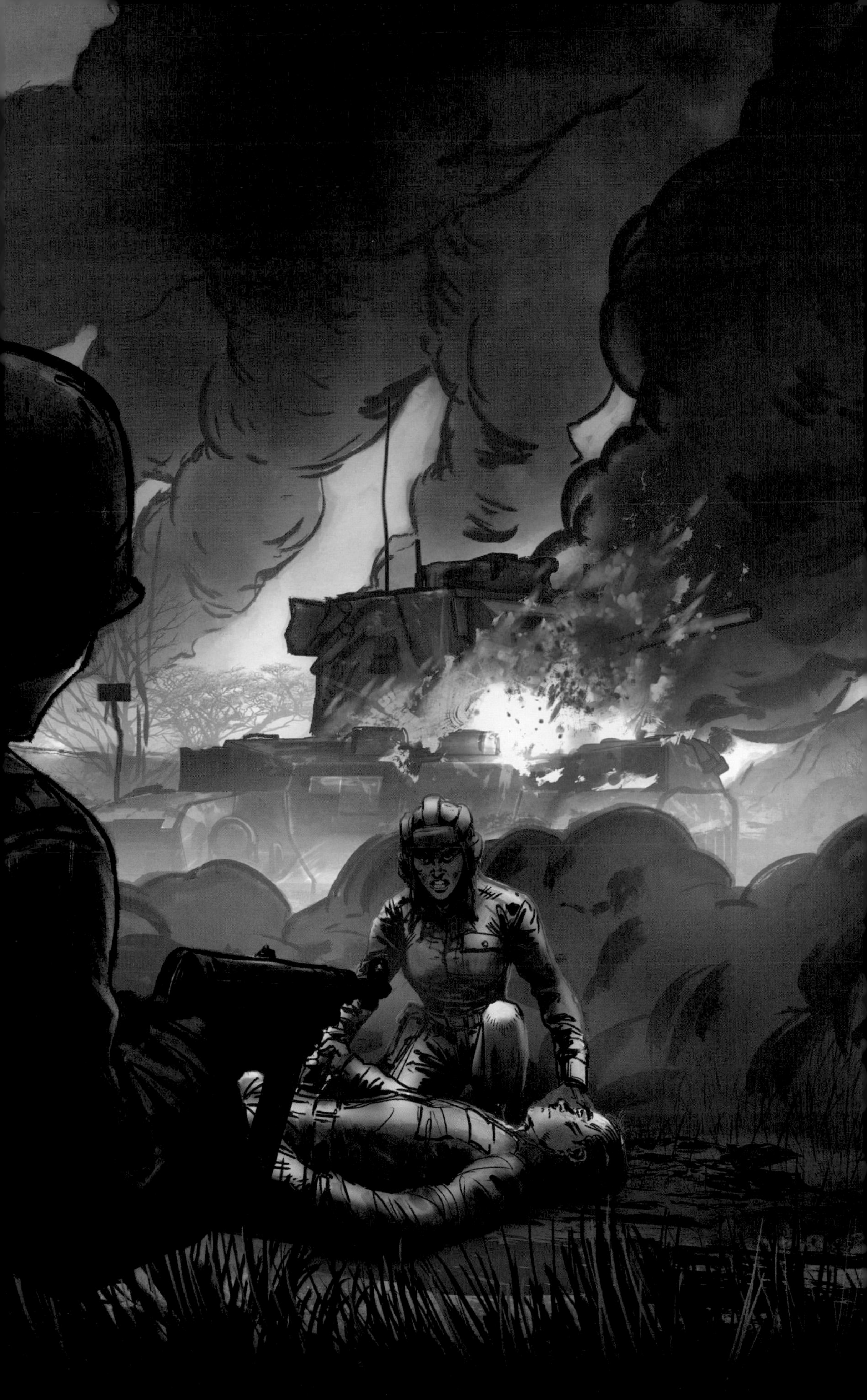

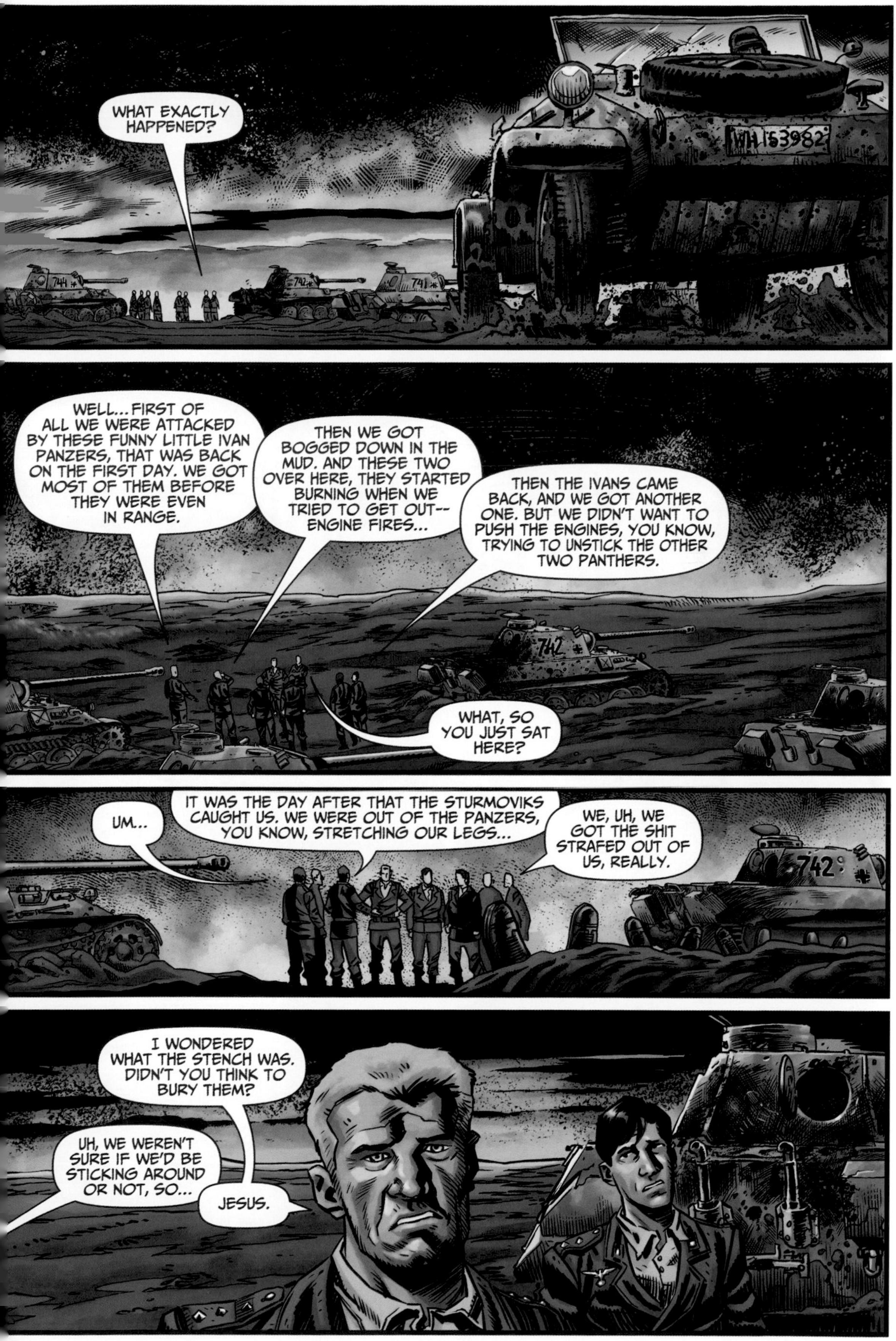
WHAT EXACTLY HAPPENED?
WELL... FIRST OF ALL WE WERE ATTACKED BY THESE FUNNY LITTLE IVAN PANZERS, THAT WAS BACK ON THE FIRST DAY. WE GOT MOST OF THEM BEFORE THEY WERE EVEN IN RANGE.
THEN WE GOT BOGGED DOWN IN THE MUD. AND THESE TWO OVER HERE, THEY STARTED BURNING WHEN WE TRIED TO GET OUT-- ENGINE FIRES...
THEN THE IVANS CAME BACK, AND WE GOT ANOTHER ONE. BUT WE DIDN'T WANT TO PUSH THE ENGINES, YOU KNOW, TRYING TO UNSTICK THE OTHER TWO PANTHERS.
WHAT, SO YOU JUST SAT HERE?
UM...
IT WAS THE DAY AFTER THAT THE STURMOVIKS CAUGHT US. WE WERE OUT OF THE PANZERS, YOU KNOW, STRETCHING OUR LEGS...
WE, UH, WE GOT THE SHIT STRAFED OUT OF US, REALLY.
I WONDERED WHAT THE STENCH WAS. DIDN'T YOU THINK TO BURY THEM?
UH, WE WEREN'T SURE IF WE'D BE STICKING AROUND OR NOT, SO...
JESUS.

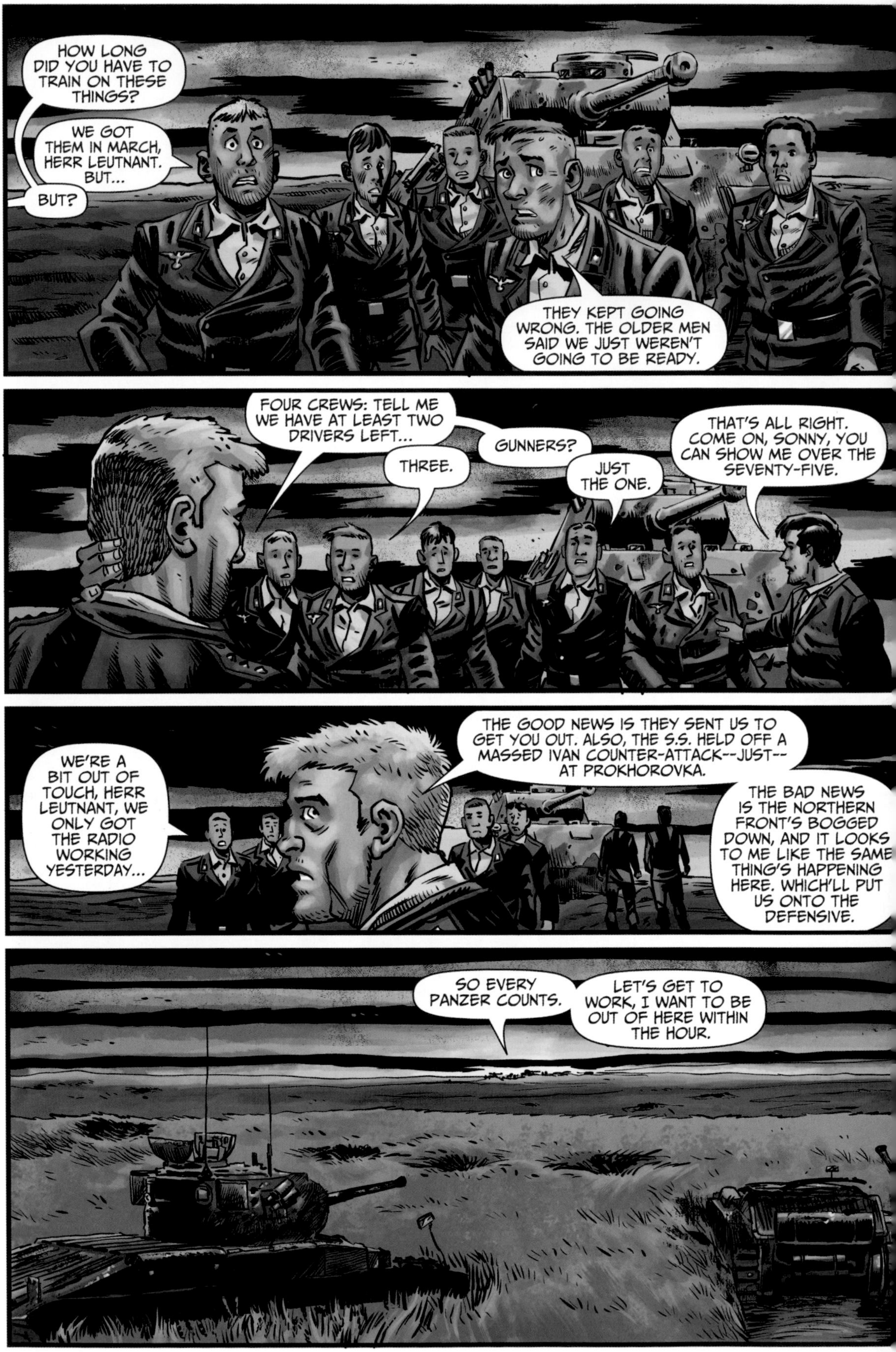
HOW LONG DID YOU HAVE TO TRAIN ON THESE THINGS?
WE GOT THEM IN MARCH, HERR LEUTNANT. BUT...
BUT?
THEY KEPT GOING WRONG. THE OLDER MEN SAID WE JUST WEREN'T GOING TO BE READY.
FOUR CREWS: TELL ME WE HAVE AT LEAST TWO DRIVERS LEFT...
THREE.
GUNNERS?
JUST THE ONE.
THAT'S ALL RIGHT. COME ON, SONNY, YOU CAN SHOW ME OVER THE SEVENTY-FIVE.
WE'RE A BIT OUT OF TOUCH, HERR LEUTNANT, WE ONLY GOT THE RADIO WORKING YESTERDAY...
THE GOOD NEWS IS THEY SENT US TO GET YOU OUT. ALSO, THE S.S. HELD OFF A MASSED IVAN COUNTER-ATTACK--JUST--AT PROKHOROVKA.
THE BAD NEWS IS THE NORTHERN FRONT'S BOGGED DOWN, AND IT LOOKS TO ME LIKE THE SAME THING'S HAPPENING HERE. WHICH'LL PUT US ONTO THE DEFENSIVE.
SO EVERY PANZER COUNTS.
LET'S GET TO WORK, I WANT TO BE OUT OF HERE WITHIN THE HOUR.

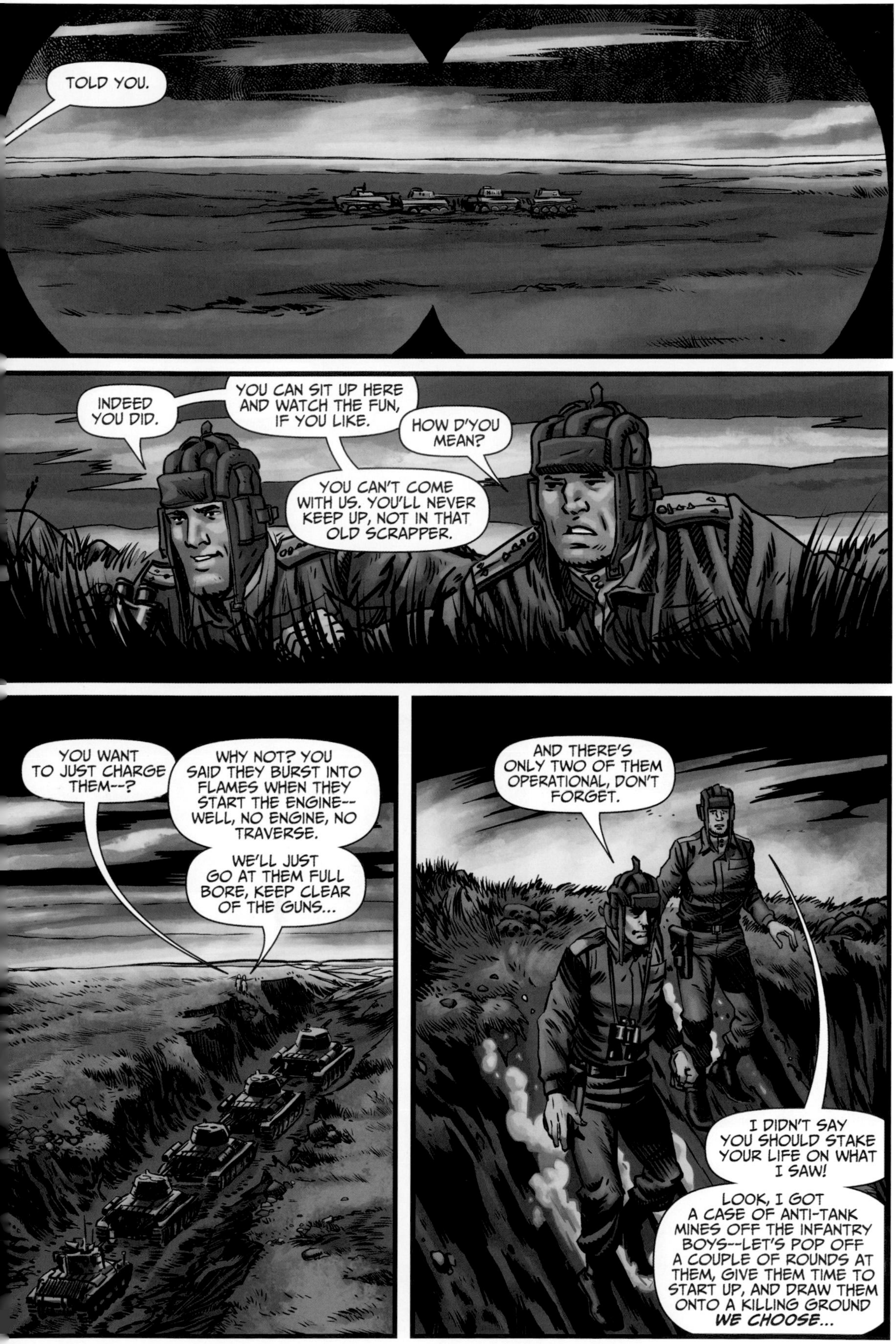
TOLD YOU.
INDEED YOU DID.
YOU CAN SIT UP HERE AND WATCH THE FUN, IF YOU LIKE.
HOW D'YOU MEAN?
YOU CAN'T COME WITH US. YOU'LL NEVER KEEP UP, NOT IN THAT OLD SCRAPPER.
YOU WANT TO JUST CHARGE THEM--?
WHY NOT? YOU SAID THEY BURST INTO FLAMES WHEN THEY START THE ENGINE--WELL, NO ENGINE, NO TRAVERSE.
WE'LL JUST GO AT THEM FULL BORE, KEEP CLEAR OF THE GUNS...
AND THERE'S ONLY TWO OF THEM OPERATIONAL, DON'T FORGET.
I DIDN'T SAY YOU SHOULD STAKE YOUR LIFE ON WHAT I SAW!
LOOK, I GOT A CASE OF ANTI-TANK MINES OFF THE INFANTRY BOYS--LET'S POP OFF A COUPLE OF ROUNDS AT THEM, GIVE THEM TIME TO START UP, AND DRAW THEM ONTO A KILLING GROUND *WE CHOOSE...*

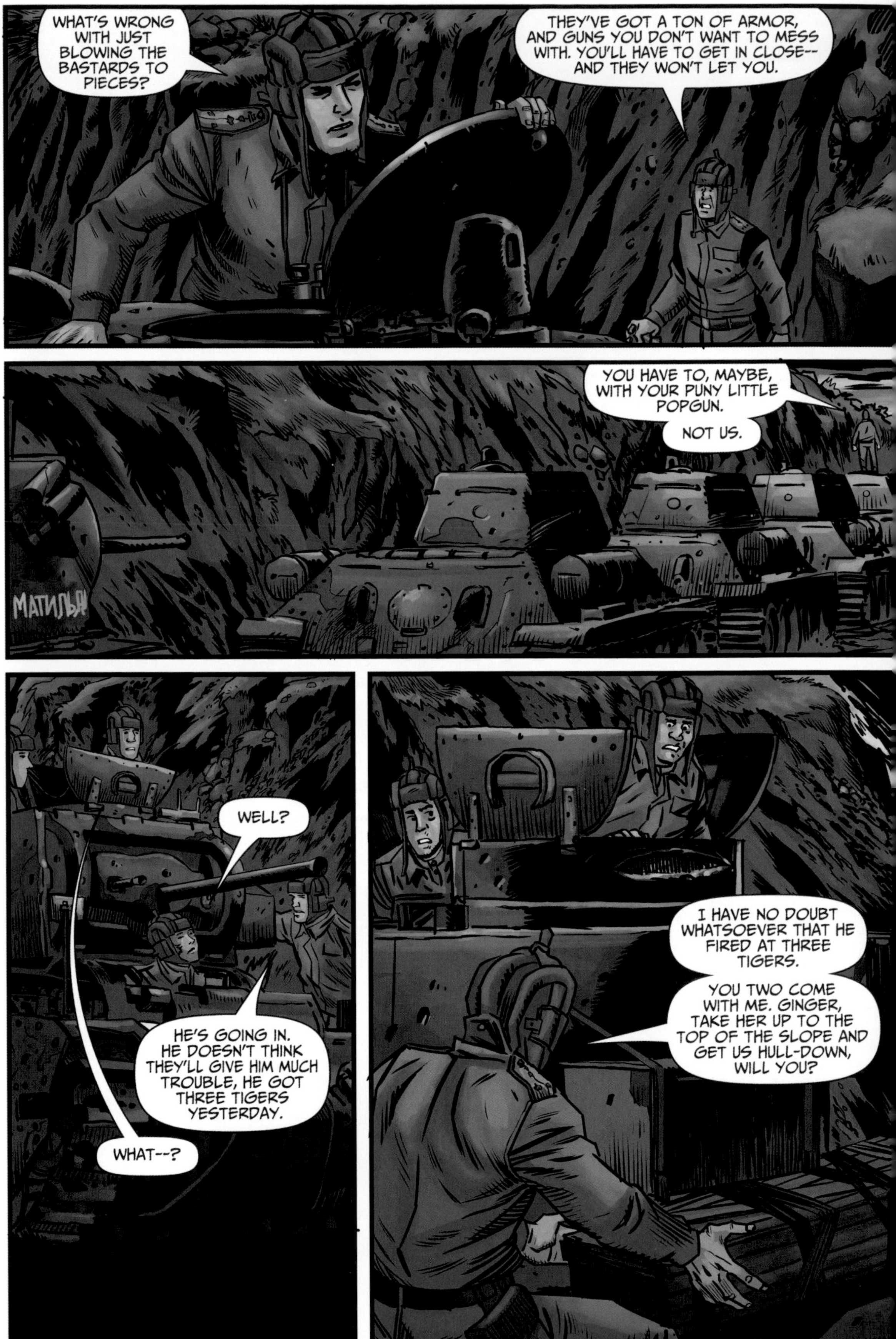
WHAT'S WRONG WITH JUST BLOWING THE BASTARDS TO PIECES?
THEY'VE GOT A TON OF ARMOR, AND GUNS YOU DON'T WANT TO MESS WITH. YOU'LL HAVE TO GET IN CLOSE-- AND THEY WON'T LET YOU.
YOU HAVE TO, MAYBE, WITH YOUR PUNY LITTLE POPGUN.
NOT US.
МАТИЛЬДА
WELL?
HE'S GOING IN. HE DOESN'T THINK THEY'LL GIVE HIM MUCH TROUBLE, HE GOT THREE TIGERS YESTERDAY.
WHAT--?
I HAVE NO DOUBT WHATSOEVER THAT HE FIRED AT THREE TIGERS.
YOU TWO COME WITH ME. GINGER, TAKE HER UP TO THE TOP OF THE SLOPE AND GET US HULL-DOWN, WILL YOU?

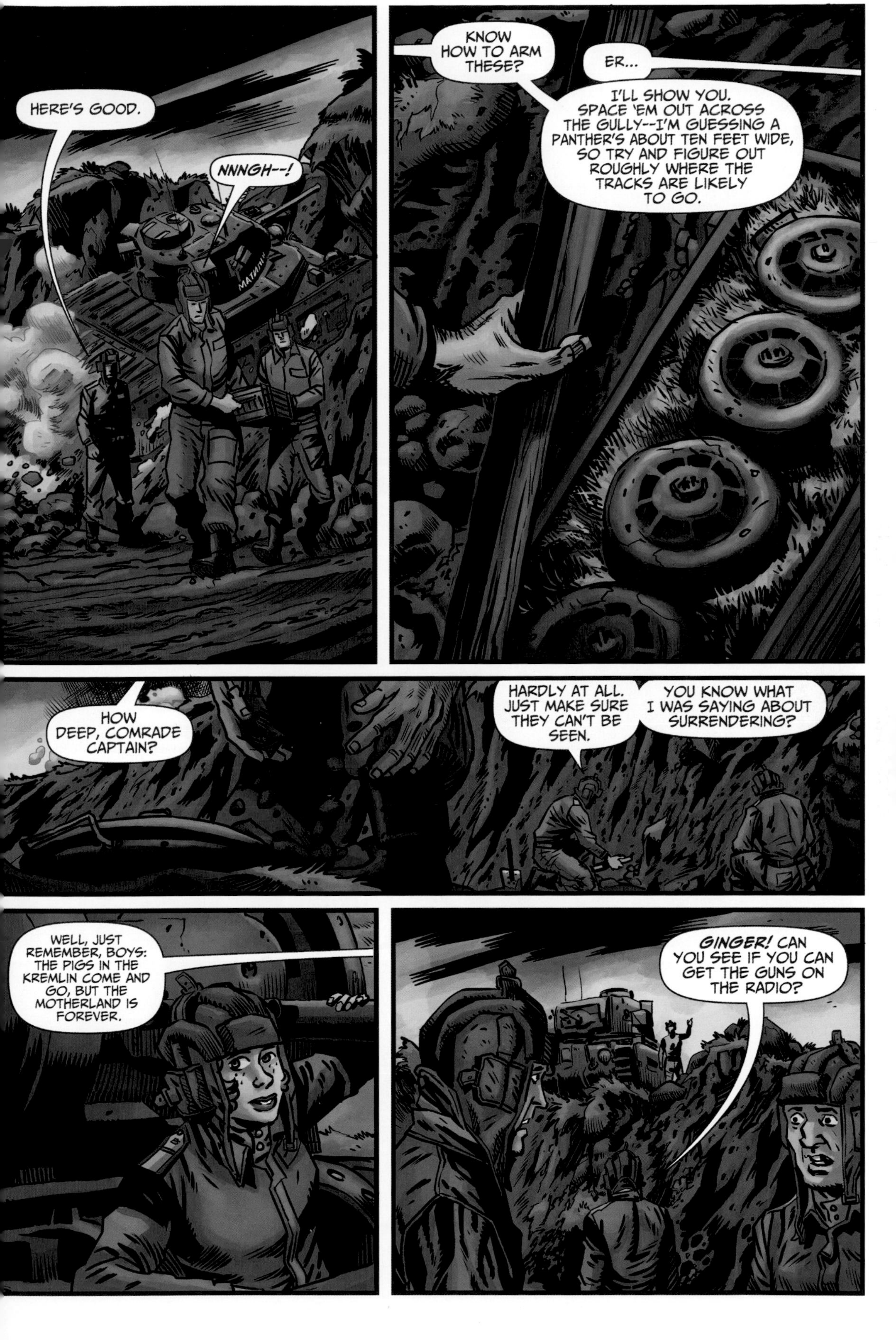
HERE'S GOOD.
NNNGH--!
MATИЛЬ
KNOW HOW TO ARM THESE?
ER...
I'LL SHOW YOU. SPACE 'EM OUT ACROSS THE GULLY--I'M GUESSING A PANTHER'S ABOUT TEN FEET WIDE, SO TRY AND FIGURE OUT ROUGHLY WHERE THE TRACKS ARE LIKELY TO GO.
HOW DEEP, COMRADE CAPTAIN?
HARDLY AT ALL. JUST MAKE SURE THEY CAN'T BE SEEN.
YOU KNOW WHAT I WAS SAYING ABOUT SURRENDERING?
WELL, JUST REMEMBER, BOYS: THE PIGS IN THE KREMLIN COME AND GO, BUT THE MOTHERLAND IS FOREVER.
GINGER! CAN YOU SEE IF YOU CAN GET THE GUNS ON THE RADIO?

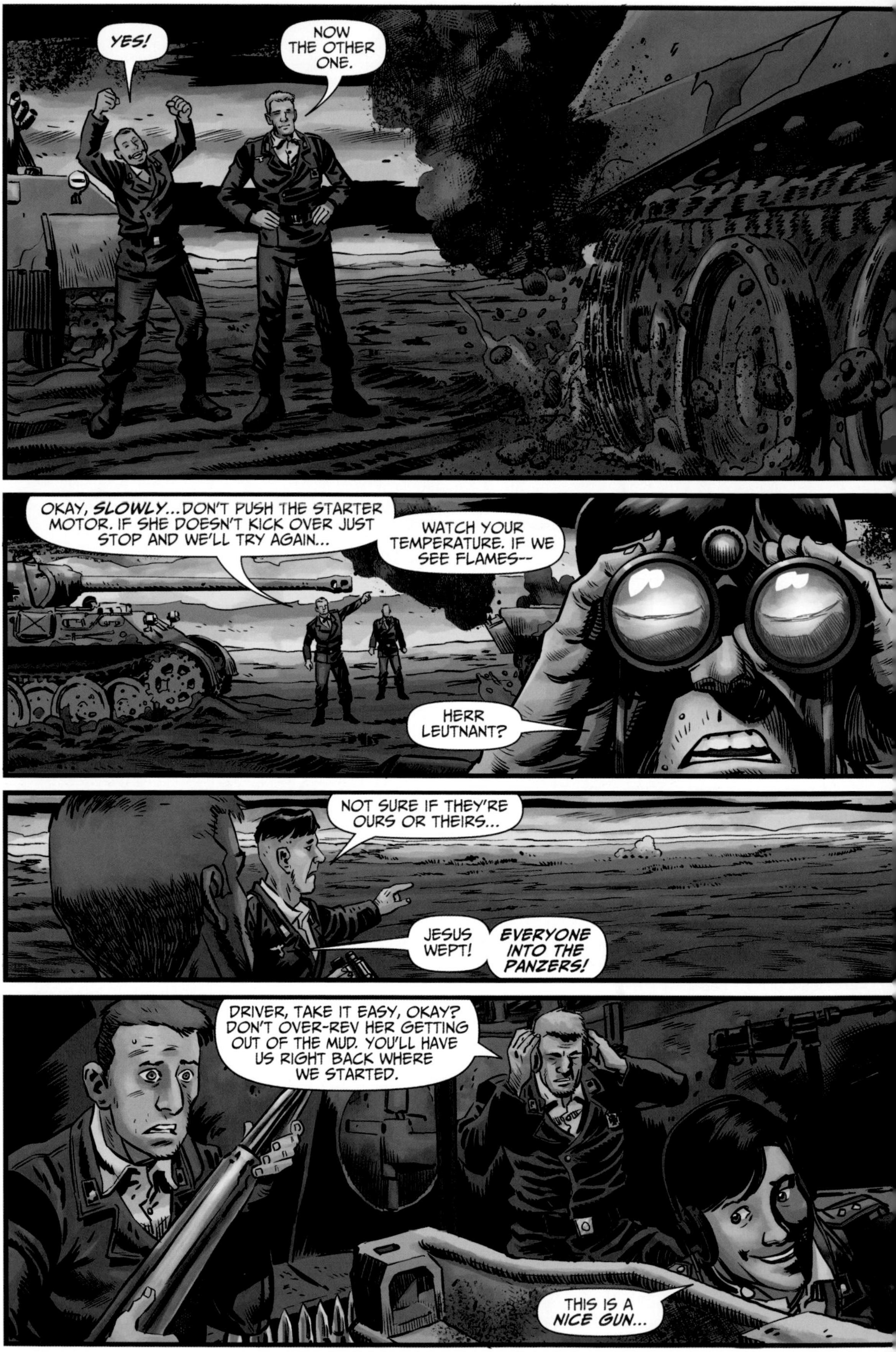
YES!
NOW THE OTHER ONE.
OKAY, *SLOWLY*...DON'T PUSH THE STARTER MOTOR. IF SHE DOESN'T KICK OVER JUST STOP AND WE'LL TRY AGAIN...
WATCH YOUR TEMPERATURE. IF WE SEE FLAMES--
HERR LEUTNANT?
NOT SURE IF THEY'RE OURS OR THEIRS...
JESUS WEPT!
EVERYONE INTO THE PANZERS!
DRIVER, TAKE IT EASY, OKAY? DON'T OVER-REV HER GETTING OUT OF THE MUD. YOU'LL HAVE US RIGHT BACK WHERE WE STARTED.
THIS IS A *NICE GUN*...

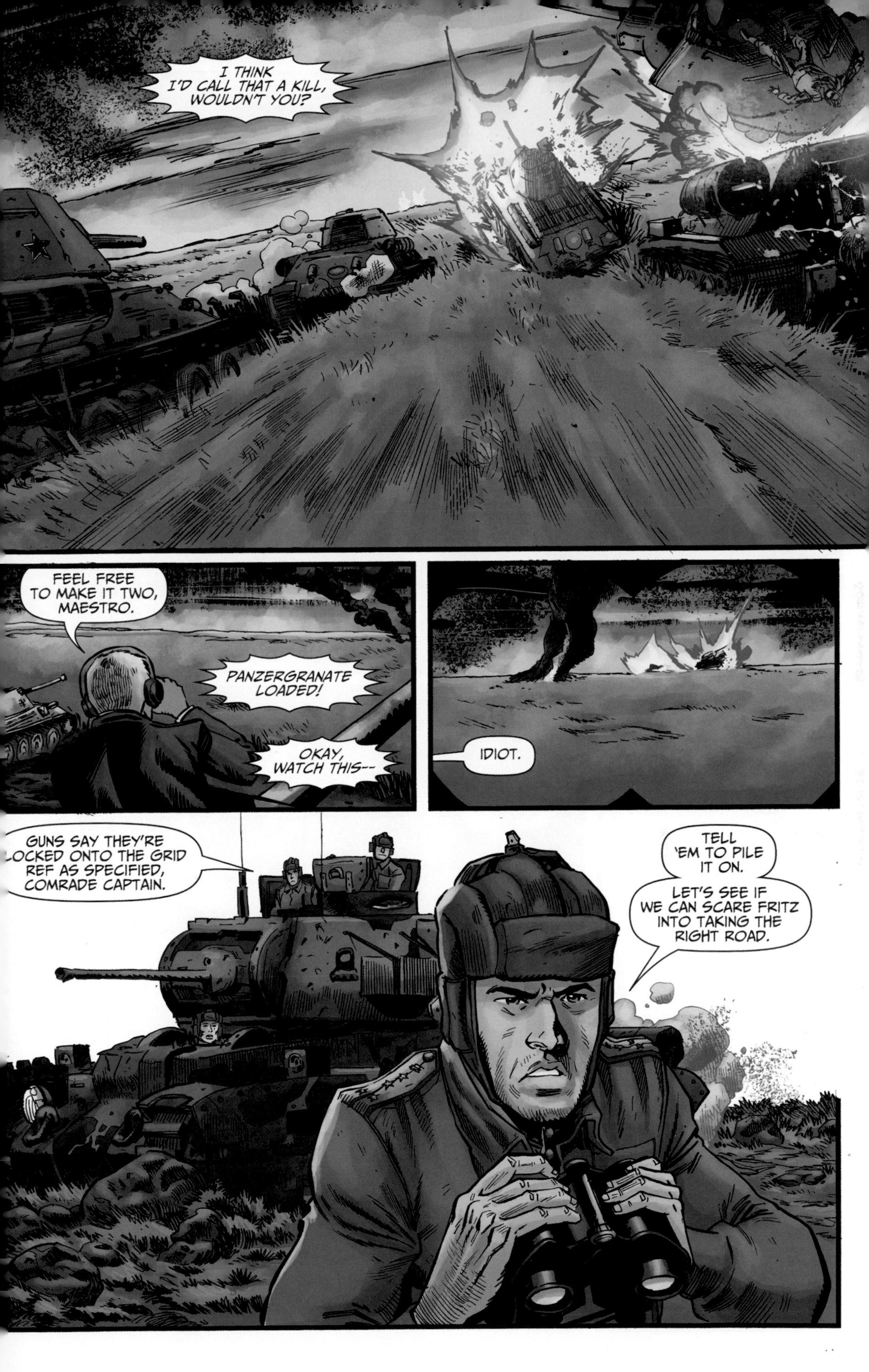
I THINK I'D CALL THAT A KILL, WOULDN'T YOU?
FEEL FREE TO MAKE IT TWO, MAESTRO.
PANZERGRANATE LOADED!
OKAY, WATCH THIS--
IDIOT.
GUNS SAY THEY'RE LOCKED ONTO THE GRID REF AS SPECIFIED, COMRADE CAPTAIN.
TELL 'EM TO PILE IT ON.
LET'S SEE IF WE CAN SCARE FRITZ INTO TAKING THE RIGHT ROAD.

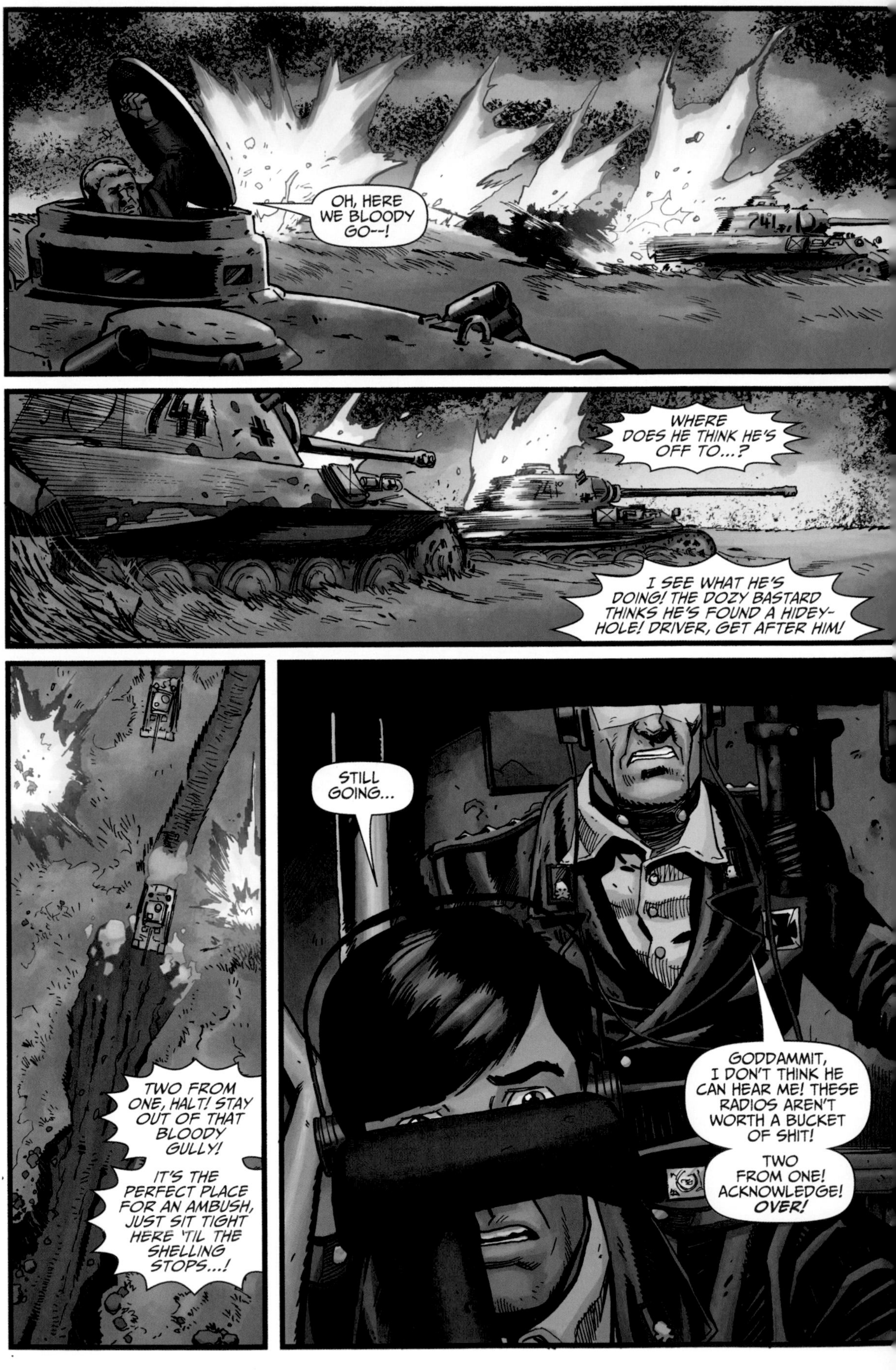
OH, HERE WE BLOODY GO--!
WHERE DOES HE THINK HE'S OFF TO...?
I SEE WHAT HE'S DOING! THE DOZY BASTARD THINKS HE'S FOUND A HIDEY-HOLE! DRIVER, GET AFTER HIM!
STILL GOING...
TWO FROM ONE, HALT! STAY OUT OF THAT BLOODY GULLY!
IT'S THE PERFECT PLACE FOR AN AMBUSH, JUST SIT TIGHT HERE 'TIL THE SHELLING STOPS...!
GODDAMMIT, I DON'T THINK HE CAN HEAR ME! THESE RADIOS AREN'T WORTH A BUCKET OF SHIT!
TWO FROM ONE! ACKNOWLEDGE! OVER!

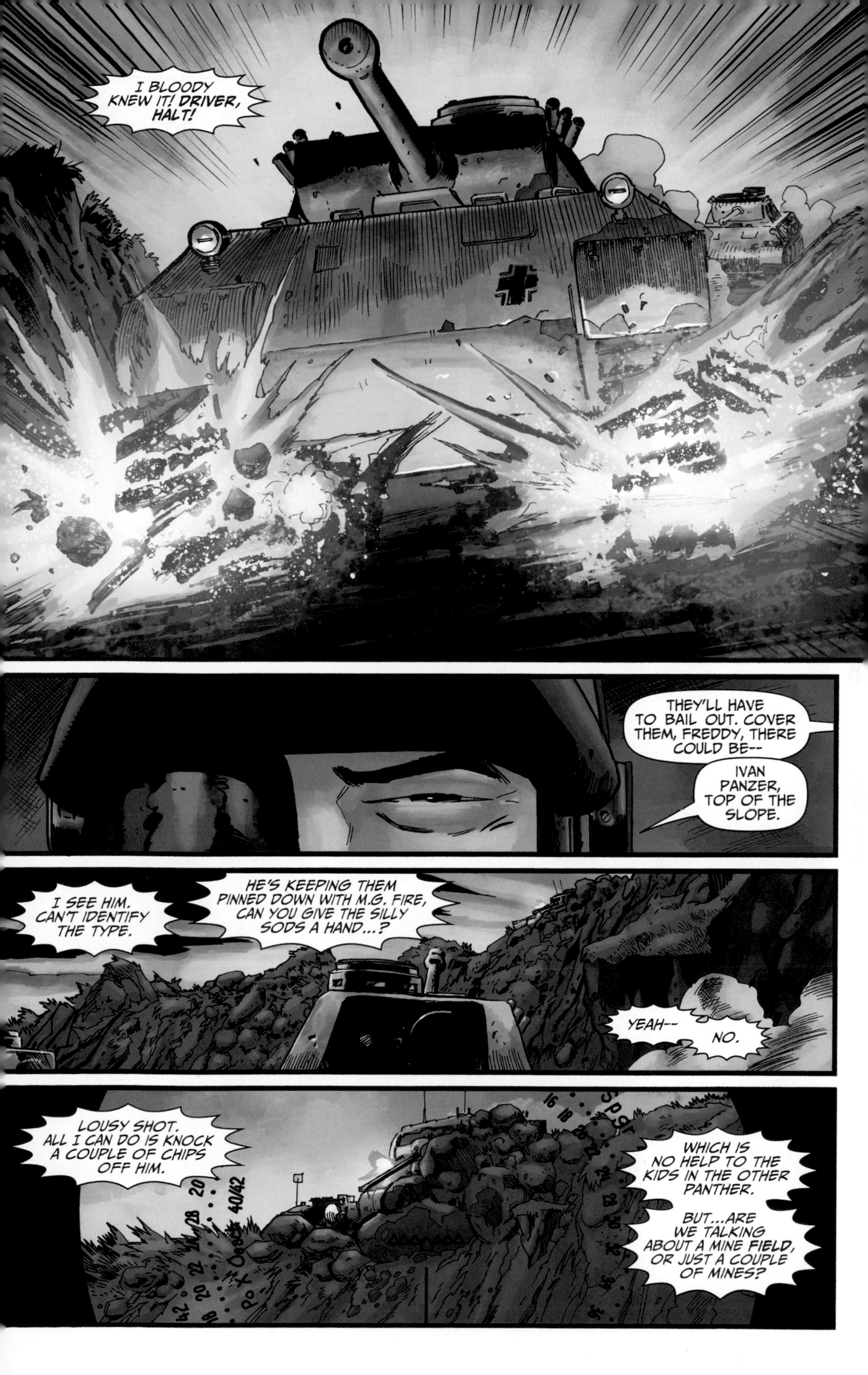
I BLOODY KNEW IT! DRIVER, HALT!
THEY'LL HAVE TO BAIL OUT. COVER THEM, FREDDY, THERE COULD BE--
IVAN PANZER, TOP OF THE SLOPE.
I SEE HIM. CAN'T IDENTIFY THE TYPE.
HE'S KEEPING THEM PINNED DOWN WITH M.G. FIRE, CAN YOU GIVE THE SILLY SODS A HAND...?
YEAH--
NO.
LOUSY SHOT. ALL I CAN DO IS KNOCK A COUPLE OF CHIPS OFF HIM.
WHICH IS NO HELP TO THE KIDS IN THE OTHER PANTHER.
BUT...ARE WE TALKING ABOUT A MINE FIELD, OR JUST A COUPLE OF MINES?

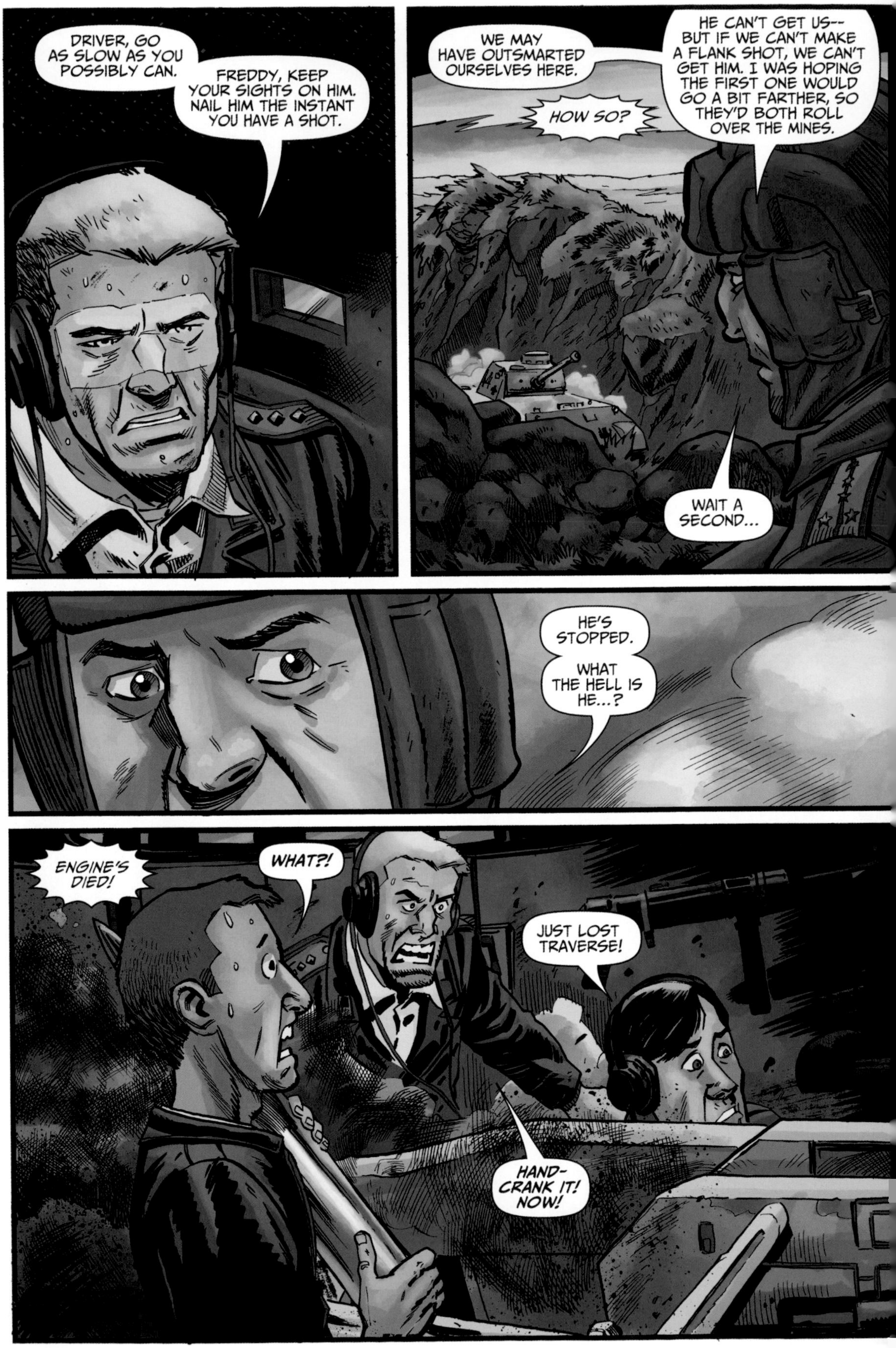
DRIVER, GO AS SLOW AS YOU POSSIBLY CAN.
FREDDY, KEEP YOUR SIGHTS ON HIM. NAIL HIM THE INSTANT YOU HAVE A SHOT.
WE MAY HAVE OUTSMARTED OURSELVES HERE.
HOW SO?
HE CAN'T GET US-- BUT IF WE CAN'T MAKE A FLANK SHOT, WE CAN'T GET HIM. I WAS HOPING THE FIRST ONE WOULD GO A BIT FARTHER, SO THEY'D BOTH ROLL OVER THE MINES.
WAIT A SECOND...
HE'S STOPPED.
WHAT THE HELL IS HE...?
ENGINE'S DIED!
WHAT?!
JUST LOST TRAVERSE!
HAND-CRANK IT! NOW!

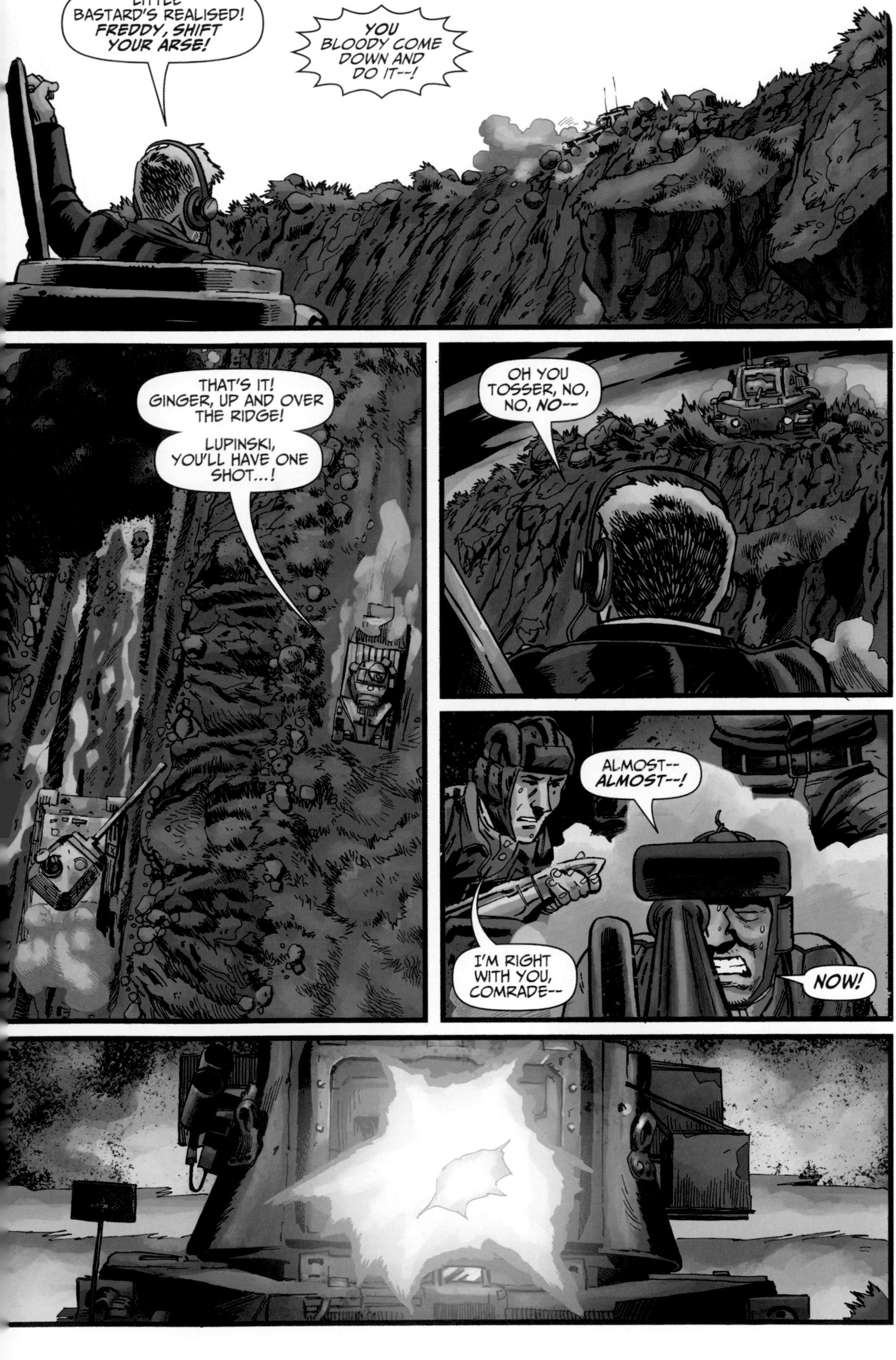
LITTLE BASTARD'S REALISED! FREDDY, SHIFT YOUR ARSE!
YOU BLOODY COME DOWN AND DO IT--!
THAT'S IT! GINGER, UP AND OVER THE RIDGE!
LUPINSKI, YOU'LL HAVE ONE SHOT...!
OH YOU TOSSER, NO, NO, NO--
ALMOST-- ALMOST--!
I'M RIGHT WITH YOU, COMRADE--
NOW!

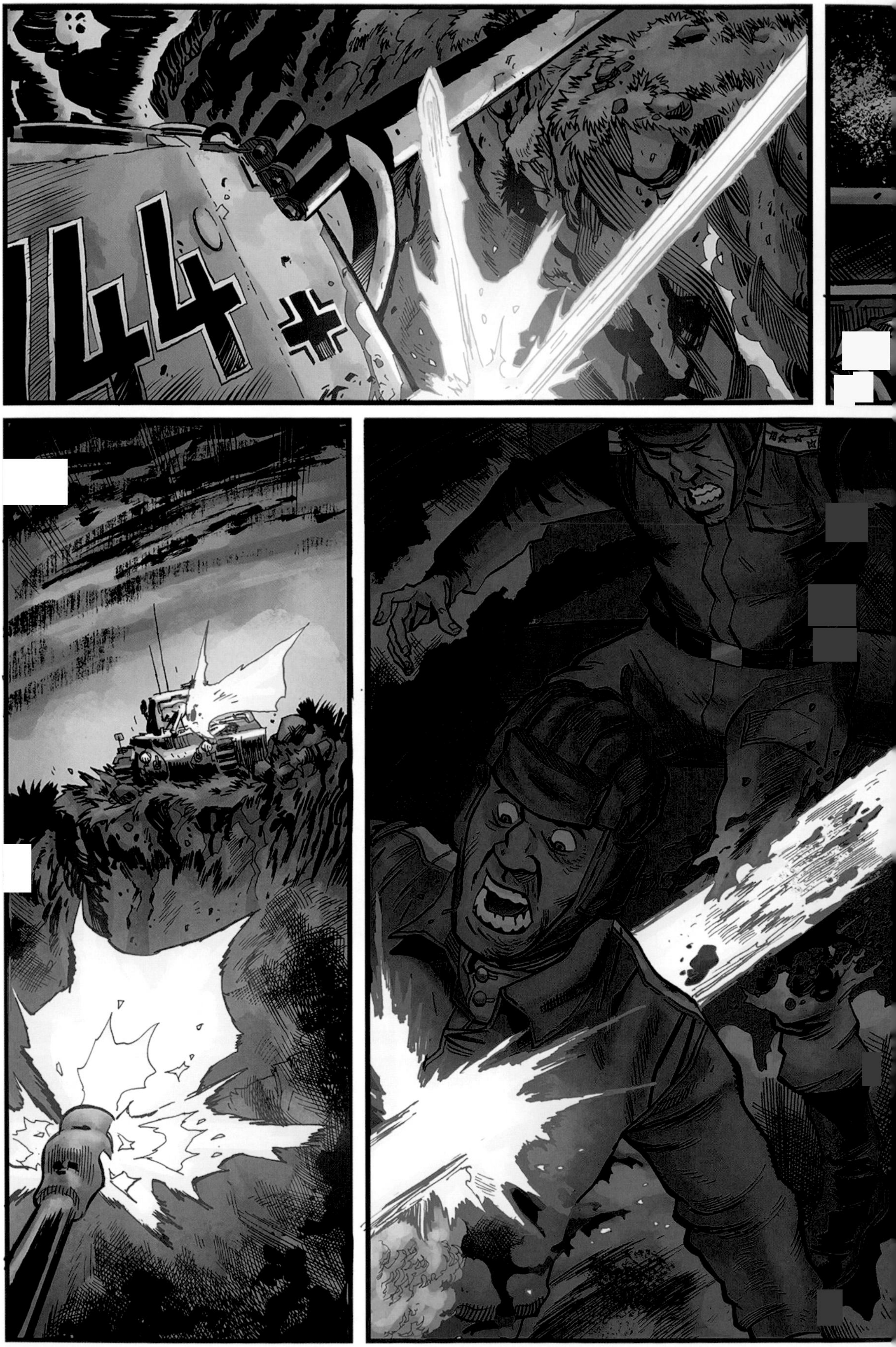

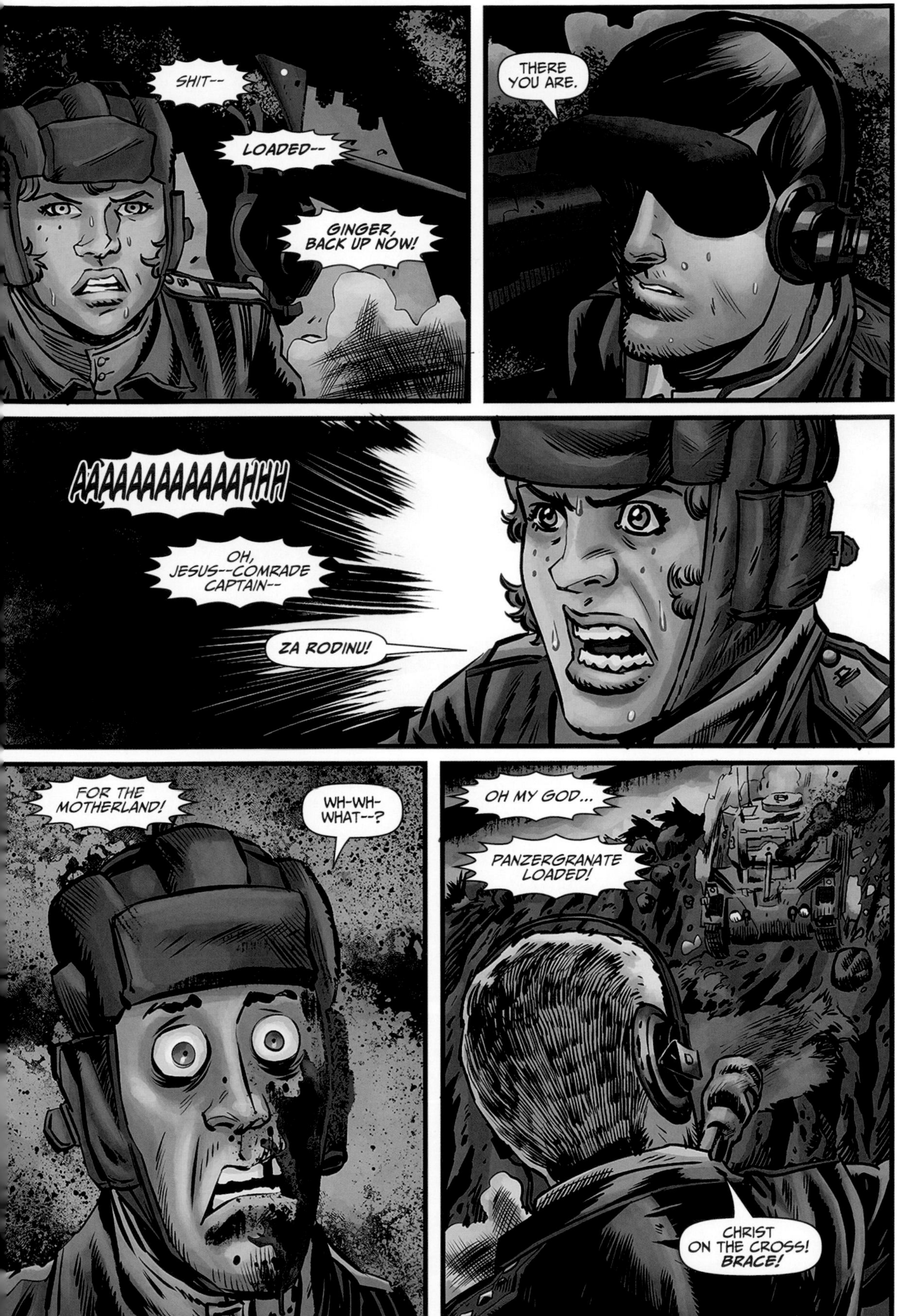
SHIT--
LOADED--
GINGER, BACK UP NOW!
THERE YOU ARE.
AAAAAAAAAAAAHHH
OH, JESUS--COMRADE CAPTAIN--
ZA RODINU!
FOR THE MOTHERLAND!
WH-WH-WHAT--?
OH MY GOD...
PANZERGRANATE LOADED!
CHRIST ON THE CROSS! BRACE!

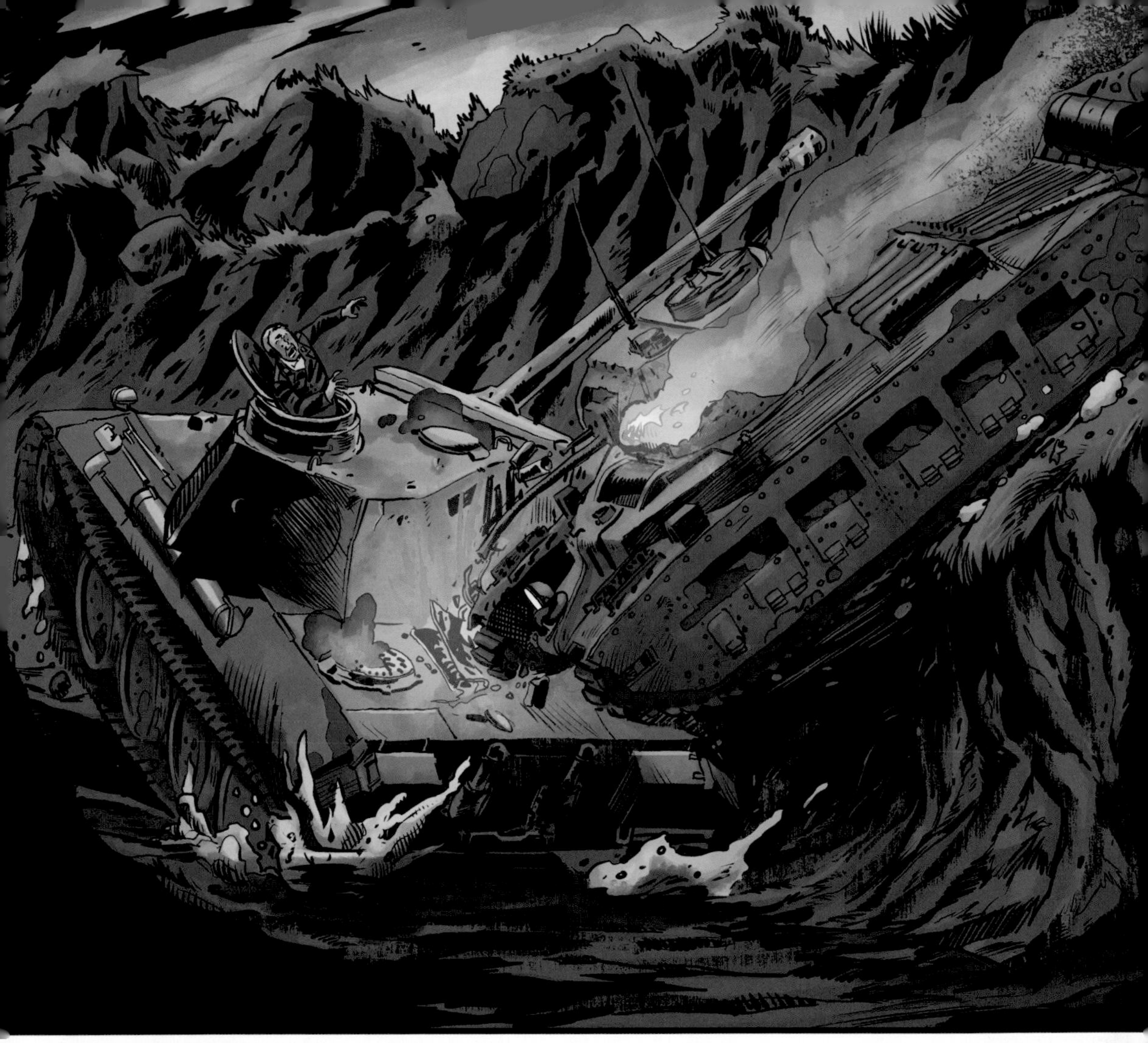
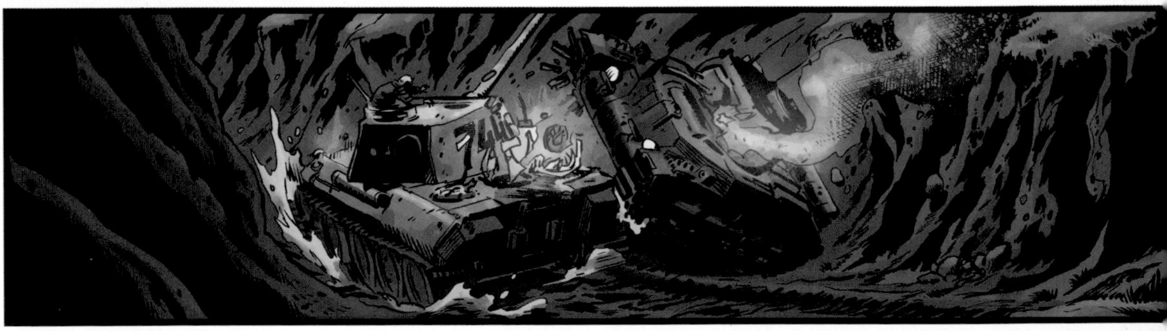
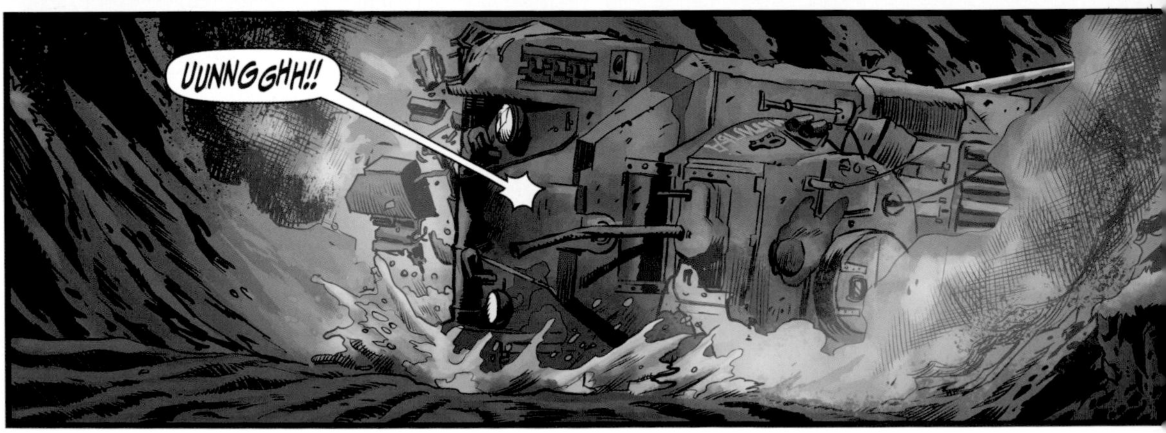
UUNNGGHH!!

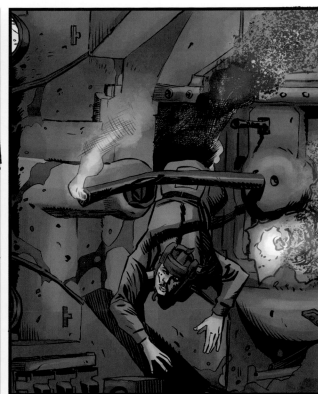

IVAN!

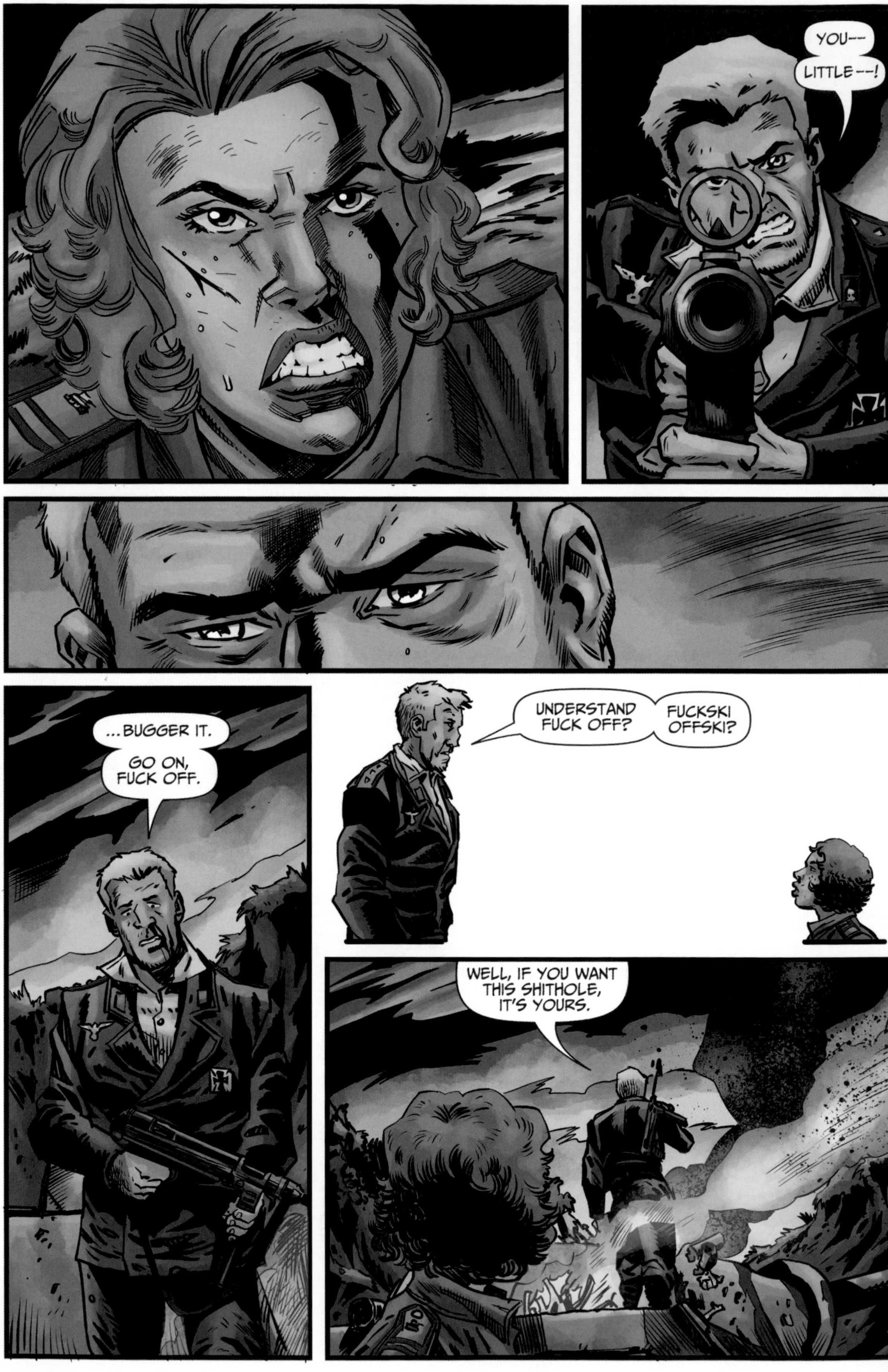
YOU--
LITTLE--!
...BUGGER IT.
GO ON, FUCK OFF.
UNDERSTAND FUCK OFF?
FUCKSKI OFFSKI?
WELL, IF YOU WANT THIS SHITHOLE, IT'S YOURS.

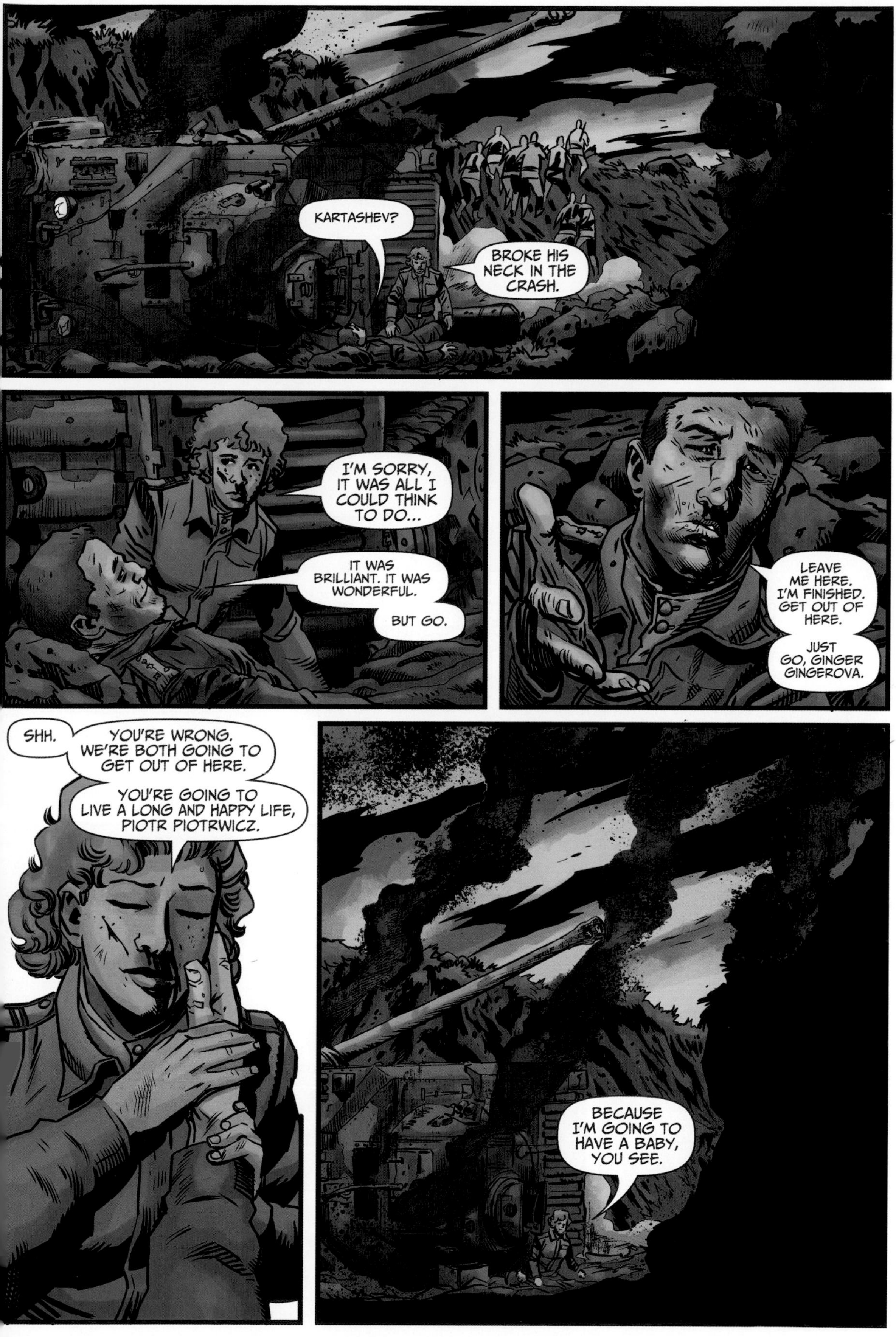
KARTASHEV?
BROKE HIS NECK IN THE CRASH.
I'M SORRY, IT WAS ALL I COULD THINK TO DO...
IT WAS BRILLIANT. IT WAS WONDERFUL.
BUT GO.
LEAVE ME HERE. I'M FINISHED. GET OUT OF HERE.
JUST GO, GINGER GINGEROVA.
SHH.
YOU'RE WRONG. WE'RE BOTH GOING TO GET OUT OF HERE.
YOU'RE GOING TO LIVE A LONG AND HAPPY LIFE, PIOTR PIOTRWICZ.
BECAUSE I'M GOING TO HAVE A BABY, YOU SEE.

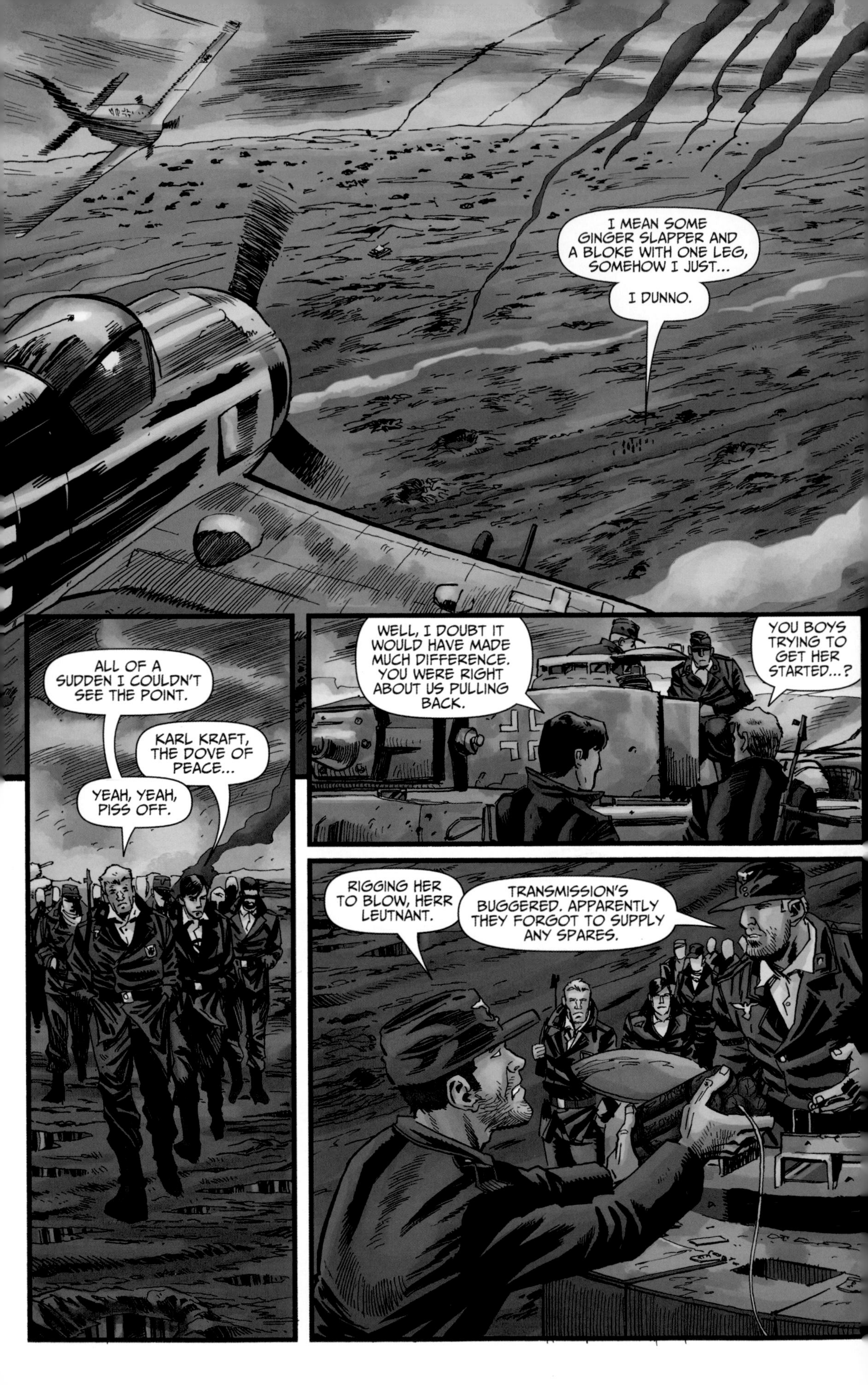
I MEAN SOME GINGER SLAPPER AND A BLOKE WITH ONE LEG, SOMEHOW I JUST...
I DUNNO.
ALL OF A SUDDEN I COULDN'T SEE THE POINT.
KARL KRAFT, THE DOVE OF PEACE...
YEAH, YEAH, PISS OFF.
WELL, I DOUBT IT WOULD HAVE MADE MUCH DIFFERENCE. YOU WERE RIGHT ABOUT US PULLING BACK.
YOU BOYS TRYING TO GET HER STARTED...?
RIGGING HER TO BLOW, HERR LEUTNANT.
TRANSMISSION'S BUGGERED. APPARENTLY THEY FORGOT TO SUPPLY ANY SPARES.

THAT'S ANOTHER THING: THIS IS THE LAST BLOODY TIME THIS IS HAPPENING TO ME, EVER.

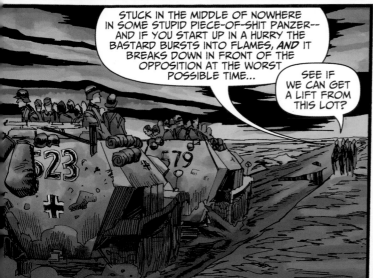

STUCK IN THE MIDDLE OF NOWHERE IN SOME STUPID PIECE-OF-SHIT PANZER-- AND IF YOU START UP IN A HURRY THE BASTARD BURSTS INTO FLAMES, *AND* IT BREAKS DOWN IN FRONT OF THE OPPOSITION AT THE WORST POSSIBLE TIME...

SEE IF WE CAN GET A LIFT FROM THIS LOT?

MARK MY WORDS, FREDDY: *NEVER AGAIN.*

AND THAT WAS THE BATTLE OF KURSK, THAT WAS.

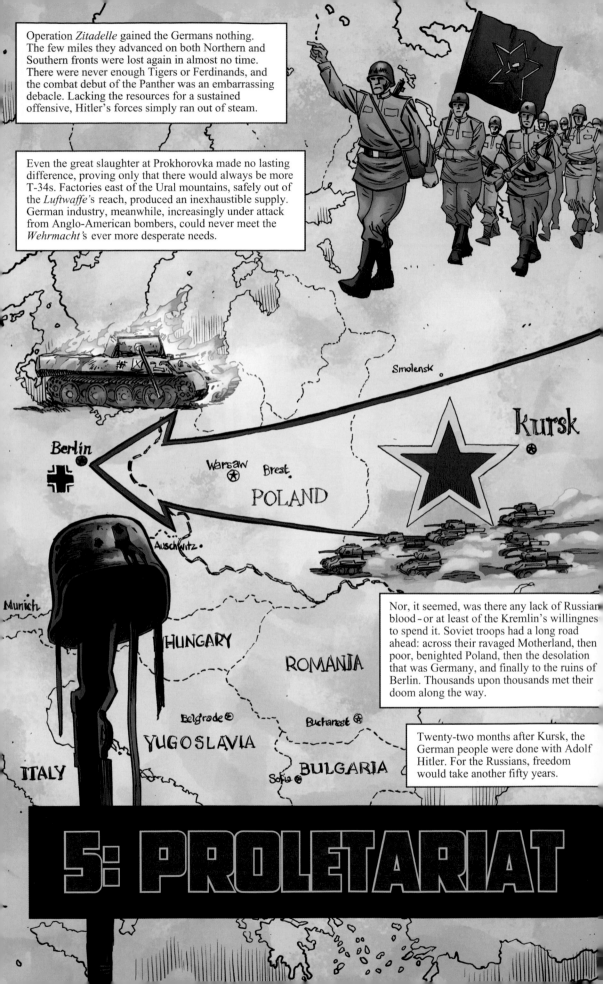

Operation *Zitadelle* gained the Germans nothing. The few miles they advanced on both Northern and Southern fronts were lost again in almost no time. There were never enough Tigers or Ferdinands, and the combat debut of the Panther was an embarrassing debacle. Lacking the resources for a sustained offensive, Hitler's forces simply ran out of steam.

Even the great slaughter at Prokhorovka made no lasting difference, proving only that there would always be more T-34s. Factories east of the Ural mountains, safely out of the *Luftwaffe's* reach, produced an inexhaustible supply. German industry, meanwhile, increasingly under attack from Anglo-American bombers, could never meet the *Wehrmacht's* ever more desperate needs.

Smolensk

Kursk

Berlin

Warsaw   Brest
POLAND

Auschwitz

Munich

HUNGARY

ROMANIA

Belgrade

Bucharest

YUGOSLAVIA

BULGARIA
Sofia

ITALY

Nor, it seemed, was there any lack of Russian blood – or at least of the Kremlin's willingnes to spend it. Soviet troops had a long road ahead: across their ravaged Motherland, then poor, benighted Poland, then the desolation that was Germany, and finally to the ruins of Berlin. Thousands upon thousands met their doom along the way.

Twenty-two months after Kursk, the German people were done with Adolf Hitler. For the Russians, freedom would take another fifty years.

5: PROLETARIAT

Sketchbook

Notes by: P.J. Holden & Isaac Hannaford

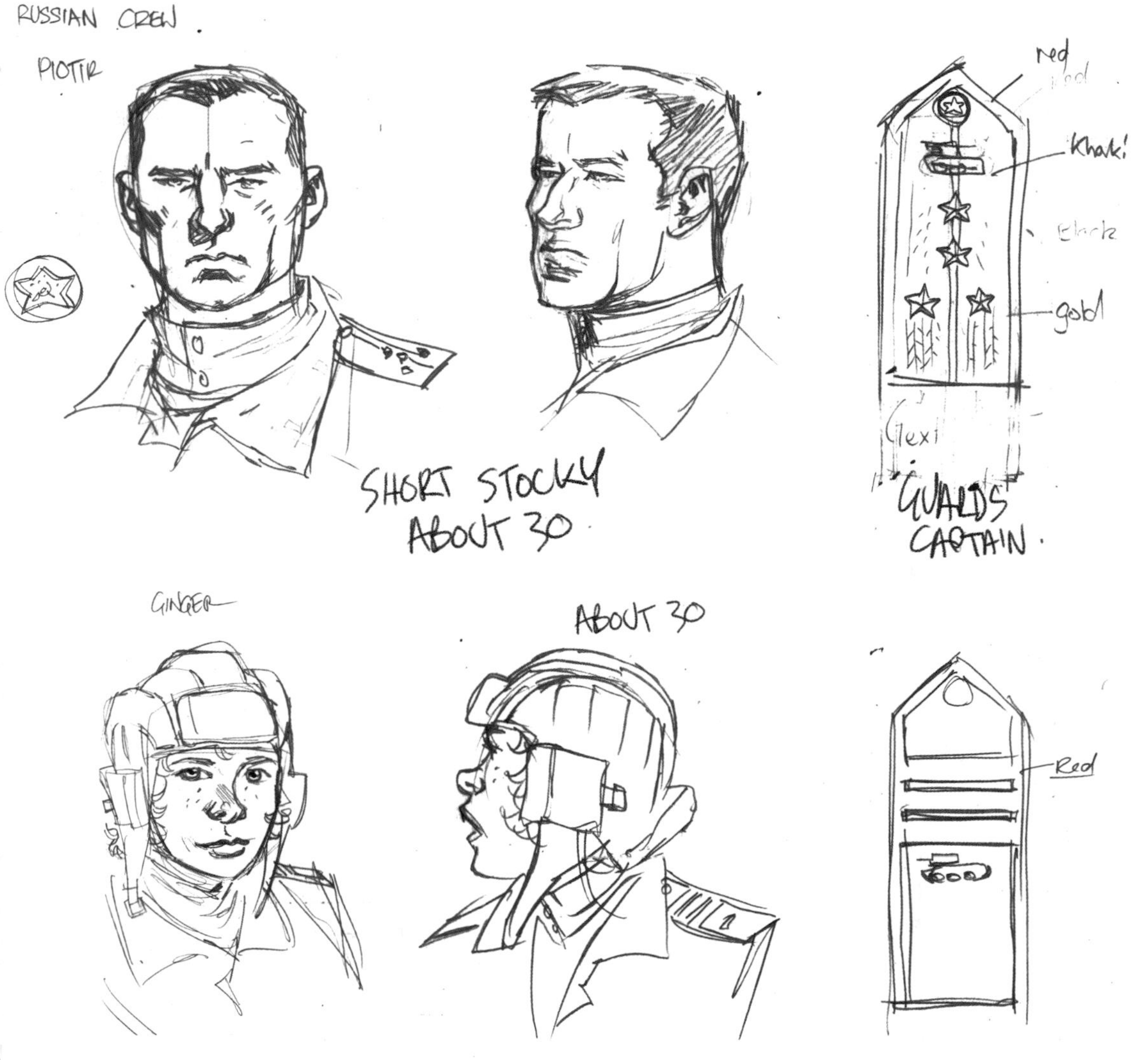
RUSSIAN CREW
PIOTR
red
Khaki
Black
gold
SHORT STOCKY
ABOUT 30
GUARDS CAPTAIN
GINGER
ABOUT 30
Red

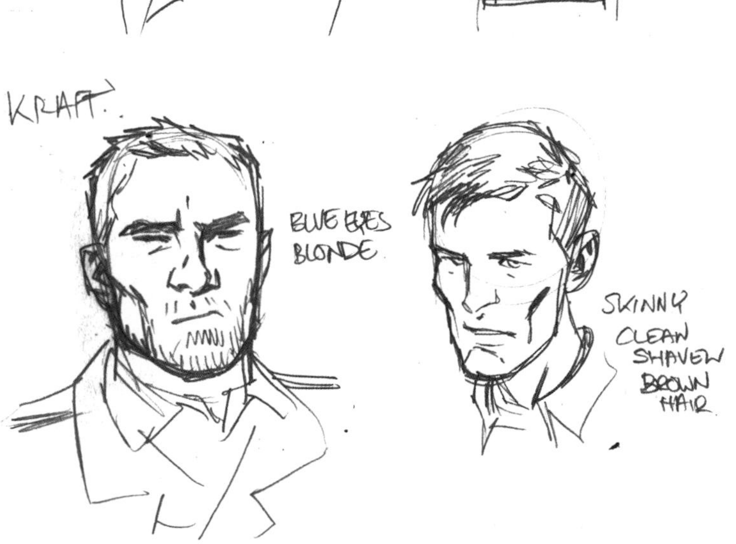
KRAFT
BLUE EYES
BLONDE
SKINNY
CLEAN
SHAVEN
BROWN
HAIR

P.J.: It's all about Tanks and People. The tanks all exist, so not much design work needed there, but then you've got to figure out the people. It's important that you can identify them quickly from just a couple of lines of the face. You'll be drawing them, often helmeted, often inside the confines of a tiny tank, so figuring out a short hand for faces was important. Piotr's nose and jawline were important (with the helmet on, his hairline vanishes). With Ginger, having that shock of red hair pushing out the sides of her cap shows both her personality and gave me more options for drawing her and keeping it obvious that it's her.

Kraft and Freddy we've met before, but here they're subtly younger.

Character designs by ***P.J. HOLDEN****.*

P.J.: Thumbnails on a project like this are as much about making sure you've got everything staged on the page in an interesting way as it is figuring out the logistics of what you're drawing. What are the vehicles? Who's speaking first? (And remember, first person to speak is on the left!) what can we see from where they are? What's the least amount you need to show to successfully communicate what's going on, while keeping it action packed and accurate?

It's like a jigsaw puzzle where someone describes the end result and now you've got to put all the pieces together (and draw them).

I'll make notes on the thumbs to ensure when I go to dig out reference I know my Stukas from my ME109s.

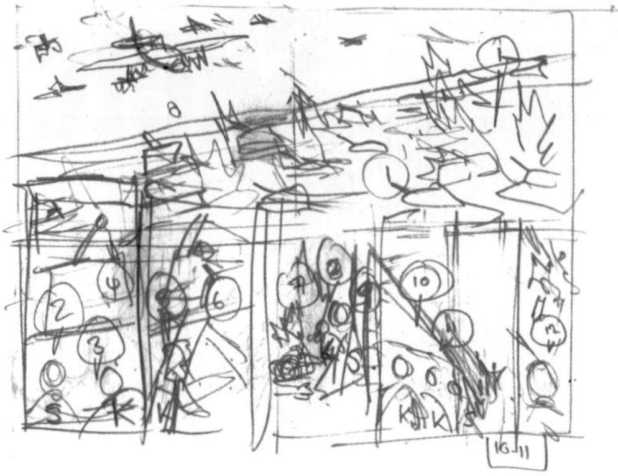

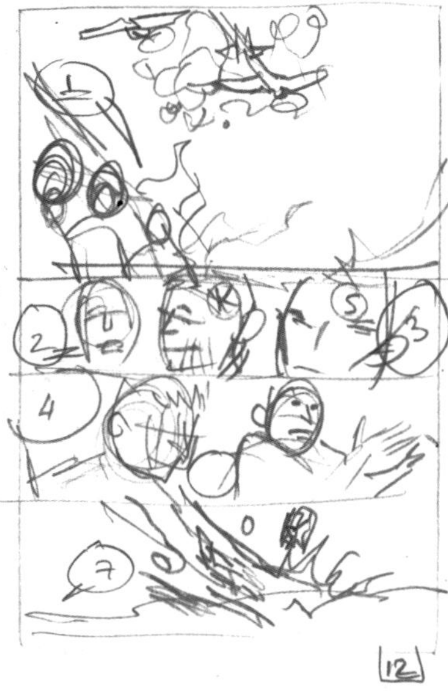
12

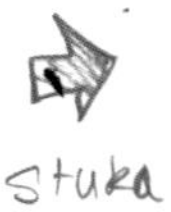
Stuka

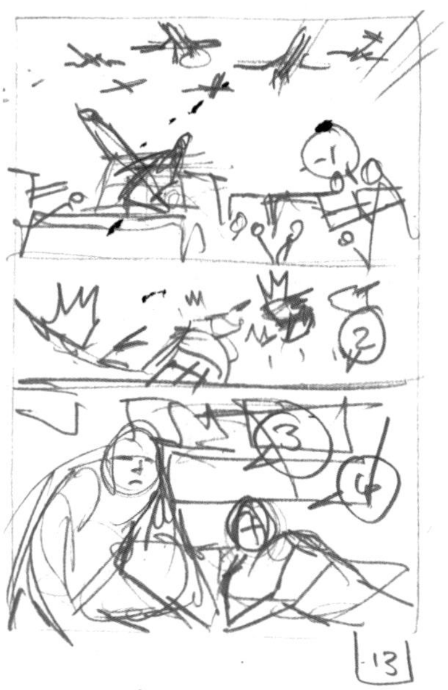
13

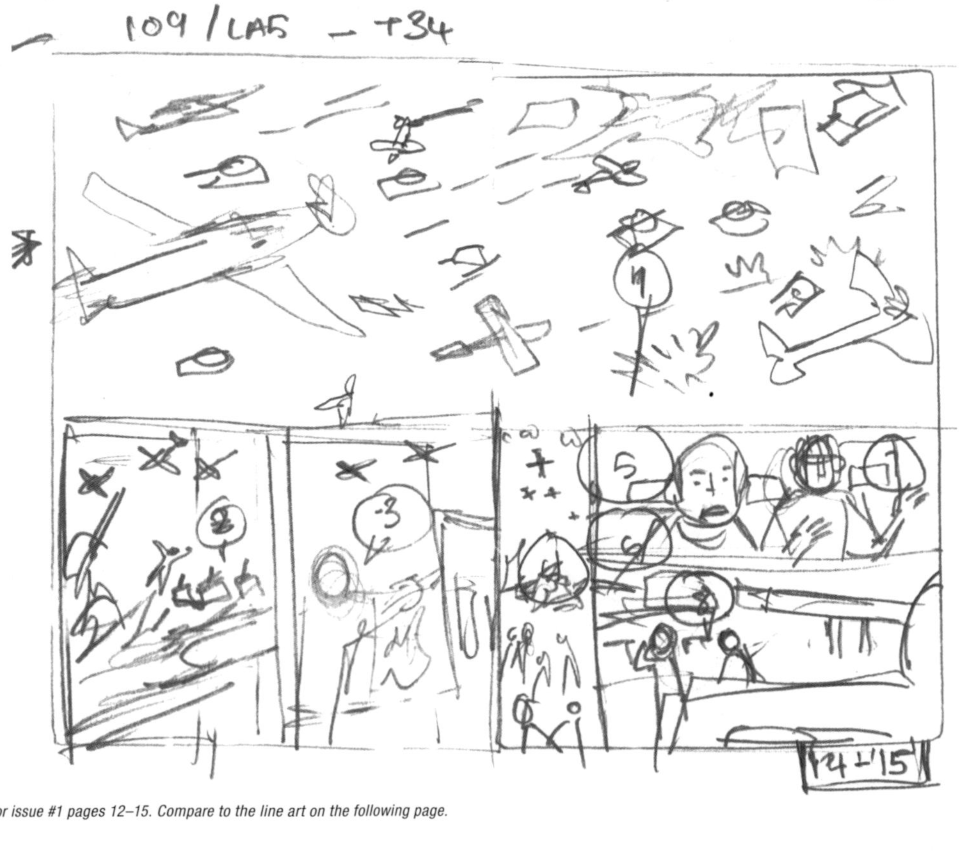
109 / LAG — T34
14-15

Layouts for issue #1 pages 12–15. Compare to the line art on the following page.

P.J.: I work both traditionally and digitally, often round robin-ing from my drawing board to my Cintiq and back again. Where you see splatter it's usually added digitally (or at least enhanced with some digital splatter).

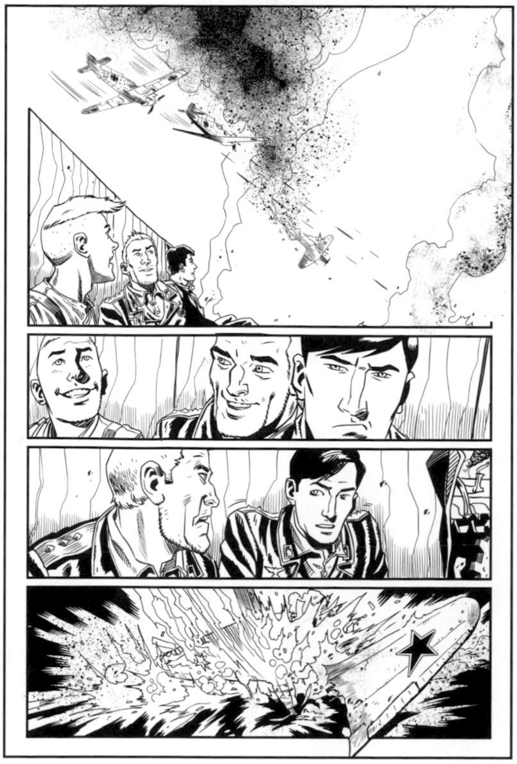

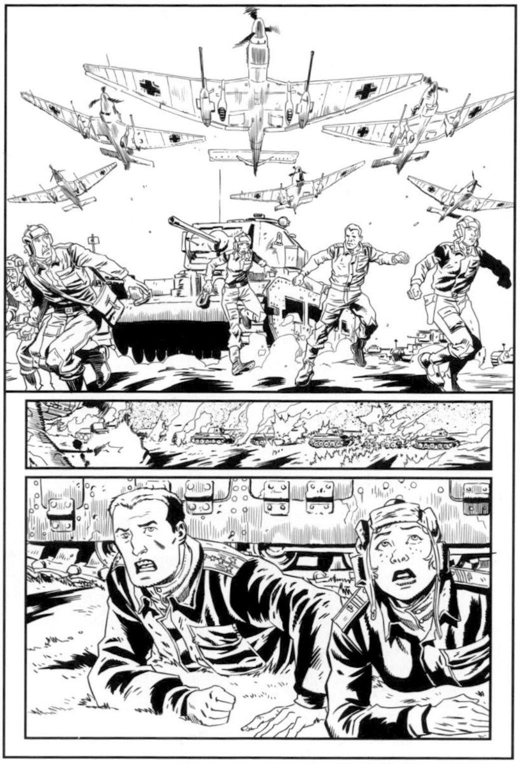

TOP LEFT: Ah the kid. The poor, poor kid. It doesn't end well for him.

TOP RIGHT: So much for the line of indestructible T34s; some tank busters taking them out and leaving our lovely Matildas as the last tanks standing.

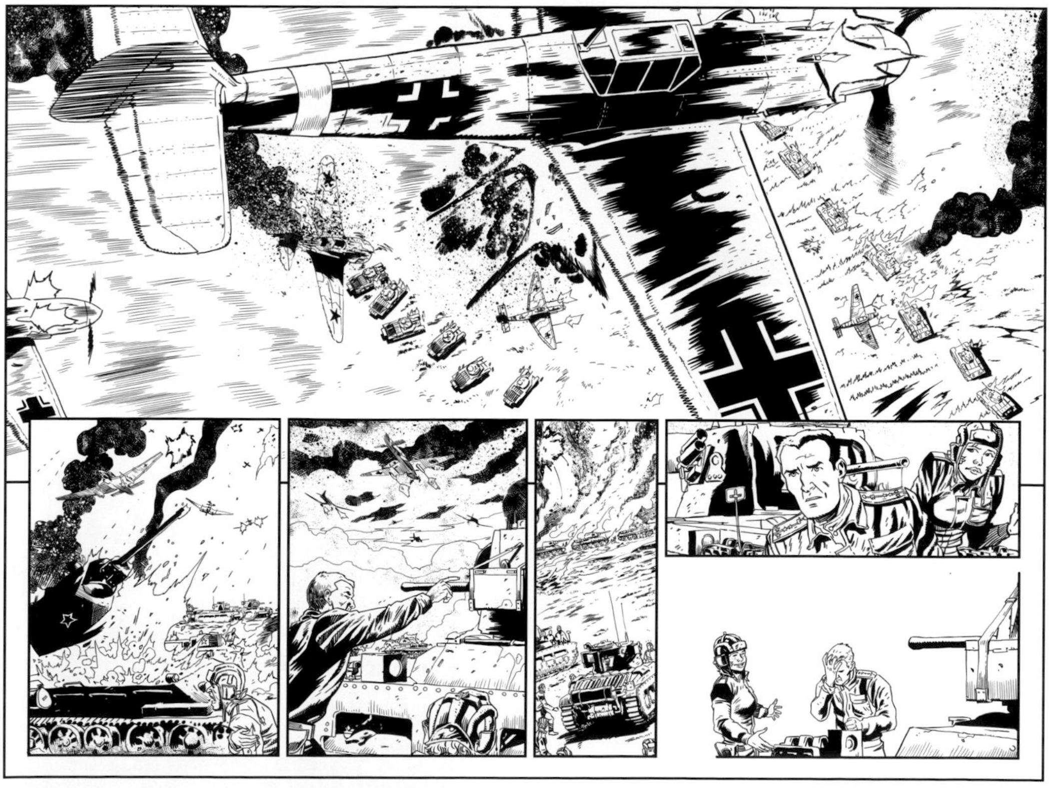

ABOVE: It's a tricky thing to get right, an extreme close up with far off action, luckily the wings of the ME109 here helped separate the Matildas from the T34s, giving us effectively two windows into what was happening on the ground. Drawing work like this, you're torn between the feeling that this is a real conflict that involved real people and should be treated earnestly and with respect, and the childlike glee you get drawing things exploding.

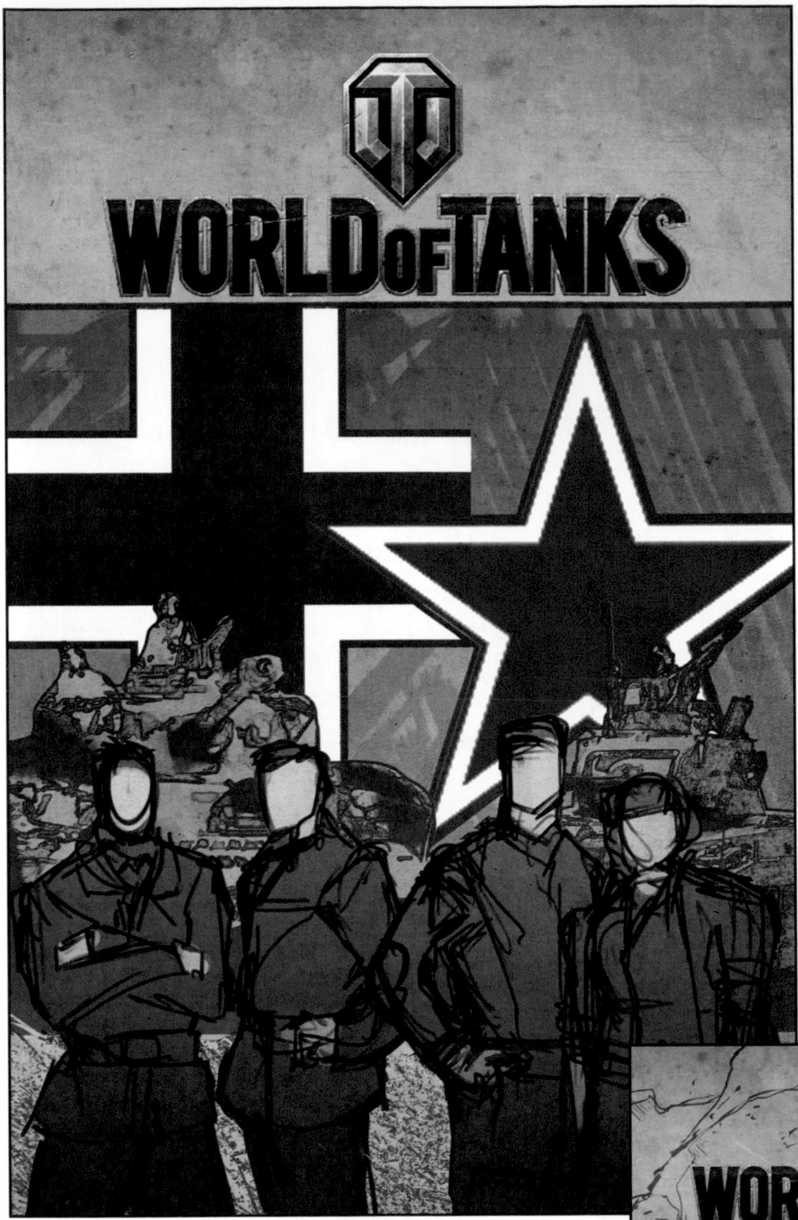
WORLD OF TANKS

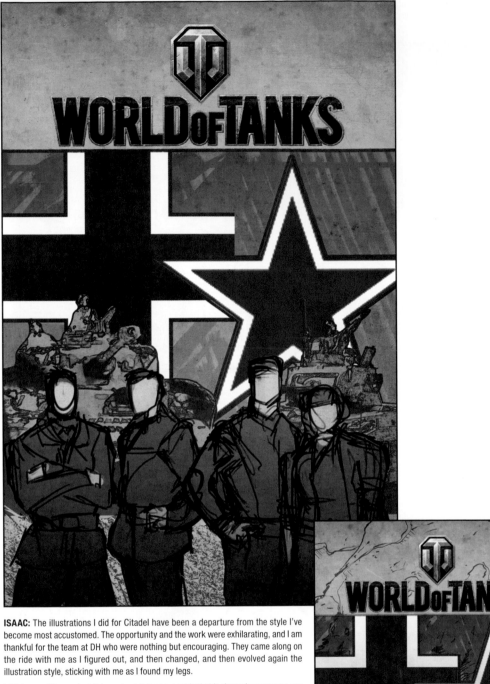

ISAAC: The illustrations I did for Citadel have been a departure from the style I've become most accustomed. The opportunity and the work were exhilarating, and I am thankful for the team at DH who were nothing but encouraging. They came along on the ride with me as I figured out, and then changed, and then evolved again the illustration style, sticking with me as I found my legs.

I think one of the coolest things about this cover set is that it shows in sequence, my thought process as the series progressed.

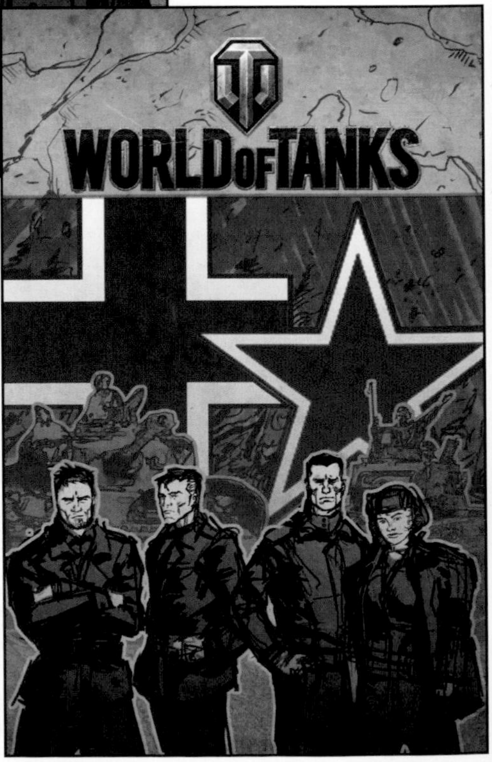
WORLD OF TANKS

Sketch and pencils for the Citadel *#1 cover by* ***ISAAC HANNAFORD****.*

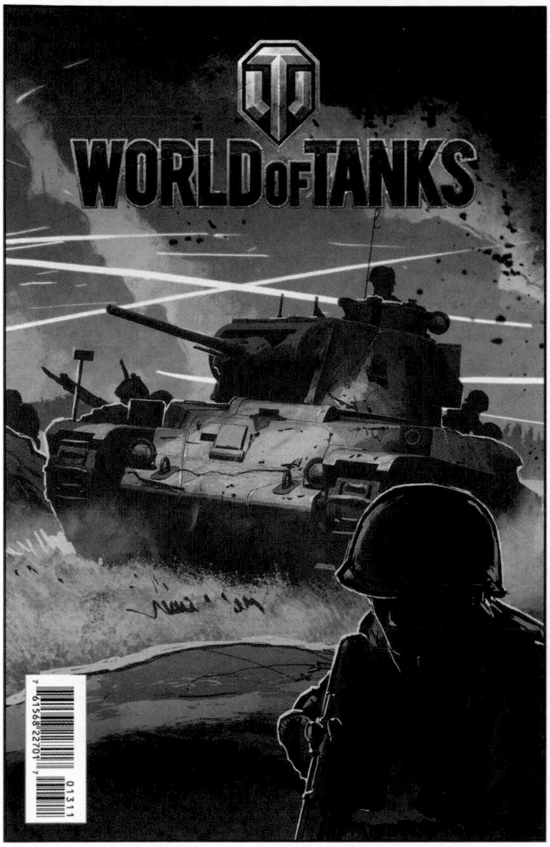
WORLD OF TANKS

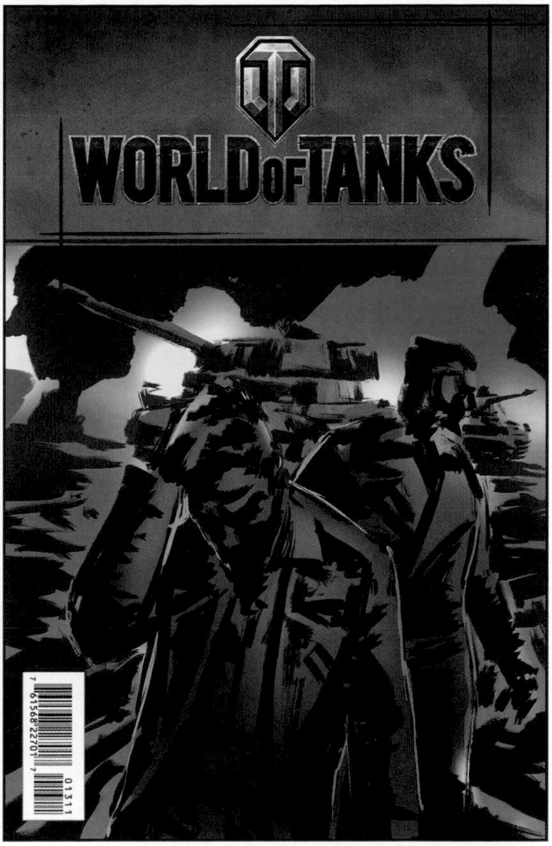
WORLD OF TANKS

Unused cover sketches for Citadel *issues #2–#3.*

BELOW: This cover sketch evolved to focus on Piotr and Ginger, telling a more personal story. I thought the Matilda looked particularly good in this illustration, much meaner than it had any right to be.

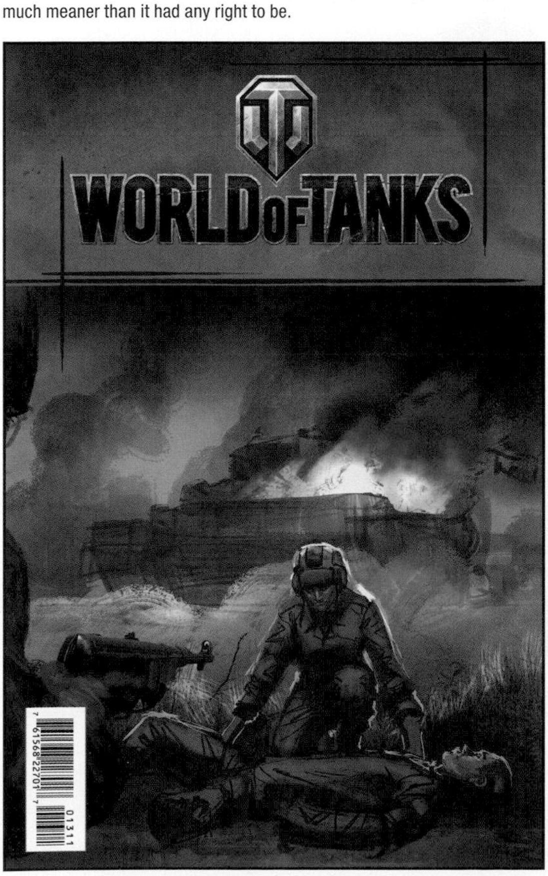
WORLD OF TANKS

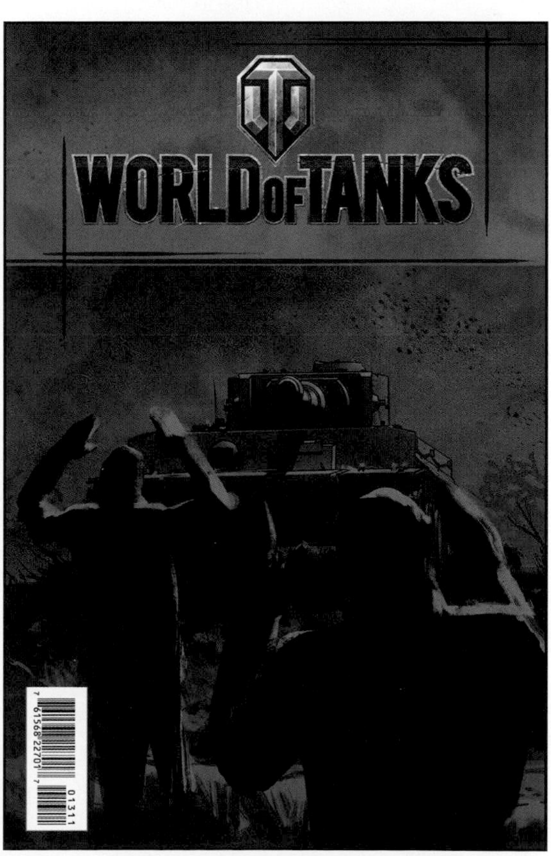
WORLD OF TANKS

Original cover sketches for Citadel *issues #4–#5.*

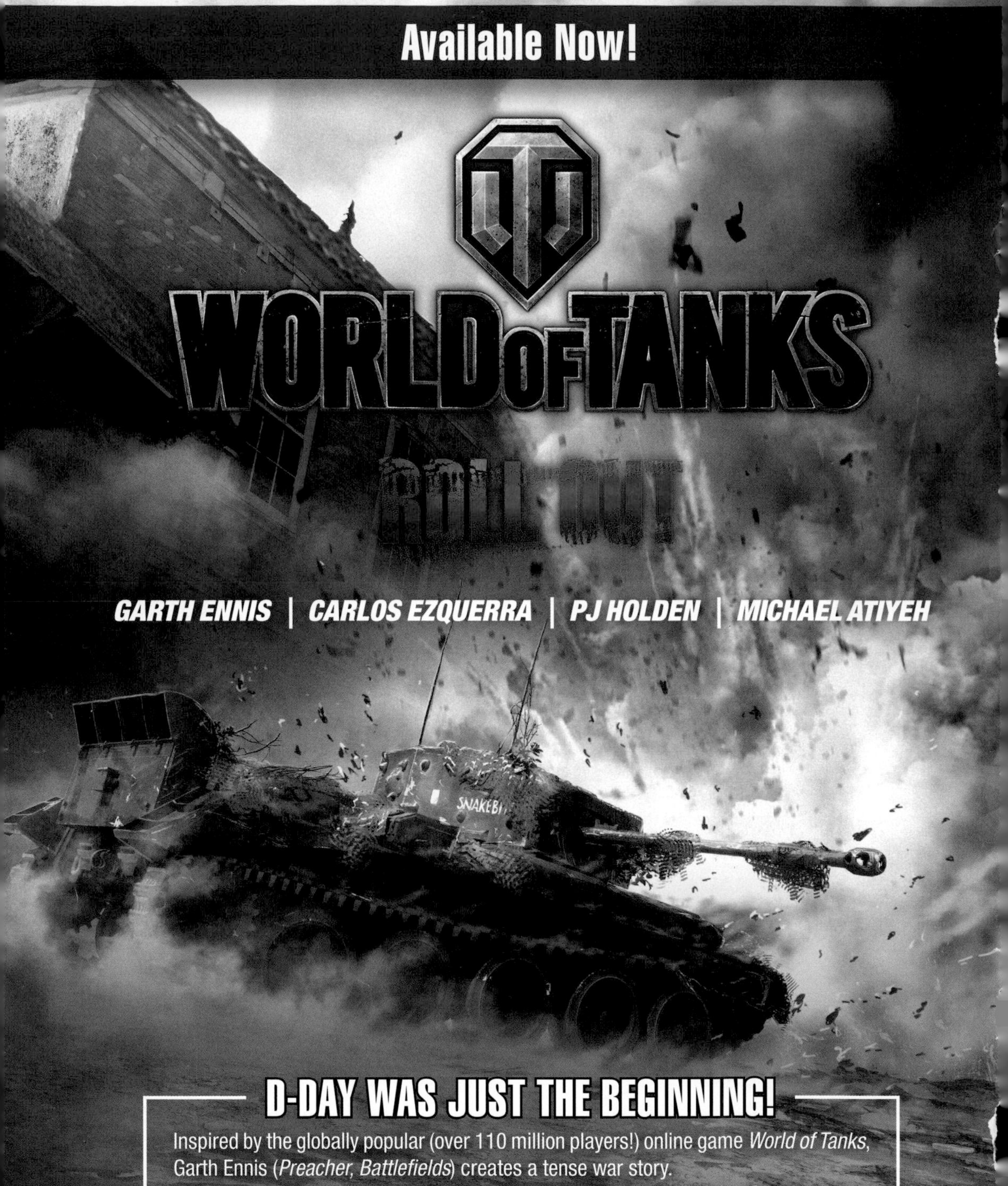

Available Now!

WORLD of TANKS

GARTH ENNIS | CARLOS EZQUERRA | PJ HOLDEN | MICHAEL ATIYEH

D-DAY WAS JUST THE BEGINNING!

Inspired by the globally popular (over 110 million players!) online game *World of Tanks*, Garth Ennis (*Preacher, Battlefields*) creates a tense war story.

 As an untested British tank crew advances into France shortly after the D-day invasion, they discover their Cromwell tank, "Snakebite," isn't quite what they were expecting. And with a veteran German Panzer unit on the hunt, the Brits will need all the luck they can get in order to survive.

Collects issues #1–#5 of the Dark Horse Comics series World of Tanks: Rollout.
$16.99 US | $22.99 CAN | ISBN 978-1-50670-060-1

AVAILABLE AT YOUR LOCAL COMICS SHOP OR BOOKSTORE

To find a comics shop in your area, visit comicshoplocator.com. For more information or to order direct: On the web: DarkHorse.com · Email: mailorder@darkhorse.com · Phone: 1-800-862-0052 Mon.–Fri. 9 AM to 5 PM Pacific Time.